If These
WALLS
Could TALK:
CLEMSON TIGERS

If These WALLS Could TALK:
CLEMSON TIGERS

Stories from the
Clemson Tigers Sideline,
Locker Room, and Press Box

Sam Blackman and Tim Bourret

TRIUMPH
B O O K S

This book is available in quantity at special discounts for your group or organization. For further information, contact:

Triumph Books LLC
814 North Franklin Street
Chicago, Illinois 60610
(312) 337–0747
www.triumphbooks.com

Printed in U.S.A.
ISBN: 978-1-62937-269-3
Design by Amy Carter
Editorial production by Alex Lubertozzi
Photos courtesy of Clemson University unless otherwise indicated

CONTENTS

FOREWORD

Clemson has had a great football tradition since its inception. Part of the reason for this is that it has always been a source of pride for the school and been a basic of the fabric of the community.

The school was founded in 1889 and had a football team just seven years later. By 1900 one of the all-time great coaches was leading the program, and he coached Clemson to three league championships in four years. That coach was John Heisman, and he set a standard through his coaching innovations and belief that the sport builds men of character.

The tradition of excellence in leadership continued when Jess Neely became the head coach in 1931. He was the first coach who saw the need for a sound infrastructure within his administration, and he was a leading force in the founding of IPTAY, the oldest scholarship foundation in the nation. IPTAY was founded in 1934, and Clemson played in its first bowl game and had its first top 20 season just five years later.

You will see in the many fascinating stories in this book that there are some common threads through history. After the 1939 season, Frank Howard, an Alabama graduate, was promoted to head coach from his assistant coach position. Each of the three winningest coaches in Clemson history are Alabama graduates who took over the reins at Clemson after serving on staff as an assistant coach.

Howard took Clemson to the Southern Conference Championship in his first year, 1940, and went on to win eight conference titles overall, two Southern Conference and six ACC titles.

I never had the opportunity to meet Bear Bryant, but I met Coach Howard at a surprise birthday party for my mom when I was a kid. My parents' friend, Bobby Hayes, was good friends with Coach Howard and brought him to my mom's birthday party. I have never forgotten meeting him. I even have a picture of my mom and dad having dinner with Coach Howard. Little did I know that years later I would be charged with carrying on the tradition he set through 30 years as head coach (1940–1969).

After Coach Howard retired, the tradition was carried on by Charley Pell, Danny Ford, and Ken Hatfield, coaches who all won ACC titles and posted top 25 seasons on a regular basis.

Of course, the highlight of the program was winning the 1981 national championship, and there is an entire chapter devoted to the players and coaches who made that happen. It set a standard that we all pursue today. It was an

Dabo Swinney

important accomplishment because it proved that the program had what it takes to be the best. That is what we all aspire to attain and it is important to work at a program that has reached the top previously.

Tradition is something all coaches evaluate when deciding on taking over a program. Programs with a winning tradition have a strong following, and this support is paramount when it comes to future success.

The 2016 season will be my 14th at Clemson, the longest I have been at any program in my coaching career. I take great pride in what this program has done for 120 years, and I take great pride in knowing we have made a contribution.

When I came to Clemson I heard about the success of the previous coaches, especially Coach Ford in the 1980s. The 1980s were the glory years. I enjoyed hearing about those stories of bowl wins over Nebraska,

Oklahoma, and Penn State, and of the conference championships, five in that decade alone. Those stories motivated me and let me know it could be done at Clemson. Now, with five straight seasons of 10 wins for the first time in school history, and five straight top 25 finishes, including three in the top 10, I am happy to report we are living through some glory years today. This is the good ole days…this is the best of times. I hope we all enjoy the journey!

This book starts with a chapter on our 2015 season, a season that finished with a school record 14 wins, a conference championship, a College Football Playoff victory, six straight weeks as the nation's top team, and Clemson's first appearance in the College Football Playoff. It was a season that included wins over top 10 teams Notre Dame, North Carolina, and Oklahoma, and a division-clinching win over 2013 national champion Florida State. It was a terrific season that kept our authors, Tim Bourret and Sam Blackman, hopping as they sought to document our accomplishments on the field through a historical perspective.

My goal is to have a 2016 season that will force them to do a significant edit to this book next year. After all…the *best* is yet to come.

Enjoy, and Go Tigers!

—Dabo Swinney

INTRODUCTION

Behind every outstanding athletic program there are outstanding people, and Clemson is not without its share down through the years.

The foundation was built with such coaching legends as Riggs, Heisman, Cody, Neely, and Howard. The legacy has continued with such names as Ford and Swinney. It has been an incredible story of how a small southern college tucked away in the northwest corner of South Carolina has become a perennial national football power.

Along the way there were many colorful people who have made Clemson great. Their legends and lore will be discussed in the following pages. A small college town has been the dwelling place for so many famous people, and their stories are all unique.

We have combined our own recollections as well as the stories that have been passed on to us, and hope to continue sharing them for years to come. What better way to do this than to create a book filled with these unbelievable but true stories. We have close to 75 years combined—more than 35 years together—of working in the Clemson Athletic Communication Office as students, graduate students, and full-time employees.

In 2009 the Clemson Athletic Communication Office was named to the Football Writers Association "Super 11" Team. The award recognized the top 11 SID offices in the nation for their service in working with media covering college football. The SID Office won the award again in 2010 and again in 2015.

We learned many of the stories about Clemson football from Bob Bradley, the Clemson sports information director from 1955 to 1989, who is a legendary figure in Clemson athletics. He was inducted into the Clemson Ring of Honor posthumously in 2005.

We hope you enjoy these stories of yesteryear and of the present.

CHAPTER 1
THE SWINNEY ERA

An Unexpected Change

The Monday morning after Clemson lost a 12–7 heartbreaker at Wake Forest on October 8, 2008, Athletic Director Terry Don Phillips called head coach Tommy Bowden to his office.

Bowden had been Clemson's head coach since 1999 and brought the program to a new level with winning seasons and bowl games in eight of nine full seasons. He also had a 7–2 record against rival South Carolina. The only year that hadn't ended in a bowl game was 2004 when a 100-yard brawl with South Carolina with five minutes left in the game forced both schools' presidents to end each team's respective seasons without a postseason.

While Bowden's teams had finished in the top 25 four times, he had not won the Atlantic Division, never mind the ACC. With a top 10 preseason ranking in 2008, most expected the Tigers to at least win the division, and privately, Phillips expected it. On this October 13 morning, Clemson was 3–3 overall, 1–2 in the ACC.

When Phillips came to the office that day, he expected that Tommy Bowden would still be his coach at the end of the day. But he felt he owed it to Bowden to tell him where he stood. After nine years as head coach, he felt it was a realistic expectation to win the Atlantic Division, and that if this was not accomplished by season's end he would make a change.

Winning the Atlantic Division would be difficult, but not out of the question. After all, just five years earlier, Bowden had worked miracles over the last four games of the season to bring Clemson from a 5–4 record to a 9–4 mark. In those last four games Clemson had beaten No. 3 Florida State, the highest ranked team the Tigers had beaten in their history, and downed No. 6 Tennessee in the Peach Bowl. It was the first time Clemson had beaten two top-six teams in a four-game period. Many members of the media felt if there had been an NCAA football tournament, Clemson would be the team you would not want to play.

So, when Phillips decided to have this talk with Bowden, he expected his response to be that he would do a midseason review of his offense (he had already announced the previous Friday he was going to make a change at quarterback from Cullen Harper to Willy Korn), and talk about what he had done in 2003.

But that was not Bowden's reaction.

With no previous heads-up that this meeting was coming, Bowden made a decision that would change the course of Clemson football for years to come. Obviously, Bowden had been thinking about the state of the program. After a strong finish to 2007 with a last-second win over South Carolina and the return of 14 starters for 2008, including "Thunder and Lightning" running backs James Davis and C.J. Spiller, Clemson was a preseason top 10 team, and expectations were through the roof.

But the Tigers had been disappointing, with a season-opening 34–10 loss to Alabama, and conference losses to Maryland and Wake Forest. The only victories had come against The Citadel, South Carolina State, and N.C. State.

When Phillips said what he had to say, Bowden responded, "Well, why don't we just make a change now?"

Phillips' eyes opened as wide as baseballs. He was getting ready to prepare for a possible change at the top in December, but not today.

Bowden then explained that he believed assistant coach Dabo Swinney would make a great head coach and that, if he was given an opportunity as the interim coach, the rest of the season he could show he could do the job. But, if they waited until the end of the year, Swinney would not have a chance.

To the general public, such a suggestion seemed odd. While Swinney was in his sixth year on the Clemson staff as wide receivers coach, he had never been a coordinator. To most, following the path to head coach after being a coordinator was the normal route. But this was not some crazy idea to Phillips. Of the 85 scholarship players on the 2008 team, Swinney had personally recruited 38 of them. He had pulled

3

off a miracle by convincing C.J. Spiller, a five-star running back whom everyone wanted, to leave the state of Florida and come to Clemson.

Whenever Phillips attended practice he found himself going to the wide receivers and watching Swinney interact with his players. He noticed a special bond between Swinney and those receivers, and many of the players at other positions. Phillips was also impressed with Swinney's work on the AARC committee, which worked with university administrators when it came to appeals for special exceptions admits. Swinney's work on that committee had a big impact on his approval as interim head coach because it gave him credibility with high-ranking university administrators when it came to the importance he placed on academics and his ability to work with the president's office and the admissions office.

After a second meeting between Phillips and Bowden at 10:30 AM that October 13, Phillips went to the staff meeting room in the McFadden Building to tell the staff Coach Bowden would no longer be the head coach. He then told Swinney to come to his office in five minutes.

That request had to stun the staff, especially offensive coordinator Rob Spence and defensive coordinator Vic Koenning. Most of the time a coordinator is elevated to interim head coach, but when Phillips told Swinney to come to his office by himself, it was apparent who the new interim would be.

A stunned Swinney sat in Phillips' corner office in the Jervey Athletic Center and listened to what the veteran athletic director had to say.

The biggest thing Phillips told him was that he wanted Swinney to be in total charge. "I told him I didn't want him to be an interim coach, I wanted him to make decisions that were his and for the good of the program. I told him he had my backing in anything he wanted to do. From the beginning I wanted to give Dabo the opportunity. I told him he would be a candidate, he would not just be an interim. Make decisions like you are the full-time coach."

And that is what Swinney did. He left Phillips' office and immediately went to the office of offensive coordinator Rob Spence and told him he was not going to be retained effective immediately. The first thing Swinney wanted to do going forward was to get Spiller more involved in the offense. At that point in the season through six games, Spiller had touched the ball on offense just 57 times, an average of 9.5 times per game. The last six games of the year (ironically, Spiller did not player in Swinney's first game against Georgia Tech on October 18) with Swinney effectively calling the plays, Spiller handled the ball 92 times, 15.3 times per game.

Swinney moved Billy Napier from receivers coach to quarterbacks coach and was involved in the play-calling. Graduate assistant Jeff Scott moved to wide receivers coach. He is still on the staff today as wide receivers coach and co–offensive coordinator.

The five days from October 13 to 18, 2008, would be the most difficult of Dabo Swinney's career. He had to meet with the team and inform them of what had happened and try to earn the respect of those players and administrators.

He did that with a team only meeting late that afternoon. He told them, "None of you owe me anything. You came to this program to play for Tommy Bowden as head coach. If you want to leave you still have your scholarship until the end of the year. But if you come to practice today, I expect you to be all-in for the rest of the year. I am going to put everything I have into this job, and I expect you to do the same."

Bowden had announced the day after the Wake Forest game that Willy Korn would become the starting quarterback in place of Cullen Harper. The team had practiced on Sunday with Bowden in charge and Korn as the signal-caller. Swinney decided not to change back to Harper. He felt the team needed a lift on offense, and he agreed with the decision.

Swinney worked 20-hour days that first week as he brainstormed ways to bring Clemson Nation together. The fan base was obviously fractured. Swinney had a sixth sense about dealing with the media from day one and held press meetings each day after practice as a way to communicate with the fan base. One of the things he did was to institute a "Tiger Walk" at the end of the team's arrival at the stadium.

Previously, the team buses pulled up right in front of the west end zone of the stadium. But Swinney had the idea to let the team off at the entrance to the Lot 5 (west end zone) parking lot, and have the team, dressed in coats and ties, walk the 100 yards through the parking lot to the stadium. He encouraged all Tigers fans to line the parking lot route and encourage the team as they entered the stadium roughly two hours prior to kickoff. The Tiger Walk was exhilarating as Swinney proved to be the Pied Piper in just five days. Fans were in the stands 90 minutes before kickoff against Georgia Tech that October 18 day.

Not everything went according to plan. Just 10 minutes into the game, Korn suffered a shoulder injury as he was struck after throwing a pass. It was back to Harper, and he responded with a pair of touchdown passes. It was a thrilling game, but the Yellow Jackets came out on top 21–17 when a questionable holding call on Thomas Austin wiped out a long pass play to Jacoby Ford.

It didn't take Swinney long to win his first game, though. After an open date, the Tigers won at Boston College, 27–21. It was Clemson's first win over the Eagles since they joined the league.

It would be the first of many Swinney accomplishments that required extensive research by the Clemson Sports Information office.

16 Months with C.J. Spiller

In May of 2003, we received word that Banks McFadden would be attending a Saturday night Clemson vs. Duke baseball game at Kingsmore Stadium. Clemson's greatest athlete of the 20th century was 86 at the time, and the opportunities to recognize the only football-basketball All-American in school history were dwindling.

So a script was given to promotions director John Seketa, who had the announcement made during the fifth-inning break to drag the infield. Banks had trouble with his hip in his later years, so we went to his seat behind home plate just before the announcement to help him stand up. When the announcement was made, it did not take long for the more than 4,000 in attendance to stand up also. It was a great, long ovation, one that put a smile on his face, and on our faces as well. It would be the last time McFadden received a standing ovation at an athletic event at Clemson, as he would pass away just two years later. When we went home that night we reflected on McFadden's greatness. Few if any Clemson fans in the stadium that night had seen McFadden play, as he had played his last athletic event (a basketball game) for Clemson in 1940. That made the ovation even greater, because it was a testament to the unprecedented level of respect he held among Clemson people.

It made us wonder if we would ever see another Clemson athlete in our lifetime held in such reverence....

January 15, 2009

The number of phone calls we received at the sports information office concerning C.J. Spiller's decision to return to Clemson or go pro after his junior year had just one comparison at Clemson—Herschel Walker's decision out of high school as to whether he would go to Georgia or Clemson in 1980. Fortunately, C.J.'s decision had a deadline, January 15. That was the last day underclassmen had to apply for the NFL Draft.

Spiller had kept his decision very close to the vest, and nothing definitive had been stated by anyone close to him. Even his closest teammates, James Davis and Jacoby Ford, didn't know what he would do. We called a 3:00 PM press conference at the McFadden Auditorium for Spiller to announce his decision on the 15th.

We arrived at Coach Swinney's office at McFadden about 15 minutes before the press conference and asked him point blank what he thought Spiller would do. He said Spiller had told him earlier in the day that he was coming back, but he wouldn't be totally sure until he announced.

A few minutes later Spiller came into the office, dressed in suit and tie. As he came, he looked like someone who was about to tell his dad something he didn't want to hear. We left Coach Swinney's office because we sensed they wanted to meet one-on-one. We waited in an adjoining room. We could not hear the discussion, but there was some serious conversation going on between Spiller and Swinney. At one point Spiller became emotional.

We went back into the McFadden Building to check on things, and the room was filling up with media and members of the team. That was another indication they didn't know either. By the time we went back to Coach Swinney's office, the meeting was finished. We asked C.J. if he was ready, and he said yes. He gave us no indication of what he was going to say. So, as we walked onto the stage in front of C.J., we had no idea what was about to take place.

Coach Swinney was in the back of the room with his kids, and we looked at him for an indication, a smile, a frown, something. But his face was blank. C.J. made few overall comments, then said, "I had to do what was best for me, things that made me happy."

That is usually the forerunner to "I am turning pro."

Instead, he reversed field like a classic C.J. Spiller kick return and said, "And for the year, 2009, I'll be here at Clemson University." The room erupted. Dabo had a big smile and was high-fiving his kids. You can look at the video on clemsontigers.com and see that Spiller kept a straight face, no smile, no feeling of relief. He told the media that his mother wanted him to turn pro and that he was projected to be a first-round draft choice by the NFL. Two more facts that would have pushed

8

most players to the NFL. But Spiller said afterward, "There was a lot of crying [when he talked with his mom about staying], but I told her something didn't feel right about leaving. A lot of guys start things, but they don't finish. I didn't want to be labeled as one of those guys."

In talking with Coach Swinney since then, he really didn't know what Spiller was going to say. When he first went in, Spiller told him he thought he needed to turn pro for his family, and that is when he started to get emotional.

"I just told him he needed to do what was best for him," said Swinney. "He finally gathered himself and said, 'Okay, I am ready.' But he still didn't tell me. So when I went into that room, I really didn't know what he was going to say."

Looking back, his return was divine intervention.

July 21, 2009

Within an hour after the end of Spiller's press conference on January 15, Coach Swinney and members of the sports information office met to discuss a plan for a "Spiller for Heisman campaign." In 1984 we did a life-size poster of William Perry, and it was a big hit in promoting The Fridge for All-American and the Lombardi Award.

Now, 25 years later, we thought it would be an old-school way of promoting Spiller for the Heisman. We planned to do the usual Internet promotion that everyone else does today, but wanted something that would be different. There was one catch to this plan: NCAA rules had changed in the last 25 years. We could no longer sell the poster to the general public. We had to give it away if we were to produce it. In these economic times, spending $10,000 on the printing of the posters was not the right thing to do. So members of our promotions department secured two sponsors, BiLo and Tom Winkopp Real Estate, and they paid for the printing cost.

Given the amount of money we raised from the sponsors, we could print 5,000. We needed 1,000 for general promotion to the national

C.J. Spiller finished sixth in the Heisman voting in 2009 despite practicing only once a week during the regular season.

media, and that left 4,000 to give away to the public. We left the give-aways up to the sponsors. Since they had paid for them, they should at least use them to drive people to their stores. We unveiled the poster on July 21, 2009, at Dabo Swinney's press conference and golf tournament at The Reserve. It was met with great fanfare locally, and *College Football Live* showed the poster on ESPN that day.

We ran into a public relations problem the day after the posters were distributed at BiLo stores throughout the upstate. Clemson fans in Columbia and Charleston didn't have access to them, and the posters were gone in a matter of hours. Of course, the furor over the poster did continue to publicize it and create more stories, which wasn't a bad thing.

September 5, 2009

For the first time in history, a Clemson player took the opening kickoff of the season the distance for a touchdown. Spiller went 96 yards for a score on the opening kickoff against Middle Tennessee State, and Spiller's season was off to a magical start.

Clemson had a 30–7 lead at halftime, and Spiller was held out the second half. At the time we thought it was due to the score and Coach Swinney's desire to rest his star for the game with Georgia Tech just five days later. But, as it turned out, Spiller had suffered a turf toe injury when someone stepped on his foot in the first half, an injury that would cause him problems the rest of the year. It was a miracle that Spiller played the next game against Georgia Tech and that he never missed a game all year. That was one big bunion, and as a result, he never practiced more than two days in any week all year.

With all that he accomplished in 2009, one has to wonder what his numbers would have been had he been healthy.

October 3, 2009

Spiller's most memorable play of the year took place at Maryland on October 3. He returned a kickoff 92 yards for a score late in the third period to pull the Tigers within three points.

It was an incredible run because, as he broke away from two Maryland tacklers at the Clemson 35, you could see he had lost his left shoe. He sprinted the last 65 yards with just a sock on his left foot. There was some historical irony in that because the last time a Clemson player had a long run in his stocking feet was also against Maryland. Kevin Mack raced 42 yards for a score against Maryland in the famous Balloon Game in November of 1983. It was Mack's last career carry in Death Valley.

Clemson won that game in 1983, but that would not be the case this day in 2009. Clemson drove into Maryland territory three times in the fourth period, but could not get into close enough field-goal range, and the Terps came away with a 24–21 victory.

The Tigers had now dropped to 2–3. Despite an impressive individual day, a dejected Spiller met with the media after the game and told them he still thought the Tigers were a top-15 team. Most thought that was a reach of a quote, but Spiller knew his teammates needed confidence and knew it was important for him as team leader to publicly express his confidence in them.

Six weeks later he would prove to be correct, as the Tigers entered the AP poll in 15th place after a sixth straight win.

October 6, 2009

There are more than 1,000 action pictures of C.J. Spiller in the archives in the sports information office. Many are dynamic shots of his greatest touchdowns, open field moves, or leaping receptions. But our favorite photo of Spiller didn't take place during a game. It took place during a visit to a retirement center in Anderson.

Spiller and most of his teammates visited the NHC Health Center on the Tuesday of an open-date week. Nathan Gray, a photographer from the *Anderson Independent* captured Spiller while he visited with Theda Anthony, 91 years young. She was holding a Tiger Paw flag in her lap and was mesmerized by Spiller, who was equally attentive to her.

Spiller was very close to his grandmother during his elementary school years. She was the one who took him to his little league football games and was a big influence on his development of core values. When she died before he came to Clemson, it was a sad day because he always wanted her to see him play in college. This picture was a great representation of the goodwill Spiller brought to everyone he came in contact with. We never saw him turn away from a fan seeking an autograph or

Spiller visits with 91-year-old Clemson fan Theda Anthony.

a picture, whether it was after a great win, a difficult loss, or a grueling practice.

In his four years at Clemson, he must have signed more autographs on footballs and jerseys than anyone in school history. One day in November we walked by after a practice as he was signing away and announced, "Would the six children in the upstate of South Carolina who don't have a signed Christmas gift from C.J. Spiller please raise your hand!"

October 24, 2009

Clemson had righted the ship a bit with a convincing 38–3 win over Wake Forest after the open date to go 3–3. C.J. had another great game with 106 yards rushing and two scores on just nine carries, including a 66-yard run that broke the game open.

But he was in need of a signature game that could get him back into the Heisman Trophy picture. A big game at eighth-ranked Miami (FL) on ABC-TV could do the trick. Spiller was always excited for a game in the state of Florida, but his level of motivation had an extra boost when he learned that his biological father, now living in South Florida, would attend a Clemson game for the first time in his career. This would be Spiller's best all-around game to date. He gained 81 yards rushing, 104 receiving, and 125 on kickoff returns, finishing with a Clemson record 301 all-purpose yards. His day included a 48-yard run, a 56-yard reception, and a 90-yard kickoff return for a touchdown.

Clemson won the game 40–37 in overtime, and Spiller was named National Player of the Week. The next Monday, he was on everyone's top-10 Heisman List, including as high as second by *Sports Illustrated*. But the most important testimony came from Edwin Pope, the legendary *Miami Herald* columnist who had been in the business for 50 years. Pope wrote, "You have hardly heard his name mentioned in the Heisman Trophy conversations yet. Disgraceful. But you will, you will."

November 7, 2009

With a three-game winning streak and national ranking, ESPN *Primetime* came to Clemson for the Florida State game.

Spiller trumped his performance at Miami with a record 312-yard effort. This one was better in the eyes of many in the media because it included a then-career-high 165 rushing yards and a come-from-behind 40–24 victory. Some national media had been critical of Spiller because he didn't have the rushing yards some of the other running backs had.

As soon as the game ended, Spiller sprinted toward the middle of the field to pay his respects to Florida State head coach Bobby Bowden. The older Bowden had recruited C.J. out of high school, and many thought he would go to Tallahassee because of Spiller's reverence for Warrick Dunn. He even wore No. 28 because Dunn was his favorite player.

After an interview with Erin Andrews, we followed Spiller into the locker room, and he virtually collapsed at his locker. No one realized how much pain he was in during that game because of his injured toe until that moment.

November 21, 2009

Clemson needed one win over Virginia on the final home game of the year to win the Atlantic Division and qualify for the ACC Championship Game. It was a great day of celebration. During pregame in a rather spontaneous action, Spiller was given an American Flag to hold at the top of the hill, and he held it as he ran down the hill for the last time. That colorful picture made the rounds on many Internet sites and newspapers across the country.

While Spiller did not have Heisman numbers on the day, his teammate, classmate, and best friend Jacoby Ford did, with a career high 211 all-purpose yards. With a comfortable lead, Swinney was able to give Thomas Austin, Ford, and Spiller final curtain calls as they exited the field. The presentation in the locker room of the Atlantic Division Championship trophy brought smiles to everyone. Finally, Clemson was going to the ACC Championship Game.

December 5, 2009

Spiller wanted an ACC championship more than anything, and it showed with his performance in Tampa, Florida, this December evening. He gained a career-high 233 yards rushing and scored a career-high four touchdowns. He finished with 302 all-purpose yards, his third 300-yard game of the year, another first in ACC history. It was not a coincidence that the only three games his father attended were the only three games in his career he had at least 300 all-purpose yards.

In the end, neither team could stop the other. It is the only Clemson game on record in which neither team had to punt, and the only college football game of 2009 in which both teams rushed for 300 yards.

But, Georgia Tech made one more drive than the Tigers and came away with a 39–34 victory. Still, Spiller was named the game's MVP, the first player on a losing side in any Division I conference championship game in history to win the award.

After the game, ACC commissioner John Swofford waited outside the postgame interview room for Spiller. He gave him a hug and said with emotion, "Young man, you are one of the greatest to ever play in this conference." That is all he said. That is all he needed to say.

December 12, 2009

While Spiller gained some more momentum for the Heisman with his performance in the ACC Championship Game, it turned out, not enough people saw it. The game was played opposite the Big 12 Championship Game between Texas and Nebraska.

Most Heisman voters tuned in to the Big 12 game to determine if they were going to vote for Texas quarterback Colt McCoy. They came away impressed with Nebraska defensive lineman Ndamukung Suh, who had an incredible 4.5 sacks in the game.

Two days after the ACC Championship Game, the Heisman Trust invited Tim Tebow of Florida, Colt McCoy of Texas, Ndamukong Suh of Nebraska, Mark Ingram of Alabama, and Toby Gerhart of Stanford to New York. Spiller was disappointed, but not devastated by not receiving an invitation. He knew he had done everything possible to be a Heisman finalist. But the Tigers had five losses on their record, too much to overcome.

The Heisman Trophy was presented the following Saturday in New York City at Radio City Music Hall to Ingram, the sophomore running back from eventual national champion Alabama. Spiller finished sixth in the voting for the Heisman, tied for the highest finish by a Clemson football player at that point.

We sent him a simple text the afternoon of the announcement. "Five months from now, all these guys in New York today will be home watching you in the same building for the NFL Draft."

In the end, only Suh would make the return trip in April.

December 17, 2009

Over the first 16 days of December, Spiller had been chosen a first-team All-American by every service, joining Terry Kinard and Gaines Adams as the only unanimous All-Americans in Clemson football history. He had been named the ACC Player of the Year, an honor that privately had been a big preseason goal for Spiller, and of course, he had a sixth-place finish in the Heisman voting.

But his most meaningful honor might have come on this day at Clemson's graduation in Littlejohn Coliseum. It was a big day for Spiller, as his entire family and many close friends from Florida made the trip to Clemson. When he walked across the stage to pick up his diploma, Clemson's board of trustees spontaneously stood in unison. That triggered an even more staccato ovation from the graduates and audience.

We had been to many Clemson graduations in the past and only recalled the board of trustees giving a standing ovation to one other student. A few years back as a student with cerebral palsy crossed the stage, the board of trustees also stood.

It was quite a tribute, one that sets Spiller apart as a student-athlete. It was recognition of his unparalleled excellence in terms of representing, not just the football team, but also the entire university. He had become the face of Clemson University.

December 27, 2009

Clemson closed out the 2009 season with a 21–13 victory over Kentucky in the Music City Bowl. Spiller reached one final accomplishment from a team standpoint in that he finally could celebrate a Clemson bowl victory. Individually, he became the only player in college football that year to score at least one touchdown in every game, and he finished his career with 7,588 career all-purpose yards, second in NCAA history.

After winning the Most Valuable Player award, he was interviewed on the field by ESPN's Holly Rowe. She asked Spiller about his decision to stay in the game and risk injury with a pro career on the horizon. "Because I love Clemson too much," said Spiller. "They were going to have to shoot me to take me out of the game. I owe it to the Clemson family. They have supported me my entire career."

April 22, 2010

The night C.J. was drafted, we were thrilled that he was taken as the No. 9 pick, just the sixth top-10 selection in Clemson history. But, with his selection, he was now officially property of the Buffalo Bills. We were no longer his media contact. While our workload was going to decline dramatically, it was a bit sad as well.

He was the most exciting, most beloved, and most respected athlete we had dealt with at Clemson.

Unless modern science develops some medicine to raise life expectancy to over 105, we won't be around 54 years from now. But I am willing to bet if C.J. Spiller happens to come back to a Clemson baseball game in the year 2070 he will get a spontaneous standing ovation.

Kyle Parker—20/20

Today more and more college athletes are graduating from high school early to start the college experience. But in 2007 it was not a common occurrence.

In January of 2008 when Kyle Parker came to Clemson and made the baseball team as a starter in the outfield, it raised some eyebrows in a positive light. When he made first-team All-ACC in a semester he should have been playing high school baseball, it was a landmark accomplishment.

In 2009, as a redshirt freshman, he quarterbacked the Clemson football team to its first Atlantic Division championship and trip to the ACC

Championship Game. He threw 20 touchdown passes for that exciting Clemson team led by C.J. Spiller. He led the Tigers to nine wins, tied for the most wins by a freshman quarterback in the nation.

The following spring he was back to baseball where he led Clemson to the College World Series with a 20–home run season. He became the first athlete in Division I history to throw 20 touchdown passes and hit 20 home runs in the same academic year. He was named an All-American in baseball and a freshman All-American on the gridiron.

Only two college athletes had even accomplished a 20/10 previously, Rodney Pete of Southern California in 1987–1988, and Josh Fields of Oklahoma State in 2003–2004.

In July of 2010, the two-sport star had to decide if he should give up college football and sign a baseball-only contract with the Colorado Rockies, who had drafted him in the first round, or return to Clemson and play football for the Tigers. A month later, he had to decide on signing a contract with the Rockies that would allow him to play football at Clemson, but that would also end his college baseball career.

Fortunately, Parker did not have to deal with these issues alone. He had the backing of his parents, Carl and Cathy Parker, who have been a guiding light to Kyle since the day he was born. "I have been blessed with two great parents," said Kyle. "My dad has been the most important person in my life when it comes to sports and my career path, and my mother has always been there for me when it comes to everything outside of sports."

When it came to the aforementioned decisions over the last three years, Carl could relate his own experiences to his son. Carl was a two-sport athlete in college as well, at Vanderbilt University from 1984 to 1987. He played football and baseball his first two years, then concentrated on football his final two years. He was drafted in the 12th round of the 1988 NFL Draft by Cincinnati and played two years with the Bengals.

"My dad's experience as a two-sport athlete in college was a big plus in helping me with these decisions the last couple of years. He had been through it himself. He handled all the negotiations [with the Rockies], and that took a big load off my shoulders."

When it comes to how to live one's life away from the diamond and gridiron, Kyle had sound advice from both his mom and dad. One need only review the story about his mother that made national headlines to see he has a great role model when it comes to perseverance and strength of character.

In 2007 Cathy Parker was watching an ESPN feature on a community in Barrow, Alaska. The community had a high teenage suicide rate. The local high school had just started a football program, and the support of the team had a positive impact on the community. But the football program did not have much in the way of facilities and had to play its games and practice on an all dirt field that was littered with rocks.

From 4,000 miles away in Jacksonville, Florida, Cathy decided she would mount a fund-raising campaign over the Internet to raise money to provide Barrow High School with an artificial surface football field. (Growing grass is out of the question that far north.)

Making contacts through the Internet, she raised over $500,000 for the school and made the arrangements to have the blue-and-gold turf field delivered and installed in time for the season opener of the 2008 season. The school was so grateful that the field is named Cathy Parker Field.

Kyle Parker helped the Tigers baseball team to the Atlantic Division title, the Auburn Regional Championship, the Clemson Super Regional title, and a third-place finish at the College World Series. He was actually drafted by the Rockies while he was playing an NCAA Tournament game at Auburn. He hit a home run in that game in helping the Tigers to victory.

Jack Leggett's baseball team finished fourth in the final polls, meaning Parker had been a leader on two top-25 teams in two major sports in the same year, something no Clemson athlete had done since Dexter McCleon in 1993–1994. Parker continued to show his leadership qualities on the gridiron in the fall of 2010. That was especially evident in another athletic event at Auburn, the Tigers' overtime contest on September 18, 2010. In the second half, he took a shot in his back when tackled by two players at the end of a running play when he was scrambling for additional yardage. Parker came off the field in obvious pain and it looked as though he was done for the night. He came off the field in a position that resembled a question mark. Redshirt freshman Tajh Boyd was warming up. But, when Auburn scored later in the quarter, Parker jumped to his feet and was ready to go, much to the surprise of the media covering the game, but not his teammates. "He is tough, tough," said tight end Dwayne Allen, now a veteran NFL tight end. "Here is a guy sitting with a million bucks in the bank, and he gets hurt. If I was in that situation, I don't know how I would have reacted."

Tajh and Sammy

Clemson had a great team in the fall of 1978. The Tigers had a great defense, but the offense featured the passing combination of Steve Fuller and Jerry Butler. They were common denominators in the greatest turnaround in Clemson history. When they were freshmen in 1975, the Tigers were 2–9, still the most losses in a season in school history.

Three years later the Tigers finished with an 11–1 record, an ACC title, and a No. 6 final ranking, the highest final ranking in Clemson history at the time. Fuller finished the year sixth in the Heisman Trophy voting, was a first-team Academic All-American and third-team All-American on the field, while Butler was a consensus first-team All-American, including the Associated Press, and was the No. 5 pick of the NFL Draft.

Their impact on the Clemson program had been immense, as the Tigers had not been to a bowl game from 1960 to 1976. Since the 1977 season, when Fuller and Butler were juniors, Clemson has been to 31 bowl games in 39 years. Now, that is an impact on a program.

Many other Clemson greats have had a significant impact on the Clemson program over the last 39 years:

The 1981 national championship team included future Ring of Honor members Jeff Davis and Terry Kinard. These two consensus first-team All-America defenders went on to induction into the College Football Hall of Fame, the only duo from the same recruiting class to make the Hall of Fame in ACC history.

And, oh, the stories of freakish athletic plays involving William Perry. The Tigers lost just one home game in four years the Fridge played in Death Valley.

C.J. Spiller was in a class by himself when it came to being an all-purpose offensive player. His 7,588 yards are still 1,700 more than any other ACC player in history. His senior year the Tigers finally reached the ACC Championship Game and his 300-yard performance in that game in Tampa will never be forgotten. When Spiller graduated in December of 2009, we all wondered if we would ever see anyone quite like him in terms of his game on the field and off the field.

But Spiller set a daily example for a true freshman quarterback named Tajh Boyd in the fall of 2009. And Spiller's performance on television and corresponding notoriety on the way to a sixth-place finish in the Heisman Trophy race that year attracted the attention of a Fort Myers, Florida, junior wide receiver named Sammy Watkins. When Watkins signed in February of 2011, Brad Scott, who had recruited him to Clemson, told us he was as exciting a player as Spiller and would bring the program to a new level. Now, five years later, the state of the Clemson program indicates that Scott is a soothsayer.

Over the last five years, the Tigers have won at least 10 games every year, a first for Clemson. The Tigers have won two ACC championships and finished in the top 25 of the final polls five consecutive years, including three top-10 final rankings. Clemson's No. 2 national finish in 2015 was the second best in school history and the 14–1 record set a school mark for the most wins in a season. The year included three wins over top-10 teams, tied for the school record for one year.

Boyd and Watkins had a lot to do with this run. Boyd started every game at quarterback from 2011 to 2013, and his 32 wins tied Rodney Williams (1985–1988) as the winningest quarterback in Clemson history. He set 57 records, including ACC marks for total offense, touchdown passes, and touchdown responsibility.

Watkins left Clemson with 27 marks, including records for receptions and receiving yards on a game, season, and career basis. His 27 touchdown receptions tied the career mark held by former teammate DeAndre Hopkins.

Boyd's and Watkins' final game together will bring smiles to Clemson fans for a long time. In the 2014 Orange Bowl vs. Ohio State, Boyd had 505 yards of total offense and accounted for all six Clemson touchdowns, while Watkins had 16 receptions for 227 yards and two scores. The receptions and yards were the most in the history of the Orange Bowl, a game that dates to 1935.

Clemson beat an Ohio State team that had finished the regular season on a 24-game winning streak. The 40–35 victory led to a No. 7 final ranking for the program, the highest final ranking since Davis and Kinard led the Tigers to the 1981 national championship.

Tony Elliott

There is no certainty Hollywood would accept the script. But if ever produced, the movie would likely be an inspiration to all that watched it. The central character experiences every human emotion, overcomes adversity, realizes dreams, and leaves the viewer smiling as the end is still unfolding. For Tony Elliott, this is no movie. For Tony Elliott, this is his life's journey.

Now Clemson's co–offensive coordinator, Elliott arrived at Clemson after previous stops at South Carolina State and Furman. As a wide receiver, Elliott lettered four times for the Tigers (2000–2003). The young coach has quite a biography early in his career, but it is his path to Clemson that amazes so many.

After lettering in football, basketball, and baseball at James Island (SC) High School, Elliott looked to Furman as the place he would continue his football career. When his plans with the Paladins did not work out, Elliott found himself at the Air Force Prep School. Still not the correct fit, Elliott arrived in Clemson in 1999, thinking his football career was over. He set his sights on an engineering degree.

Convinced by a member of the football team to walk on, Elliott did just that. It did not take long for Elliott to make an impact as he earned a letter in the 2000 season covering kickoffs. Elliott went on to play in 44 games in his career, including four as a starter in 2003. He had two career touchdown receptions, each against Georgia Tech.

Elliott's impact on his teammates and the entire program cannot be measured by statistics. By his senior season of 2003, Elliott had been named the team's "most respected player" in a survey conducted by the *Anderson Independent*. Both players and coaches recognized Elliott's work ethic and leadership. He was named a co-captain of a team that finished 9–4, ranked No. 22, and recorded a win over the highest-ranked opponent in Tigers history—a 26–10 victory over No. 3 Florida State.

In the hotel prior to the South Carolina game that season, Clemson players gathered for one last team meeting before heading to the stadium. It was the weekend before Thanksgiving, and team chaplain Darren Bruce asked each senior player to stand and state something for which they were thankful.

In an unforgettable speech, Elliott thanked his teammates for being his extended family. He told the story of how as a young boy in California, he was in a car accident with his mother and sister. Elliott spoke of the horror of that day as his mother tragically died in the accident. He explained the difficult circumstances involving the relationship with his father, and how he moved east to live with his aunt. Elliott shared with his teammates that while many of them had mothers and fathers traveling to watch them play, he did not. Elliott said his teammates *were* his family. *They* were what he was thankful for.

No one moved or made a sound. Most players never knew the story Elliott had just shared. He concluded by assuring his teammates that the Gamecocks would get his best effort that night and asked that they do the same. The meeting ended in silence.

Clemson won 63–17.

Elliott graduated from Clemson in 2002 with a team-high 3.55 GPA in industrial engineering. Upon leaving Clemson, he put his degree to use and found work as an industrial engineer with Michelin in nearby Anderson. Few could have predicted Elliott would later be reunited with the position coach from his senior season, current Tigers head coach Dabo Swinney.

In 2006 Elliott ventured into college coaching when he joined the South Carolina State staff as an assistant and helped the Bulldogs to consecutive 7–4 seasons in 2006 and 2007. In 2008 Elliott joined Furman's staff, where he worked for three seasons under head coach Bobby Lamb.

Lamb was replaced by Bruce Fowler in December of 2010, and the new Paladins head coach decided to retain Elliott on the Furman staff. However, when Swinney called Elliott the next month, extending an offer to join the Clemson staff, the former Tigers co-captain could not refuse. "I was working as an engineer, but I felt the Lord led me into coaching," said Elliott. "Once I started, I dreamed about Clemson as my ultimate opportunity in coaching."

The offer had special meaning also. When Elliott's mother was killed in front of him during that auto accident in California, the accident took place on Sycamore Drive. Elliott took Swinney to the scene of the accident while they were in California at a convention.

When Swinney was ready to offer Elliott the job, he told him to come over to his house. Swinney lives in Clemson on Sycamore Drive. "I wanted to offer him the job at my house on Sycamore," said Swinney. "I knew that the accident in California had to be the most horrible day of his life. I wanted something great in his life to now happen on Sycamore Drive."

Elliott's coaching career at Clemson is off and running. Clemson has won at least 10 games every year he has been at Clemson, and that includes the 2015 season when the offense he coordinated with Jeff Scott set countless records and became the first offense in the ACC to gain at least 4,000 yards passing and 3,000 yards rushing.

The Legend of Deshaun Watson

It didn't take long for Deshaun Watson to become a legendary figure at Clemson. There was much fanfare when the five-star quarterback recruit committed to Clemson and head coach Dabo Swinney on signing day of 2012 when he had just completed his sophomore football season. He was the most highly recruited signal-caller to sign with Clemson since Steve Fuller in 1975.

There was a tie to Fuller from the start. Watson had worn No. 4 at Gainesville High School in Georgia and wanted to wear that number at Clemson. The only problem was that the number had been retired in honor of Fuller, who was a first-team Academic All-American and third-team AP All-American on the field in 1978. He had led the Clemson resurgence in the late 1970s, including a No. 6 final ranking in 1978 with an 11–1 record.

Swinney had developed a friendship with Fuller and asked about letting Watson wear No. 4 with a special patch. Swinney had seen Michigan honor Tom Harmon's No. 98 a couple of years back by having quarterback Devin Gardner wear 98 with a patch that had Harmon's name on it. Swinney pointed out that the patch would be shown on television and rekindle the memories of Fuller's career, something that had happened with Harmon's career at Michigan.

Fuller agreed with the concept, and thus Watson today has No. 4 on his back with the Fuller patch on his chest.

As a freshman in 2014 he had some memorable moments early in the season. There was a laser touchdown pass to Charone Peake on his first career drive at Georgia. He came off the bench to gain nearly 300 yards of total offense at No. 1 Florida State in his third career game.

He then threw six touchdown passes, a Clemson record, and gained 463 yards of total offense in his first career start against North Carolina. The next week he accounted for four more scores, including a breathtaking whirlybird touchdown run against N.C. State.

Injuries slowed his run to freshman All-America honors as he was limited to just 29 plays over six games between October 11 and November 22. Watson suffered a knee injury against Georgia Tech 18 plays into a game, his first start after suffering a hand injury against Louisville on October 11. While there was speculation about Watson's injury at Georgia Tech, he did not tear the ACL in Atlanta. But he did in practice leading up to the South Carolina game of November 29.

When told the news, Swinney figured his star freshman had no shot of playing against the Gamecocks, who had beaten Clemson five consecutive years. It looked like the Gamecocks jinx might continue. But, after meeting with Clemson doctors and trainers, and presented with a special brace that would in effect act as his ACL, Watson went to Swinney one afternoon and told him he could play.

Swinney met with the Clemson medical team, and they assured him the brace would be effective and that he could not hurt the knee any more. The decision was made to let Watson give it a go.

He started the contest and was effective early. Twice he limped off the field to the concern of Clemson faithful, but his only problem was the knee brace was too tight. There was nothing more wrong with his knee. When he returned each time, it only heightened his legendary status. *Is this kid bionic?*

Deshaun Watson reached legendary status when he quarterbacked the Tigers to a victory over South Carolina in 2014 despite playing with a torn ACL.

In the first half he threw a 53-yard touchdown pass to roommate Artavis Scott and actually scored on a one-yard run himself. Clemson led 21–10 at the half. In the second half he added a 70-yard scoring pass to Scott on a flip pass and scored a second touchdown run. He completed 14-of-19 passes for 269 yards and two scores and added 13 yards rushing and two more scores on the ground for the day.

Clemson ended the streak with a 35–17 victory. As Clemson fans celebrated on the field, Swinney conducted his postgame press conference and told the world Watson had done all that playing with a torn ACL.

It was not a common occurrence, but two Clemson quarterbacks had a history of performing well with a torn ACL. Mike Eppley played the entire 1983 season with a torn ACL, but still finished third in the nation in passing efficiency, the highest finish in that statistical category in Clemson history. Clemson finished with a 9–1–1 record. Tajh Boyd, Clemson's starting quarterback from 2011 to 2013, had played his senior year of high school with a torn ACL and led his team to the state title in Virginia.

Watson comes by his ability to deal with pain and give his best in every area from his mom. Deann Watson is a strong woman who contracted cancer of the tongue when Deshaun was in high school. She spent six months in the Emory Hospital in Atlanta. She went through the treatment and rehabilitation while Watson was going through the football season so it was a tough time for the entire family. Deann's sister has been a great help through the entire ordeal.

But, by the time Deshaun came to Clemson, his mother had made great progress. Her speech is still affected, but she still made it to all of Clemson's games in 2014, Deshaun's freshman year, and still came to games he could not play in due to injury. She wanted the family to show support for the team even though her son was injured.

Dealing with adversity was important for Watson during 2014 when he suffered a shoulder injury in spring practice, injured a hand against Louisville, and eventually suffered a torn ACL at the end of the season.

He sat out spring practice of 2015 as the knee recovered, and there was much speculation as to whether he would be full strength for the beginning of the 2015 season. Head coach Dabo Swinney had no doubt he would be ready. "Deshaun does everything the right way and with the greatest effort, and that was the same way in his rehabilitation. He was always ahead of schedule in his recovery because he was so focused on getting back on the field."

Watson began the season with efficient performances in Clemson wins over Wofford and Appalachian State. He ran the ball only 11 times for 39 yards in those two games, but threw for 442 yards and five scores. Those stats were good at the time, but he would do that in a single game by the end of the season.

In the third game he ran 12 times for 54 yards against Louisville, and the Tigers finished with a 20–17 Thursday night victory.

That set up the epic game with Notre Dame on October 3. It was time to unleash Watson the runner, and the Tigers offensive coaches did that on the first play of the game when he ran for 38 yards. Playing in a torrential downpour, Watson showed his ability as a leader and led Clemson to a 24–22 victory over the sixth-ranked Irish.

The nationally televised prime-time victory brought Clemson to a new level and a No. 6 ranking. The wins continued, including triumphs at Miami and N.C. State when the Tigers scored 114 points over the two games.

Watson's ability as a runner continued to show, and he had at least 100 yards rushing in five of six games at one point. That included 131 yards in the ACC Championship Game against North Carolina, and 145 yards against Oklahoma in the College Football Playoff semifinal game.

After claiming the ACC championship, Watson was named a finalist for the Heisman Trophy. On the trip he was allowed to bring two family guests, his mother and his aunt. It was the first trip to New York for all three. It had been a goal of Watson's to bring his mother and aunt to New York for that award.

The highlight of the trip took place on the Friday night before the award ceremony when the Heisman foundation took the finalists and their entourage on a double-decker bus tour of New York City. Watson sat in the front row of the top deck with Stanford finalist Christian McCaffrey, while Watson's mom and aunt sat in the other two front-row seats. All four were sitting forward with a prime view of New York the entire two hours.

Watson shocked many when he showed up at the Heisman ceremony at the PlayStation Theater wearing a bright red suit. Red? The primary color of Clemson rival Georgia? But he explained to all that he wanted to honor his home town, Gainesville, Georgia, and their football program for giving him his start.

Watson finished third in the Heisman balloting, the highest finish for a Clemson player in history. Derrick Henry of Alabama took the award home. Watson had a landmark season for sure. He won the Davey O'Brien Award and the Manning Award as the top quarterback in the nation and also took home the Archie Griffin Award, an honor presented by the Columbus, Ohio, Touchdown Club in February. It is given to the top player in college football after the bowl games.

One must wonder how the Heisman voting would have gone if the bowl season was included. All Watson did in the bowl season was lead Clemson to a 37–17 victory over Oklahoma in the Orange Bowl by throwing for 187 and rushing for 145 more. He then threw for 405 yards and rushed for 73 more in the National Championship Game against Alabama, a game the Crimson Tide won 45–40.

He finished the season as the only quarterback in history with at least 4,000 yards passing and 1,000 yards rushing. Watson had proven himself on the national stage, the biggest game of the season. While the Tigers did not close the deal, Watson brought great respect to his game and to the Clemson program. His performance was one of the best against a Nick Saban–coached team.

As we write this book, Watson still has at least one more season in a Clemson uniform. It will be interesting to see how far his legend grows.

2015: A Season for the Ages

The 2015 Clemson football season ranks among the best in school history. It was the best in many areas, including victories. Clemson finished with a 14–1 record, was ranked No. 2 in the final polls, and played in the College Football Playoff National Championship Game.

Records were set in all areas, and they were set against one of the toughest schedules in school history. The Tigers finished with five wins over teams that won at least 10 games, the most in school history and the most in the nation. There were eight wins over teams that finished with a winning record and only Alabama had more across the country. The only goal they did not reach was winning the national championship, something the 1981 team did accomplish with a 12–0 record.

Here are some of the storylines, in chronological order, that made the 2015 season special:

Dealing with Death

In the middle of August, while preparing for the 2015 season, head coach Dabo Swinney had to deal with the death of his father, Ervil Swinney. Father and son had a distant relationship when Dabo was young but had reconciled and were close late in his dad's life. In fact, in the summer of 2015, Ervil spent three months living at Dabo's home as he went through chemo treatment.

Swinney gave his dad's eulogy in Pelham, Alabama, in mid-August, and it was a long, heartfelt, and emotional eulogy from Swinney, who grew up in the town where his father worked for many years in the local hardware store. It was also where he died, working at his desk in the store. He told how much his dad was looking forward to the football season, and he had a picture of his dad cheering on the Tigers at a game the previous year in his office.

One game Ervil was looking forward to was the Notre Dame game on October 3. He really wanted to see his son coach against the team that had been the most famous in the country when he was growing up.

So, when Swinney had the game clinched, he went to one knee as the rain poured down. He appeared to be emotional in those final moments. In the postgame interview, he revealed that he was thinking of his dad and how happy he would be looking down from heaven.

Mike Williams One and Done

The first touchdown of the 2015 season was scored by junior receiver Mike Williams on a four-yard touchdown pass from Deshaun Watson. As he made his second catch of the opening offensive drive of the season he crashed into the goal post at the east end zone of the stadium.

He lay still near that post after making the catch.

Medical personnel came to the field, and it was determined that a neck brace needed to be applied and that Williams needed to be taken from the field on a stretcher. Further tests revealed that Williams, Clemson's top returning receiver from 2014 in terms of yardage, did not have a spinal injury, but he did have a crack in his neck.

The injury ended Williams season, and he was forced to watch Clemson's incredible run from the sideline. But he will return for 2016 and hopes to lead the Tigers' receiving corps back to the national championship game.

Jay Guillermo to the Rescue

Jay Guillermo had a difficult spring of 2015. He suffered from sleep apnea, depression, and high blood pressure. The problems led to too much alcohol, tremendous weight gain, and a meeting with Coach Swinney in January.

Guillermo, who was listed as the backup center at the time, told Swinney he needed to leave school and get his act together. If he didn't, he might not come back. He had had some suicidal thoughts. Guillermo went home to his family in North Carolina and received great guidance from experts in the field, and most importantly, his grandfather, Ron Greene, a former high school football coach.

Guillermo made great progress psychologically and physically. He got back in shape by chopping wood in the forest, and by the summer contacted Swinney and asked if he could come back.

He did and worked back into the team activities. By August he was back at practice. By the third game of the year he was in the starting lineup.

Returning two-year starter Ryan Norton suffered a knee injury in the second game of the year against Appalachian State and Guillermo got the nod at starting center for the first ACC game at Louisville. He responded and was named ACC Offensive Lineman of the Week in three games at midseason. He was the first three-time Clemson selection since 2009 when Thomas Austin was chosen. That was fitting since Austin had been a player Guillermo idolized, hanging his picture on his bedroom wall in his youth. He was named second-team All-ACC at the end of the season.

Now Guillermo looks to be Clemson's emotional leader on offense for 2016.

A Win for the Ages

Clemson and Notre Dame had not played in Clemson's Memorial Stadium since 1977. That November 12 the Irish trailed by 10 points entering the fourth quarter. But Joe Montana led a comeback, and Notre Dame won 21–17. It was the only close game Notre Dame played over the last nine games of the season on its way to winning the 1977 national championship.

Now, as No. 6 Notre Dame came to Clemson in 2015 to meet the 11th-ranked Tigers, the game had the same feel. This would be a game that would have an impact on the national championship as both teams were undefeated entering this October 3 game.

A hurricane was in the area, and there was talk about moving the time of the game, but with *ESPN College GameDay* in town and the weather forecasters deeming the game safe enough to play, the night game went on as scheduled.

Clemson got off to a great start behind Deshaun Watson and the play of defensive end Shaq Lawson, who had 3.5 tackles for loss in the first quarter. But, just as the Irish had done in 1977, Notre Dame made a fourth-quarter comeback. Clemson had a 21–3 lead entering the final period, but the Irish cut the margin to 24–16 with nine minutes left and had the ball with under two minutes remaining.

The Irish then scored on a touchdown pass from DeShone Kiser to Torii Hunter Jr. (son of the major league baseball player) with just seven seconds left. The Irish went for the tying two-point conversion, but Carlos Watkins, Kevin Dodd, and Ben Boulware combined to stop Kiser on the attempt, and Clemson sealed the victory.

In one of the great media notes in history, Clemson linebacker B.J. Goodson had two defensive takeaways in the fourth period. It was the first time since 1979 that a Clemson player had forced two takeaways in the fourth quarter of a game Clemson won by seven points or less. When it happened in 1979 Terry Kinard did it, ironically against Notre Dame—the last time the two teams had played.

Dabo Swinney coached the Tigers to the College Football Playoff Championship Game in 2015. An October win over Notre Dame put Clemson in the title picture.

After the game, in an interview with ESPN's Heather Cox, Swinney told the national television audience, "This game was BYOG, Bring Your Own Guts." It was a comment that went viral, was turned in to T-shirts, and was the Tigers' calling card the rest of the season.

This Defense Might Be Okay After All

Clemson moved up to No. 6, replacing Notre Dame in the national polls the next week. While the media gave Clemson great credit for its win over Notre Dame, many of them thought the Tigers would be upset by Georgia Tech the next week.

Tech had been ranked in the top 10 in the preseason and was still ranked that high before losing two weeks earlier at Notre Dame. Now Clemson was trying to win the round-robin between the three schools.

Tech had been a Clemson killer in recent years, at least in games played in Atlanta, where Swinney has never won as head coach. Tech was also the team that had beaten Swinney at Death Valley in his first game as Clemson coach in 2008.

But this 43–24 victory on October 10 was another example that this Clemson team was different. This was not a team that would have a letdown after a thrilling victory over the winningest program in the history of college football.

Clemson's offense exploded for 33 points in the first half and finished the game with 537 yards of total offense, including 265 yards passing by Watson. But this day belonged to a Clemson defense that allowed Georgia Tech just 71 yards rushing. This was the vaunted Yellow Jackets running attack that had averaged nearly 300 yards a game. But Clemson's defensive effort held Georgia Tech to the second fewest by a Paul Johnson–coached team.

Dominating Like 1981

With a 6–0 record and a No. 6 ranking by both polls, some were starting to make comparisons between this Clemson team and the 1981 national champions. There were already many similarities between the two teams. Both teams had started the season with wins over Wofford by similar scores, each on September 5. Both had quarterbacks with single-digit numbers who were natives of the state of Georgia and came from cities just 35 miles apart.

The 1981 Clemson team was captained by Jeff Davis. Now his twin sons were linebackers on the 2015 team. The same goes for Bill Smith, whose son, Cannon, was on the 2015 Clemson team.

Then came the seventh game of the season at Miami. The game was played in Miami, the city where Clemson had won the national championship with a victory over Nebraska in the Orange Bowl. Clemson played perhaps its best game of the season, considering Miami would finish 2015 with eight wins. The Tigers scored 21 points in each of the first two quarters for a 42–0 halftime lead.

The two teams had exchanged verbal jabs during pregame warmups, and Swinney held his team on the field for the first few minutes of intermission so there would be no altercation as the two teams went to the locker rooms.

Those pregame verbal spars had obviously fired Clemson up in taking this dominant lead. Clemson won the game 58–0, tied for the largest margin of victory in an ACC game in Clemson history. It tied the record of 58 points (82–24) against Wake Forest in, you guessed it, 1981.

Finally Beating the Seminoles

Only one player on the current Clemson team had experienced a win over Florida State. That was redshirt graduate student Charone Peake, who had played as a true freshman in Clemson's 2011 victory at Clemson.

The winner of this game had been the Atlantic Division champion every year since 2008, and with both in the top 20, this would be the case again in 2015.

Clemson had been ranked No. 1 in the nation according to the first College Football Playoff poll the previous Tuesday evening. After doing an interview on the ESPN Bus with fellow Alabama graduate Rece Davis, Swinney said upon exiting the bus, "Well at least I will be ranked No. 1 by someone for a week in my career."

It would be a habit by the end of the season.

Dalvin Cook got Florida State off to a great start with a 75-yard run in the first 45 seconds of the game. But Clemson's defense did not allow a touchdown the rest of the game.

Watson showed his abilities as a runner like never before with 107 yards rushing on 16 attempts, and Wayne Gallman added 103 yards and the game-clinching touchdown in the fourth quarter of Clemson's 23–13 victory.

Record-Setting Seniors

Senior Day was special when the Tigers defeated Wake Forest on November 21 at Memorial Stadium. The 33–13 victory gave Clemson an

11–0 record for the season, including an 8–0 mark in ACC play. It was the first time Clemson won eight ACC games in a season. It was the 43rd win for the senior class, breaking the record of 42 set by the 2014 seniors. It also gave this group a record for wins over ACC teams in a four-year period and in home games. It was Clemson's 16th straight home win, also a school record. On the day, Clemson gained 552 yards of total offense, the seventh straight game the offense had gained at least 500 yards, an all-time-record school streak.

One of the highlights of the day took place during pregame when senior Daniel Stone proposed to his girlfriend when he reached the sideline after rubbing Howard's Rock and running down the hill for the last time.

She said yes.

The World's Largest Pizza Party

Clemson finished off the regular season with a 37–32 win over rival South Carolina in Columbia, the Tigers' first win in Columbia under Dabo Swinney.

The next Saturday the Tigers headed to Charlotte to take on North Carolina, a team that had made even more of a resurgence than Clemson. The Tar Heels had been just 6–7 the year before, but had risen to 11–1 overall, including an 8–0 record in the ACC. It was the first meeting of two 8–0 teams in ACC Championship Game history.

But the Tigers had a lot more to lose than the ACC championship. Clemson was ranked No. 1 in the nation in all three polls, including the important College Football Playoff poll.

The pregame predictions called for a high-scoring game, and the two teams did not disappoint as the Tigers came away with a 45–37 victory. Clemson gained 319 yards on the ground and 289 yards through the air as Wayne Gallman had a career-high 187 yards rushing and Watson followed with 131. Artavis Scott had his best game in a month with seven catches for 96 yards and a score.

The next day, a Sunday, Clemson held a pizza party for 30,000 people. During a press conference earlier in the season, Swinney was asked about his team's No. 1 ranking. He told the media that the ranking didn't mean anything, but if his team is No. 1 on December 7, the day the committee announced its final rankings, he would have pizza for everyone in Death Valley. "We will have the biggest pizza party you ever saw."

Swinney might not have thought out the entire commitment he made, but director of athletics Dan Radakovich backed Swinney up, and arrangements were made with a local pizza distributor to provide a slice of pizza for all who attended.

The Fake Punt

The College Football Playoff committee made Clemson the No. 1 team in the rankings for the sixth straight week and matched the Tigers in the Orange Bowl with No. 4 seed Oklahoma.

A lot of Clemson fans were disappointed when the pairings were announced because the Tigers had humiliated the Sooners 40–6 the previous year in the Russell Athletic Bowl. Think the Sooners would be fired up for this one, a game that had 10 times the meaning of the previous year?

Oklahoma was a much better team in 2015, and they were much stronger at quarterback with Baker Mayfield, who had better stats in some categories than Watson during the regular season and had made the Football Writers Association All-America team ahead of Watson.

There were some words between the two teams in media interviews. Things came to a head when 25 players from each team attended the Orange Bowl Luncheon the day before the game. When both teams were dismissed, but before coaches and administrators left the luncheon, the two teams got into an argument. The Oklahoma players had already boarded their bus, and one of them shouted something and gave a gesture to Shaq Lawson. Lawson responded, and some of the Clemson players joined in. Others, including senior leader Eric Mac Lain, stood back and just laughed.

No Oklahoma player left their bus and no Clemson player entered the Oklahoma bus. No punches or even pushes were exchanged. There was just an exchange of testosterone.

On gameday Oklahoma took an early lead. Clemson gained the momentum back on the play of the year by the Tigers. Trailing 7–3 with the ball on the Oklahoma 44, Dabo Swinney called a fake punt on fourth-and-4 called "UCONN." The play was a pass from punter Andy Teasdall to defensive tackle Christian Wilkins, who played high school football in Connecticut. The 31-yard play gave Clemson a first down, and a subsequent touchdown.

Clemson shut out the Sooners in the second half on the way to a 37–17 victory and a berth in the National Championship Game against Alabama.

51–0 When Leading Entering the Fourth Quarter

The College Football Playoff National Championship Game against Alabama at the conclusion of the 2015 season was a dream matchup for Clemson head coach Dabo Swinney. An Alabama graduate who has a piece of the old AstroTurf Bear Bryant walked on at Legion Field in Birmingham in his garage, this was the only way to end this magic season.

Alabama was coached by Nick Saban, who had a summer home in Florida in the same area as Swinney. They had actually gone fishing and played golf together the previous summer, never knowing they would be matched in the National Championship Game seven months later.

Derrick Henry started the scoring with a 50-yard touchdown run. That was predictable, as he had just won the Heisman Trophy a month earlier. Clemson responded with two touchdown passes from Watson to Hunter Renfrow, one of 31 yards and one of 11 yards. That was not predictable, in that Renfrow was a walk-on who played high school football a year earlier. He beat two four-star defensive backs on the plays.

The game was tied at halftime 14–14, and Clemson had a 24–21 lead entering the fourth quarter. At the end of the third, ESPN showed the following graphic: "Clemson has won 51 consecutive games when leading entering the fourth quarter."

It was the all-time television announcer jinx.

The game turned in the fourth quarter when Saban gambled and called for an onside kick after it had kicked a field goal to tie the score at 24–24. "We hadn't stopped them, and their quarterback had been outstanding," said Saban. "We had to do something to change the momentum."

That play in fact did change the momentum, and Alabama scored on its next possession. The teams exchanged four fourth-quarter touchdowns, including a 95-yard kickoff return by Kenyan Drake, a play that gave the Tide an 11-point lead for the first time.

Alabama won 45–40, but the Tigers had gained a lot of national credibility. In particular Watson had become a household name as he passed for 405 yards and rushed for 73. The 478 yards of total offense set a record for a national championship game, and the Tigers gained 550 yards as a team. It was a game for the ages, one that enhanced the heritage of Clemson football history.

The following chapters document many of the other great performances and legends that have made Clemson one of the top programs in the nation.

CHAPTER 2
HOW IT ALL STARTED

The Meeting That Started Football

On a still, balmy, September night in 1896, on the young and undeveloped Clemson College campus, a group of cadets met in the barracks to discuss the feasibility of organizing a football team to represent the all-male military school. Other state schools had football, and the question was raised—why not Clemson?

From this group, three students were appointed to consult engineering professor Walter M. Riggs as to the management of a football team and to ask his aid as coach. It was only appropriate Riggs would coach the Clemson Tigers. Riggs originally came to Clemson from Auburn. He graduated with top honors in 1892 with a BS degree in electrical and mechanical engineering. At Auburn, he was captain and catcher of the baseball team as well as the manager and left end of the football team. He also served as class president and was the director of the glee club. Upon his graduation at Auburn, Riggs was an assistant to the president of the college until 1896, and then he made his trek to Clemson.

Walter Riggs could easily be called the father of Clemson Athletics. He coached the football program at Clemson, not only because he had football experience, but he was also one of only two people on the Clemson campus to have ever seen a football game when the sport started in 1896. (The other person was Frank Tompkins, who played in the backfield on Clemson's first team in 1896.)

The interest in Clemson football dates to the founding of the college. Clemson University was established in 1889, and just seven years later the school had a football team. Only Miami (FL) and N.C. State started programs sooner after their founding, among current ACC schools.

Walter Riggs Comes to Clemson

In an article written by Walter Riggs several years after he helped found the football program, he describes his arrival at Clemson:

In 1896, Clemson College was quite a different looking place to what it is now. The campus was more or less covered with underbrush. There were no well-defined paths and very poor roads. There was only one barracks and only three other principle buildings, the Main Building, the Chemical Laboratory, and the Mechanical Hall. The Agricultural Laboratories and classrooms were in the main building. The post office was a little one-room wooden house to the right of the road as you pass the Mechanical Hall, and about halfway between the road and the Calhoun Mansion. On the grass field in front of this little post office, football had its beginnings.

When leaving Auburn, I had "sworn off" from athletics. But when the fall of 1896 came around and the Clemson boys wanted to get up a football team, the "call of the wild" was too strong, and again I found myself in a football suit, and the single-handed coach of the first Clemson football team.

There was only one man in college who had ever seen a football and that was Frank Tompkins. The players had to be taught everything. They had never seen a gridiron or a football game, and had no idea what to do or how to stand.

The first game was with Furman University in Greenville, and it was the first time the Clemson eleven lined up on a full-sized gridiron. Furman, who had been playing since 1889, was confident of victory—Clemson won the game 14 to 6.

In looking back over a service of several years, I regard the introduction of intercollegiate football into Clemson College as one of the most valuable steps in the development of the institution. Long before its graduates could spread its fame as an institution of learning, its football teams had made the name of Clemson College known and respected throughout the nation.

In a well-rounded college life, play is just as indispensable to healthy growth as is work. Athletics should not interfere with studies, nor should studies exclude athletics, each should have a proper and legitimate place in the thought and life of the students.

Riggs stepped down as football coach after the first season because the players wanted him to devote all of his time to being a professor in the engineering department. Clemson athletics and Riggs, however, could not be split. Although not given the title, Riggs also was the equivalent of an athletic director, managing money and making contracts with other teams as he served as president of the Athletic Association.

Riggs could easily be called a loyal man, as he answered the need of the Clemson football team again in 1899. The Clemson Athletic Association was low on money and could not afford to hire a coach. So Riggs once again answered the call of the school and became the coach of the 1899 team for free.

Riggs later became president of Clemson on March 7, 1911, and on October 2, 1915, a new football stadium with other athletic facilities was named in his honor as Riggs Field. It is currently the home of the Tigers soccer teams. In two years of coaching the football team, Riggs guided the Tigers to a career record of 6–3.

After starting the Clemson program and coaching the team in 1896 and 1899, he headed the Clemson Athletic Association and was a key administrator of the Southern Intercollegiate Athletic Association (an early southern athletic conference with several schools as members).

The First Game

There is something to be said about the "old college try."

On October 5, 1896, Clemson began practice on a 50-by-200-foot field in front of the college. It is believed that this field was located where the Walter Cox Plaza is located today (the area between Tillman Hall and the Trustee House) on campus.

The first football team had training rules to be followed to the letter. They were as follows:

1. Will report promptly to all practices prescribed by the coach unless physically disabled or prevented from attending on account of college duties.
2. That in any of the above instances, we will report the facts beforehand, when possible to the coach.
3. That we will not, without the consent of coach and trainer, eat anything at any time except at the training table; will not drink an alcoholic beverage or spirituous liquors or soda water.
4. Will not use tobacco in any form or engage in any form of dissipation.
5. Will retire not later than 11:00 PM unless permission is granted by coach and trainer or prevented by college duties.
6. Will obey the directions of the coach and captain on the field of play as before specified, and use our influence to promote discipline both on and off the field of play.

Practice continued, and as one description put it, "A hardy group of early Tigers who cared little for their skin and bones turned out for practice and began enthusiastically slamming each other to the rock-strewn practice field."

Without any capital, the team's first equipment was personal property, but other necessary equipment was purchased with money, which was willingly contributed by members of the faculty and student body.

Equipment in the early years consisted of very little padding except at the knees and elbows. Tightly fitting and laced leather or canvas jackets were the main bodily protection against the crashing effects of mass plays and left little for a tackler to grab. A few had nose and shin guards. Due to the lack of helmets and head protection, they wore long hair to protect the head.

After gruelling practices, the first-ever Clemson gameday finally arrived. On October 31, 1896, Clemson traveled to Furman more than likely by train. This was the first time that many of the Clemson players had seen a full-sized gridiron.

George Swygert, center on the first Clemson football team, recalls the Furman game and the first season as follows: "With Professor Riggs as our coach, we got in shape fairly well. Our first game was with Furman, the biggest men I have ever seen, and believe it or not we won that game! We had a few trick plays. One was when the play ended near the sidelines, our lightest end would hide the ball under his sweater, and as the two teams moved toward the center of the field for the next play, he appeared to be injured, then when things were clear, he would make a bee-line for the goal. This worked maybe once a game; it worked against Furman our first game."

Very few details of the Clemson-Furman game are known, but it is known that Charlie Gentry scored Clemson's first touchdown in history. The Tigers defeated Furman 14–6 at Greenville, South Carolina.

Clemson's upset win over Furman was a monumental milestone for the school. Furman was considered at the time an experienced team having played the game since 1889 (the year Clemson was founded).

A member of Clemson's first football team, Shack Shealy was the head coach of the Tigers in 1904. He holds the distinction of being the only former Clemson player to coach his alma mater. Shealy coached Clemson one year and guided the Tigers to a 3–3–1 record overall, which included wins over Alabama, Georgia, and Tennessee.

CHAPTER 3
HEISMAN AT CLEMSON AND OTHER EARLY HEROES

Bringing Heisman to Clemson

Before he came to be known as one of the best coaches in college football history, John Heisman was a tomato farmer somewhere in Texas. President Riggs once recounted how he brought Heisman back to football:

> In the spring of 1894, I was a graduate manager of the football team at Auburn. It fell to my lot to find a coach for the season of 1895, and as the University of Pennsylvania had that year one of the most successful as well as originial teams in the East, I wrote to Carl Williams, the Penn '94 captain, asking him to suggest a suitable man. He replied, recommending J.W. Heisman, an ex-Penn player, and an old coach of his while at Oberlin. He did not know Heisman's whereabouts at the time, but he had his home address.
>
> After several weeks, I got into communication with Mr. Heisman, finding him in Texas engaged in raising tomatoes. It seems that he was only an indifferent farmer and, having sunk about all of his capital in the tomato venture, he was glad to go back to his old love, and we readily came to terms. The salary was, as I remember it, in the neighborhood of $500.00, and we thought that figure high.
>
> I shall never forget my first impressions of Heisman while I met him at the depot in Auburn. Looking at his rather small stature and begrimed as he was with the travel stain of a long journey, I could not but feel that we had again made a mistake in the selection of a coach—we had made several before.
>
> But it did not require many days of practice to show that the Auburn team was in the hands of a master, and with the decisive defeat of the University of Georgia at the Exposition Grounds, which closed our season of 1895, we felt that in Heisman we had found the right man.

I left Auburn that winter to ally myself with Clemson College, then the newest of the A and M colleges. No football had ever been played there and only one student had ever seen the game played. There on a little field only one-third size, overlooked by the white-columned homestead of the great John C. Calhoun, the first football scrimmage took place in the fall of 1896.

From that first kick, it was a four-year struggle to lay a foundation that might enable me to realize an ambition that I had cherished ever since leaving Auburn, to get Heisman at Clemson. By 1899 the Clemson football team had risen steadily until its material was equal to that of any southern college, and the time had come to put on the long-planned finishing touch. I went to Birmingham to compete with Auburn of Heisman's services, and came back with a contract.

During the four years that Heisman had coached at Clemson, I have not missed 10 practices nor a single match game. I have had no closer person or athletic friend than Heisman, and I know his methods thoroughly, therefore I feel that in speaking of him both as a man and as a football coach I am speaking from an actual and intimate knowledge. As a coach there is no other like Heisman.

Heisman at Tigertown

A name synonymous with not only the early years of Clemson football but the collegiate game is John Heisman. A stern disciplinarian, he expected his players to be of high character and performance both on the football field and in the classroom.

Heisman's ingenuity in originating plays was one of his strong points. He usually had something new up his sleeve for every game. It is said he used everything in the book and a lot that was not. Coach C.R.

John Heisman coached at Clemson from 1900 to 1903. He led Clemson to an undefeated season in 1900. The famed Heisman Trophy is named in his honor.

"Bob" Williams said it availed little to case one of Heisman's games, for he rarely used the same trick twice. As he often introduced new plays before each game, he had little use for players that could not quickly learn his signal system and remember the intricate and changing plays. This eliminated much otherwise eligible material.

Heisman used very few substitutes (three or four, at most), even with the 35-minute halves. This may have been due to scarcity of first-class material, or the expense of travel and upkeep and extra equipment. Also the rules of the game limited return to the game. A player had to have stamina to remain in for the full 70 minutes of the game.

Heisman coached the Tigers from 1900 to 1903 and was responsible for putting the Clemson name in the annals of the great early collegiate teams. He invented the hidden-ball trick, the handoff, the double lateral, and the flea flicker. He pioneered the forward pass, originated the center snap (previously, the center would roll the ball on the ground to the quarterback), and coined the word *hike*.

Heisman took Clemson to a 19–3–2 record in his four seasons. His .833 winning percentage is still the best in Clemson history. He was also the Clemson baseball coach from 1901 to 1904.

Clemson was a powerhouse during his tenure and was a most feared opponent. His secret was that he depended on smart, quick players rather than large size and brawn. Another favorite Heisman story was the speech he used to make before a season began. Heisman would face his recruits holding a football. "What is it?" he would sharply ask. Then he would tell his players, "A football is a prolate spheroid, an elongated sphere—in which the outer leather casing is drawn up tightly over a somewhat smaller rubber tubing." Then after a long pause, he would say, "Better to have died as a small boy than to fumble this football."

Heisman broke down football into these proportions: talent, 25 percent; mentality, 20 percent; aggressiveness, 20 percent; speed, 20 percent; and weight, 15 percent. He considered coaching as being a master-commander, a dictator even. According to Heisman, the coach has no time to say "please" or "mister," and "he must be occasionally severe, arbitrary, and something of a czar."

On November 29, 1900, Clemson defeated Alabama 35–0, which allowed Heisman's team to finish the season undefeated with a 6–0 record. This was Clemson's first undefeated team and was the only team to win all of its games in a season until the 1948 squad went 11–0. The

Tigers only allowed two touchdowns the entire 1900 season and were the Southern Intercollegiate Athletic Association champions.

Clemson opened the 1901 season with a 122–0 win over Guilford. The Tigers averaged 30 yards per play and a touchdown every 1:26. The first half lasted 20 minutes, while the second half lasted only 10. Legend has it that every man on the Clemson team scored a TD in this game.

The Guilford captain was so distraught over the way his team had played. "We missed everything today, tackles and blocks. One thing we won't miss is the train back home."

More Heisman Stories

In 1902 the trick of all tricks was played on Georgia Tech and their followers by John Heisman, who told the story:

> We had already won a couple of games, and word drifted to Clemson that Georgia Tech would spare nothing to beat us. When the train with the Clemson team, bag, and baggage arrived in Atlanta the day before the game, the Tech supporters made it a point to entertain our players royally.
>
> The Tech supporters marveled at the ease with which they were able to get our players to sneak out that night and participate in the wild parties around town. There was quite a lot of eating and drinking, and the more the Clemson men indulged in such pastime the more were the Tech men willing to back with money their belief that they would win the next day. Boy, did we clean up the Tech money. Clemson won 44–5. The Tech people wondered at the hardiness of the Clemson men after a night of revelry, until they discovered that Coach Heisman had sent a bunch of bohunks to Atlanta with the team's equipment and kept the varsity at Lula, Georgia, a small town some miles from Atlanta, the night before the game.

In the Furman game on October 24, 1902, Clemson defeated Furman 28–0. But how Clemson set up one touchdown was quite interesting.

Heisman made use of the handoff or lateral slightly backward pass, as the forward pass was against the rules in that day. It seems that an oak tree stood a few feet inside the sideline on the Furman playing field, which for sentimental reasons had not been removed. Observing this, Heisman instructed the quarterback, "If a line of scrimmage occurrs near this tree, signal for a lateral pass, from one back to another back to pass or run between the tree and the sideline." The ruse worked so well, a long gain was made that set the stage for a touchdown.

On November 27, 1902, Clemson played in the snow for the first time in a game against Tennessee. The Tigers won the game 11–0 and claimed the Southern Intercollegiate Athletic Association (SIAA) crown. The SIAA had several southern colleges and universities as members, including many current ACC and SEC teams.

Heisman is the only Clemson coach in any sport in school history to win an athletic event and win a lady's hand in marriage on the same day. On October 28, 1903, Heisman coached the Tigers to a 24–0 win over N.C. State in a game played at the Fairgrounds in Columbia, South Carolina. Later that day, he married the former Evelyn Barksdale in the same city. That actually might not have proven to be a good day in Clemson football history. According to legend, Evelyn liked the bright lights of Atlanta better than the small-town atmosphere of Clemson. At the end of the 1903 season, Heisman left Clemson for Georgia Tech.

In his final season of 1903, Clemson defeated Georgia Tech 73–0 on October 17, 1903. Clemson rushed the ball 55 times for 660 yards, while Tech ran the ball 35 times and collected 28 yards. The second half was shortened to 15 minutes.

The man, whose name graces the famous trophy that each year honors the best player in college football, holds the distinction of building the foundation of Clemson's football tradition.

Clemson's "First Bowl Game"

On November 24, 1903, Clemson participated in its "First Bowl Game." The game between Clemson and Cumberland was billed as the game to decide the "Championship of the South," as the winner would be the champion of the SIAA. The SIAA crown was a formidable title in the day, as "there were many collegiate powers prowling the playing fields of the South."

Although it was not officially a modern postseason extravaganza similar to what football fans enjoy today, the 1903 Clemson-Cumberland game had some of the criteria of being Clemson's first bowl game.

Clemson was considered the best in the Atlantic Coast region that season, as the Tigers had defeated Georgia, Georgia Tech, N.C. State, and Davidson. The only loss came at the hands of North Carolina. Clemson had outscored its opponents 156–11, including a 73–0 win over Georgia Tech.

Cumberland was considered the best team in the western part of the southern region, as it had defeated powers such as Vanderbilt, Tennessee, and Sewanee, and had scored 304 points.

Originally, the two teams' seasons would have drawn to a close in early November, but the interest surrounding college football to decide which was the best football team in the South could not be ignored by players on both sides, not to mention the fans. The result was Clemson and Cumberland officials agreeing to meet on November 26, in Montgomery, Alabama.

As with today's bowl games, a contract was signed, and the game was to take place at a neutral site and on a holiday, Thanksgiving Day. The contract, drawn up just two weeks before the game, stated that the contest was to be played at Oak Park in Montgomery. The game was to begin promptly at 3:00 PM and end at 5:00 PM sharp.

The game had added significance, as it was the Tigers' first opportunity to solidify itself as a southern power, as this was only the eighth year Clemson had fielded a football team.

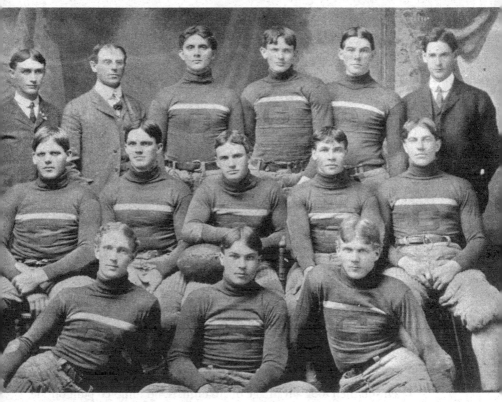

The 1903 Tigers were named Champions of the South.

It would be a battle of Cumberland's backfield of giants charging the Clemson line and a battle of Clemson's smaller, swifter backs making long runs around the end. The average height and weight of the Clemson starting 11 was 5′9½″ and 163½ pounds. Cumberland was the bigger team, as the average height and weight was 5′11″ and 172 pounds.

Some interesting notes on some of the members of Clemson's 1903 football team included: halfback Fritz Furtick and Jock Hanvey were also track stars for the Tigers; quarterback John Maxwell was the catcher on the Tigers baseball team; right end Hope Sadler was Clemson's record holder in the broad jump and the 440-yard dash; left end C.V. Sitton was named All-Southern end on the 1902 team and was recognized as the best college baseball pitcher in the South and later pitched in the majors for Cleveland in 1909; J.A. Forsyth, a right guard, had played every down for the last three years as a Tiger; and J.A. McKeown was Clemson's largest player on the 1903 team, as he was 6'2" and weighed 194 pounds.

Cumberland dominated the game in the early going, as the Bulldogs jumped to an early 11–0 lead. Cumberland's first score was made by line plunges eight minutes into the game. Fullback E.L. Minton scored from a short distance, and M.O. Bridges kicked the extra point, giving Cumberland a 6–0 lead (touchdowns were worth five points then, while extra points were worth one point). Four minutes later, Cumberland struck again as halfback J.A. Head crossed the goal line and M.O. Bridges failed to convert on the extra point.

After a 10-minute halftime, Cumberland kicked off to Clemson. The Tigers' John Maxwell took the ball at his own 10-yard line and raced 100 yards to score Clemson's first touchdown of the game (the fields were 110 yards in length in 1903). The extra point was no good, and Cumberland led 11–5.

Clemson then took advantage of a Cumberland fumbled punt on the Bulldogs' 35-yard line late in the game. With less than a minute to go in the contest, darkness hovered over the field and the hundreds of spectators who had braved the cold afternoon were quiet, anxiously awaiting the last play of the game. Clemson had one last chance, and of course Cumberland was expecting a trick play.

"Twenty-five, eighty-six, three, fourteen—hike!" rang out Maxwell's voice as he gave signals for the last play. After the ball was centered, a Clemson man dressed in a gold jersey was seen with the ball unexpectedly running up the middle through Cumberland's defense for 35 yards and into the end zone with little if any interference.

Fritz Furtrick, the Tigers' right halfback, had scored the tying touchdown by simply running up the middle over center as time expired. Jock

Hanvey kicked the extra point (as two-point conversions were not legal at that time). The game was over and Clemson and Cumberland had tied 11–11. The Tigers were co-champions of the south and the SIAA. It was the third conference title for Clemson as the Tigers had won the 1900 and 1902 championships.

When word reached Clemson that the game had ended in a tie, the Clemson students and local townspeople built a bonfire and paraded around campus. Then came the dispute for the coveted game ball. The ball always goes to the winning team, but the score was a tie. Captain Suddarth of Cumberland insisted on Captain Sadler of Clemson taking the trophy, while Captain Sadler was equally as insistent that Captain Suddarth should have the ball. A compromise was finally reached after 10 minutes. The ball would go to Patrick J. Sweeny, the policeman, who had been efficiently guarding the entrance to the sidelines by warning the media, substitutes, and fans to "get down in front" so the spectators could see the game.

The shared title would be bittersweet, as this turned out to be John Heisman's last game as the Tigers' head coach—he accepted Georgia Tech's head coaching job later that night. Heisman concluded his Clemson coaching career with a player scoring on the last play of his final game.

From this touchdown play on a cold, Thanksgiving afternoon in Montgomery, Alabama, a bowl tradition was started, and Clemson established itself not only as a southern power but as a national power when bowl games are played.

Jim Lynah—A Second Chance

An early Clemson football star, Jim Lynah made the most of his second chance. Lynah was born in Charleston, South Carolina, and grew up in Savannah, Georgia. He was a two-year starter for head coach John Heisman at right end for the Tigers in 1900 and 1901. The

1900 team was Clemson's first undefeated team and also SIAA champion. The Tigers were 6–0 that season and rolled over teams, winning by scores of 64–0 (vs. Davidson), 51–0 (South Carolina), 39–5 (Georgia), 35–0 (Alabama), 21–0 (Wofford), and 12–5 (Virginia Tech), surrendering just 10 points the entire year. The 1901 team finished 3–1–1, and Heisman's Tigers defeated Guilford 122–0 and Georgia 29–5.

Lynah was about to graduate from Clemson in June of 1902. To add merriment to the occasion of his upcoming graduation, he and some others "borrowed" a turkey from Clemson professor William Shannon Morrison's farm. They had a fine celebratory turkey dinner at the expense of the bird owned by Professor Morrison. The guilty participants were caught, and Lynah, the ringleader in this prank, was expelled from school the week before graduation.

In the fall of 1902, Lynah enrolled at Cornell and began college again where he was regarded as one of the top players in the East and captained the 1904 team under Hall of Fame coach Pop Warner. He played primarily the position of quarterback and was a member of the Quill and Dagger society as well as Sigma Phi. He was described as a "powerful runner who was dangerous with the ball."

After graduating from Cornell in 1905, with a degree in mechanical and electrical engineering, Lynah joined the construction department of the E.I. DuPont Company as an electrical engineer. In 1922, 20 years after he was to have graduated from Clemson, the class of 1902 had a reunion, and the school presented Lynah with a diploma from Clemson. In the registrar's office, he is indicated as having received a bachelor of science degree in engineering.

That same year he started work at General Motors in Detroit, Michigan, and for the next several years proved to be an ingenious asset for the company. At GM, Lynah directed the general purchasing and manufacturing staffs, and at the young age of 48, he retired to his Savannah home in 1929.

A year later he was appointed chairman of a committee for the expansion and development of the College of Engineering by the Cornell University Board of Trustees. In 1935 Lynah was named the first full-time director of athletics at Cornell and served in this capacity until 1944.

While Athletic Director at Cornell, Lynah still had time to perform a major service for his country. In July of 1940, with World War II already started in Europe, he took a dollar-a-year job as coordinator of speci-fications for the nation's huge national defense program serving under William S. Knudson, chairman of the National Defense Commission. Also during World War II, Lynah ran the Brunswick Shipbuilding Company in Brunswick, Georgia.

During his tenure, he put Cornell athletics on a sound financial basis. He took the lead in organizing what became the Eastern College Athletic Conference (ECAC). He instituted the plan for a central office of the ECAC and became its first chairman. He was also a strong pro-ponent for a stronger Ivy League. The ECAC is a college athletic confer-ence comprising schools that compete in 19 sports. It has 303 member institutions in NCAA Divisions I, II, and III. Most member schools are in other conferences as well, but through the ECAC they are able to par-ticipate in sports that their main conferences do not offer. Its headquar-ters are located in Centerville, Massachusetts, on Cape Cod.

In 1948, Lynah was named chairman of the NCAA enforcement panel, which became known as the "NCAA Sanity Code." He played a key role in the investigations of alleged violations of the code by any of the member universities and colleges. Fearless in his convictions, he took a strong stand on control of recruiting and devoted many years to improving procedures of the NCAA.

Lynah organized Cornell's department of athletics, physical educa-tion, and women's physical education into a single department. As chair-man of a university committee for the development of athletic facilities, he set plans in motion that brought about Moakley Club House at the

Cornell Golf Course, Teagle Hall, and an indoor ice skating and hockey rink, which was completed in 1957 after Lynah's death in February 1956 and was named in his honor. Lynah Arena at Cornell is an iconic building that is used by Cornell's hockey teams.

Lynah was also a significant proponent in forming the Ivy League in football, established nearly six months after his death in 1956. He is a charter member of the Cornell Athletic Hall of Fame and was named to the Greater Savannah Athletic Hall of Fame posthumously in 1978.

Each year the ECAC awards the James Lynah Distinguished Achievement Award. The award is bestowed annually to a maximum of four former ECAC athletic administrators who have achieved outstanding success in their respective careers or have made great contributions to intercollegiate athletics, the NCAA, and the ECAC.

LYNAH AND GUYON

Jim Lynah is one of the two players known to have played for two of the most famous and legendary football coaches to ever pace the sidelines, John Heisman and Pop Warner. The other player that both men coached also had Clemson ties. Joe Guyon played for Warner at the Carlisle Indian Industrial School in 1912 and 1913 and later played for Heisman at Georgia Tech in 1917 and 1918, including the Yellow Jackets' 1917 national championship team. Guyon was a Native American who had attended Carlisle with the great Jim Thorpe, the greatest athlete in the first 50 years of the 20th century, according to the Associated Press. He also had the distinction of playing both pro football and baseball. An injury in baseball ended his playing career, and so he came to Clemson as a coach. He was the Tigers' head coach in baseball and boxing during the late 1920s and early 1930s. Guyon is a member of both the National Foundation Football Hall of Fame and Pro Football Hall of Fame.

For many years, a fund established by Lynah was awarded to Clemson students with high scholastic rating and possessed outstanding qualities of character and leadership. The award was given in memory of the distinguished professors who were teaching at Clemson when the 1902 class were undergraduates. This list of professors included William Shannon Morrison, the owner of the turkey that Lynah stole in 1902.

A newspaper article by *Savannah News Press* sports editor Frank Tilton summed up Lynah's life this way: "When Lynah died the morning of February 24, 1956, at his residence, he left behind a splendid record of achievement in all that he endeavored to do, whether it was serving his fellow man, or country's business, cultural, or national affairs, or promoting the integrity of sports."

Frank Shaughnessy, Clemson's Most Interesting Coach

Every year on April 15, Jackie Robinson Day is celebrated across major league baseball. As part of the celebration, every player wears No. 42 in his honor, a unique number to all the current players because it is retired by every club. Robinson's career is regarded as the most significant in baseball history by many historians because he was the first to break down racial barriers during the 1940s. A onetime Tigers coach played a pivotal role in helping to tear those barriers down.

A Notre Dame graduate in 1905, Frank Shaughnessy was a star back at Notre Dame and still holds the school record for the longest scoring play, a 107-yard, midair fumble return (fields were 110 yards long in those days) against Kansas in 1904. He also starred in baseball and track and field for the Fighting Irish.

He played minor league baseball in Ottawa, Canada, in 1906 but wanted to coach football. In the fall of 1906, he secured a position as the head coach at Welsh Neck High School in Hartsville, South Carolina.

Clemson head coach Bob Williams took note of his football experience at Notre Dame and asked him to come to Clemson the week of the Georgia Tech game to help the Tigers prepare for John Heisman's squad.

Clemson upset the Yellow Jackets 10–0 in the final game of that 1906 season, a big victory in a rivalry that was as strong then as it is today because Heisman had left Clemson suddenly after the 1903 season to become head coach of the Yellow Jackets. This was Clemson's first win over Georgia Tech since Heisman left.

Clemson administrators were impressed with Shaughnessy's impact on the Tigers team that week and offered him the head coaching position when Williams resigned after the 1906 season. Shaughnessy accepted and led Clemson to a 4–4 record in 1907, beating North Carolina and Georgia Tech, a second straight win over Heisman, in the season finale.

A star baseball player at Notre Dame, Shaughnessy stayed on and coached the Clemson baseball team in the spring of 1908, then got a call from the Philadelphia A's and manager Connie Mack, still the winningest manager in major league history. Mack offered Shaughnessy a major league contract, and he resigned from Clemson after the baseball season ended.

Shaughnessy batted an impressive .310 in his limited action as a reserve outfielder with Philadelphia in 1908. Among the players he competed against was Hall of Fame Detroit Tiger and future all-time hits leader Ty Cobb.

Despite the solid stats as a reserve outfielder, Mack traded Shaughnessy for a minor league player named Frank "Home Run" Baker, who would go on to lead the American League in home runs four different seasons and was inducted into the Hall of Fame in 1955.

Shaughnessy's baseball career ended in 1909 when he decided to go back to coaching. Between 1909 and 1936, he coached college football in the fall, mostly at McGill University in Canada, and minor league baseball in the summer, mostly with the Dodgers organization.

In 1915 McGill did not have a football team because of World War I. As a result, Shaughnessy was asked to serve as head coach of the Ottawa Senators of what is now the NHL. Improbably, he coached Ottawa to the finals of the Stanley Cup before losing to Vancouver.

After coaching baseball at the minor league level for 27 years, he was named president of the International League, the highest level (Triple A) in the minors. He held that position from 1936 to 1960. During his career, he invented a playoff system that is used by most professional sports leagues today. At that time, only the two best teams in each minor league played each other for the title. Shaughnessy thought it would hold interest in the season for more players and more fans if more teams qualified for the playoffs. He adopted the Shaughnessy Playoff System for the International League that allowed four teams, just under half the league, to make the playoffs.

However, Shaughnessy's most important contribution during his career as president of the International League took place in 1946, when he joined with longtime friend and colleague Branch Rickey in facilitating Jackie Robinson's move into professional baseball. Shaughnessy had worked for Rickey in the Dodgers organization as a minor league coach in Syracuse, New York. So, when it came time to place Robinson in the minor leagues prior to his move to the parent Dodgers club, he was assigned to Montreal, an International League team. Rickey knew that Shaughnessy would look after Robinson in his pursuit to become the first African American to play in the majors.

"He's the best player in minor league ball," Shaughnessy said of Robinson in 1946 when he first came into his league. "He's also the smartest. I see where some people don't think he will hit because he didn't hit Bob Feller on a barnstorming tour. How many hitters have any success against Feller? I'll put my money on Robinson." That public support helped move Robinson along, and he was in the majors to start the 1947 season.

Shaughnessy retired from his International League post in 1960 and died in 1969 at the age of 86. There have been some great Notre Dame football players and some great Clemson football coaches. But none had a more interesting career than Frank Shaughnessy.

Mr. Touchdown, Bertie Cecil "Stumpy" Banks

Bertie Cecil "Stumpy" Banks holds the distinction of earning five varsity letters from Clemson as he played from 1915 to 1919. The reason he got to play the extra year is that he missed part of one season due to his service in World War I.

He actually was part of the program for six seasons as he entered Clemson in 1914 and played on the freshman team that fall. He came to Clemson as a 5'5", 105-pound running back. By the time he graduated, he'd gained 50 pounds. He was also the starting catcher on the Tigers baseball teams in 1918 and 1919.

On the football field he scored five touchdowns against Furman on October 13, 1917, in a 38–0 Tigers victory and set the school record that is still in existence today. He also caught two touchdowns against South Carolina on October 26 in Clemson's 27–0 win. He was the captain of both the 1918 and 1919 teams.

Banks was one of six brothers to graduate from Clemson. After graduation, he was a mainstay at all Clemson games as he manned the sideline chains for 35 years. This included all of the games with South Carolina on Big Thursday in Columbia. He started the first-down chain duties in 1920 and missed only three games until his death in 1961.

Banks was named all-state three years and All-Southern in 1919 by the legendary John Heisman. He was listed on the All-Clemson team covering the period from 1896 to 1935. In 1975 he was inducted into the Clemson Athletic Hall of Fame.

Robert C. "Daddy" Potts—Clemson's First NFL Player

The first player to play for Clemson and go to the NFL was Robert C. "Daddy" Potts. Potts was a three-time football letterman at Clemson from 1917 to 1919. He took an interesting route on his way to the pro ranks as he first attended graduate school at Washington and Lee in Lexington, Virginia, after graduating from Clemson in 1920. While at Washington and Lee, Potts again played football and was a standout wrestler.

The first game Potts ever saw was a game he played in as a ninth grader at Fort Mill (SC) High School in 1912. Nobody on the Fort Mill team had ever seen a football game, for that matter, and they were beaten 72–0 by Winnsboro. The Fort Mill team began to understand the game as the season progressed and actually won a rematch with the same Winnsboro team at the end of the season.

It was already apparent that Potts might have a future in football, as he was the largest player on that Fort Mill team. He was dominant on both sides of the ball, and after a stellar prep career; he was on his way to Clemson on an academic scholarship, as those were the days before IPTAY and athletic scholarships.

At Clemson, Potts started at left tackle for head coach Edward "Jiggs" Donahue. During the three years, the Tigers went 17–6–2, including a perfect 3–0 record against rival South Carolina. Potts was named to the all-state team in 1918 and 1920 and was also on the All-Southern team in 1920. Potts was a teammate of Clemson Athletic Hall of Fame members Bertie "Stumpy" Banks, Frank "Boo" Armstrong, and James "Susie" Owens.

It was during his time at Clemson that Potts received the Nickname of "Daddy." The 1920 edition of *Taps* had this description of Potts: "'Daddy,' our term of endearment, implies the sense of strength and leadership, and to say that he deserves it is putting it mildly."

After graduating from Clemson in 1920 and studying at Washington and Lee until 1923, he moved to Florida to work as an engineer. While working in central Florida, Potts was asked to play on local football teams that scrimmaged nearby professional teams. These scrimmages and training sessions were similar to today's spring training for major league baseball teams in Florida.

At the end of one of the training sessions, Potts was signed by the NFL's Frankford Yellow Jackets. They were a team based out of the Philadelphia suburb for which they were named. The franchise would eventually become the Philadelphia Eagles.

Nineteen twenty-six was the only year Potts played professionally. He definitely picked the right year to play, as Frankford went 14–1–2 and won the NFL championship. This was well before the Super Bowl. The league champion was crowned based on the win-loss record achieved in the regular season. On the way to the championship that year, Frankford beat George Halas and the Chicago Bears.

Against the highly regarded New York Giants, Potts intercepted a pass and almost returned it for his only career touchdown before being tackled on the 2-yard line. The 14 wins by Frankford in 1926 were the most in the regular season by an NFL team until 1984, when the San Francisco 49ers had a record of 15–1.

Potts was a tackle on that Yellow Jackets team and got to play against NFL legends Jim Thorpe, Red Grange, and Curly Lambeau during the championship run. At 235 pounds, Potts was the heaviest player on the team, and at age 28 he was the second oldest player behind only coach Guy Chamberlain, who also played.

A teammate of Potts' on those Yellow Jackets teams was Houston Stockton from Gonzaga. There would be another famous Stockton to come out of Gonzaga named John, the longtime Utah Jazz point guard who was the grandson of Houston.

After his lone professional football season, Potts moved to Whiteville, North Carolina, and married Blanche Dyson. After World War II they moved to Loris, South Carolina, where they opened Potts Jewelry Store. Potts was very active in Loris, and returning to South Carolina enabled him to keep up with the Tigers and travel to Clemson games when possible.

"Daddy" Potts was the foundation for the Tigers' tradition of sending players to the NFL. He was an ambassador for Clemson in many ways other than just being the first Tiger to play in the NFL. Potts passed way in August of 1981 just prior to Clemson winning the football national championship. Somewhere, Daddy Potts was looking on with a very big smile—his Tigers were the champions.

E.J. Stewart—An Innovator in College Football

The 44-year-old Edward James Stewart served as head coach at Clemson in 1921 and 1922. He also made stops at other noted schools during his career. Stewart played football and baseball at Scio College and played football, basketball, baseball, and ran track at Western Reserve University. He was the first athlete there to win letters in all four sports in the same school year at Western Reserve. Upon his graduation, he played, organized and served as head coach of the Massilon, Ohio, professional football team.

He began coaching college athletics at Mount Union College in Alliance, Ohio, and in 1907 papers rated his team as the strongest in the state. The basketball team of his coaching was without a doubt the best in Ohio. In 1909 Stewart left Mt. Union College and was named head basketball coach at Purdue University. After four consecutive losing seasons, the first-year coach directed Purdue to an 8–4 season and a second-place finish in the Big Ten Conference.

Clemson's E.J. Stewart is thought to have been the first coach to use communication between the press box and the sidelines to get a better view as coaches do today.

He coached at Oregon State (then Oregon Agricultural College) in 1911 and won the Pacific Coast Championship in basketball his first season. He built the football, basketball, baseball, and track programs, and the Oregon State Aggies ranked athletically with the best of the Pacific Coast.

Stewart left Oregon State and was hired as the head football and basketball coach at the University of Nebraska. At Nebraska, he led the Cornhuskers football team to a combined record of 11–4 in 1916 and 1917. They also won the Missouri Valley Conference title both seasons. As the Cornhuskers basketball coach for three seasons, Stewart compiled a 29–23 record. He gave up the positions when he left to serve in World War I.

After leaving the service, he entered the automobile business as president and treasurer of the Stewart Motor Company. Because of the economic conditions at the time, he decided to go back into coaching, this time he took a job at Clemson.

In the spring of 1921, Stewart coached the baseball and track teams while conducting spring football practice. In the fall, Stewart's football team went 1–6–2, but he improved to a 5–4 mark in 1922.

It was in the 1922 season that Clemson had its first homecoming game, a 21–0 loss to Centre on September 30. He coached the track teams in 1922 and 1923. He was also the head basketball coach in 1922 and 1923 and had a 19–19 record for both years. In 1923, he had an 11–6 mark.

He was also signed to coach a third year at Clemson, but a larger school, the University of Texas, came calling, and he moved on to coach their football team for four seasons. At Texas his teams finished 8–0–1 (1923), 5–3–1 (1924), 6–2–1 (1925), and 5–4–0 (1926). The 1923 and 1925 teams finished second in the Southwest Conference.

After his stint at Texas he went to the University of Texas at El Paso (then the College of Mines and Metallurgy of the University of Texas) for two seasons, 1927 and 1928. In 1927, he had a 2–2–2 record, and in 1928 he finished with a 3–4–1 mark. Stewart was tragically killed in a hunting accident in Texas on November 18, 1929.

Stewart is believed to be one of the first coaches to use communication from the press box or top of the stands to the field while the game is in progress. Eastern coaches, such as those at Harvard, thought that they had come up with the idea in the late teens and early '20s. The idea of using a telephone during a football game was evolved by Stewart during his regime at Oregon State. He first tried it during the Oregon–Oregon State game in 1913 and used the telephone plan repeatedly in subsequent important contests on the Oregon State schedule.

After he went to Nebraska to assume the head-coaching position, he revived his telephone scheme during the Nebraska-Syracuse game on Thanksgiving Day, 1917. Seated on the top of a covered stand at the north side of the Nebraska field, a vantage point that enabled him to get a better view of every play and player than if he were on the sideline,

Stewart used a telephone in passing information to his aides on the Cornhuskers bench.

It is not known if he used this technique at Clemson or not, but everyone around the country on all levels of football uses this system today.

Stewart seemed to enjoy his days at Clemson and remarked about the school and the wonders of the student body support in a letter to the student newspaper, *The Tiger*: "I know that Clemson is filled with a spirit that cannot be conquered, and I know that they are given the most devoted backing possible. The student body and alumni pick the teams up and make them win against odds that are seemingly against them. I know of no other school in the country whose men fight harder and more whole-heartedly than the Clemson Tigers."

O.K. Pressley, Clemson's First All-American

The record book never gives the complete story. Although it typically lists the accomplishments of former greats in various categories, it never tells of an athlete's character, integrity, leadership, dedication, or his love for the game and Clemson. Those accomplishments are etched in the minds of family, friends, and those they have touched during their lives.

Former Clemson football great O.K. Pressley is listed in the Clemson record book as the Tigers' first football All-American in 1928. The Tigers archives also tell of him being All-Southern in 1928 and captain of the first Clemson football team to win eight games in a season (1928). He was a unanimous choice for all-state honors in 1928, and named to the All-Southern team. But most importantly, according to family and friends, he was also an All-American in the game of life.

"O.K. Pressley was like his initials—he was O.K.!," said Henry Asbill, who was an end on the Clemson teams in the late 1920s. "O.K.

was a dedicated player. He played the game because he loved football and his school. He would help his team play better and harder by encouraging us. He would yell to us on defense, 'Lets go, boys, let's hold them here, we can do better than that,' or, 'Good play.' He never complained if he got hurt."

O.K. Pressley was the starting center and linebacker on the Clemson varsity football team from 1926 to 1928. Back in those days, a player participated on both offense and defense. He was named third-team All-America, according to Newspaper Enterprise of America, John Heisman, and Walter Trumbull.

"He was a great player and person. He gave it his all," said Bob McCarley, who was a running back on the Clemson teams in the late 1920s. "He was an inspiration to all of us. He played clean and was a good sportsman who represented Clemson well. We all admired him."

"A better center than captain O.K. Pressley of Clemson is hard to find," said former South Carolina head coach Billy Laval.

Pressley was a dedicated family man, as his son, Kirk, explains, "My father was a great father and an All-American in every aspect of his life."

O.K. Pressley almost did not make it to Clemson, as his brother, Tom, tried to get him to go to Wofford with him and play football. Tom got off the train at Spartanburg and tried to convince his brother, but O.K. insisted he needed to go to Clemson. After he had gone 10–15 miles up the track toward Clemson, he almost jumped off the train and ran back to Spartanburg, but something inside of him told him to go on and be a Tiger—thus beginning one of the greatest football careers ever at Clemson.

When O.K. arrived at Clemson, he began playing for the local YMCA team. Too modest to tell of his high school exploits, he remained on the YMCA team until the Clemson varsity coaches discovered him.

The YMCA team and varsity would scrimmage quite often on Bowman Field in front of Tillman Hall. He was playing defensive tackle in the first scrimmage, and he was an instant star. At first, the varsity put their best blocker on him, and then they started double- and triple-teaming him, and he was still making tackles.

The Clemson varsity team claimed he was stealing their signals, and Pressley challenged the varsity team to have their huddles at Tillman Hall, then come and play. A star had been found, and immediately he was asked to join the Clemson football squad.

Pressley was not only a great football player, but at times served as trainer, publicist, and friend—anything to help the Clemson Tigers win. As a trainer, Pressley helped team doctor Lee Milford. "It was in the South Carolina game in 1928 on the opening kickoff that two of our boys ran together, and both of them had severe cuts over their eyes," recalled Pressley in a 1983 interview.

"They could barely see out of them," said Pressley. "Dr. Milford came running out on the field and said, 'We got to take these boys out.' Those were the days when you couldn't substitute. If you left the game, you were finished for the day. We didn't have anybody else to put in the game. I told him to give me some tape so I could work on one while he worked on the other. We patched them up so they could see out of their eyes and remain in the game."

Pressley acted as a publicist when he kept the Winthrop University campus informed of the Tigers' exploits, especially his hometown girlfriend and later wife. (Winthrop was consided Clemson's sister school in those days, as Clemson was all-male, and Winthrop all-female.) Still in pads after a ballgame, he would walk to the Western Union office and send a telegram to her at the Winthrop campus and tell of the Clemson fortunes. Several Winthrop students would wait anxiously for the news of the Tigers.

O.K. loved his teammates and was willing to share with them as any good friend would. The day before an Auburn game, the players went downtown in Auburn, Alabama. O.K. Pressley had 50¢ for the trip and bought a banana split for 25¢. Pressley insisted on 12 spoons so his teammates could share in this special and unusual treat. It must have had some special power, as Clemson upset Auburn 6–0. It was in this game that Pressley suffered a severe hand injury.

He was in a great deal of pain on the train trip back home, but he never complained. He would miss the next game against N.C. State, and he was going to be held out of the 1928 South Carolina contest. In the South Carolina game, the Gamecocks were driving. O.K. Pressley knew he could help his team, but head coach Josh Cody did not want to play him because of his injury. South Carolina kept driving. O.K. went to Cody and begged to be put in, but the coach said firmly, "No." South Carolina was on the Tigers' 10-yard line. O.K. looked at the coach with pleading eyes.

Cody looked at O.K. and then looked at the field with an approving nod of the head, as if to say, "Please go in and stop the Gamecocks." Pressley charged out onto the field. On the first play, he tackled the South Carolina player for an eight-yard loss. The next play, Pressley tackled the South Carolina ball carrier for a seven-yard loss. The next two plays, Pressley tackled the Gamecocks' runners for a five- and seven-yard loss respectively.

It was probably the greatest one-man defensive stand in the history of Clemson football. Pressley must have given the Tigers a charge, as Clemson defeated the favored Gamecocks 32–0. Both teams had come into the game with undefeated records of 5–0.

College graduation in 1929 didn't end Pressley's football-playing days, as he entered the Marine Corps and served as a player/coach for seven years. He went on to become a much-decorated military figure before he retired with 20 years of service to his credit in 1949 and returned to his native Chester County. He taught in the public schools there for several years and retired to his farm near Chester.

Pressley was honored at Clemson in 1983, more than 50 years later, by being inducted into the Clemson Hall of Fame, along with other Clemson greats. Pressley died on September 22, 1984.

Clemson's first All-America football player continued to be an All-America player long after his Clemson career and made his mark in many people's record books.

Josh Cody Leads Clemson to Success

Although a lot of changes have taken place in college athletics since Josh Cody paced the sideline as head football and basketball coach in the late 1920s and early 1930s, some principles he stressed should never change.

After leaving Clemson after the 1930 season with a 29–11–1 record, Cody coached at Vanderbilt, Florida, and Temple, which was his final stop in coaching and administration. At one time or other, he coached both the football and basketball teams at those schools.

Cody played football at Vanderbilt. He remains the only Commodore to earn All-America honors three times (1915, 1916, and 1919). The 1920 Vanderbilt graduate was selected as an All-Time All-American by the Football Writers Association. The Commodores had a 23–9–3 record, as he was a devastating lineman on both sides of the ball under legendary head coach Dan McGugin.

On occasion, he played in the backfield and was both a great passer and drop-kicker. He once converted on a 45-yard drop-kick against Michigan. As one teammate recalled, "He would tell the running backs on which side of him to go, and you could depend on him to take out two men as needed. He was the best football player I've ever seen."

Cody also played basketball, baseball, and was on the track team at Vanderbilt, earning 13 varsity letters in all. And, if this were not enough, he was a lieutenant in World War I in 1917 and 1918.

Another teammate who witnessed his greatness once said, "He was a farm boy and he had no polish, but he was very honest and sincere. He didn't have a scholarship—we had none in those days—but he had a real

Josh Cody coached Clemson's first All-America player, O.K. Pressley, and had a perfect 4–0 record vs. South Carolina.

job. He cleaned the gym every day, cleaned up the locker rooms and the showers, and tended to the coal furnace after practice."

There was also much documentation to his toughness. Teammates remember that he did not like to wear pads, so he cut up an old quilt and sewed it into the shoulders of his jersey.

Upon graduation, Cody started his coaching career at Mercer in 1920 as coach of all sports and athletic director. In 1923, Cody came back to Vanderbilt as head basketball and baseball coach, and as an assistant in other sports. In 1926–1927, the Commodores finished 20–4 and won the Southern Conference basketball title under his tutelage.

In his first year as head football coach at Clemson (1927), he led the Tigers to a 5–3–1 record, then guided Clemson to back-to-back 8–3 seasons in 1928 and 1929. Cody was a popular man among the Clemson student body. He was nicknamed "Big Man" because of his large stature. According to one account, when he was seen on campus and the name "Big Man" was yelled, he would turn and wave and smile the largest grin. He loved and respected the students at Clemson, and they loved him.

This probably was best exemplified when it was rumored he was leaving after three years at Clemson. To show their appreciation for his fine record (including a then 3–0 mark against South Carolina), the students, faculty, and staff acted quickly and took up a collection to buy him a brand-new black Buick, and presented him this new car in front of the steps at Tillman Hall on May 6, 1929.

He would stay for two more years after this kind gesture. In 1930 the Tigers finished with an 8–2 mark in his final football season at Clemson, the first time in history the Tigers had won eight games in three consecutive years.

Cody is the only coach in Tigers history with at least two seasons' tenure who never lost a football game to South Carolina. He also defeated Furman three straight seasons, had a 13–0–1 home record, and had a 72 percent winning mark overall, fourth best in Clemson history. He also coached Clemson's first All-American, center and linebacker O.K. Pressley. He coached the basketball team for five years and led the Tigers to a 16–9 slate in 1930. During the 1928–1930 seasons, he guided Clemson to a 22–4 mark at home on the hardwood.

Upon leaving Clemson, Cody returned to Vanderbilt as an assistant football coach and head basketball coach. He was the head football coach and athletic director at Florida from 1936 to 1939. In 1940 Cody was a line coach at Temple and was appointed head basketball coach in 1942. He held that post until he became athletic director in 1952. During his tenure as basketball coach, Cody racked up 124 victories and guided the Owls to the NCAA Tournament in 1944, the first NCAA Tournament appearance in the history of the program. That team reached the Elite Eight of the tournament. In 1955, he coached the football team at

Temple after the original coach resigned on the eve of the season. The Owls were winless that year (0–8), but Cody never complained, and instead stressed, "They were improving and trying hard."

During his career, Cody had a few guiding principles he developed that he thought were important. At that time, Cody had African Americans playing at Temple on the basketball team. When asked before the NCAA Tournament what he would do if segregation became an issue and his team could not stay in the same hotel or eat in the same restaurant, he simply replied, "We will not play in that city. We go together as a team or not play at all."

Such was Cody—he loved his players and respected them, and they did the same. "I've always tried to treat a player the way I'd expect my son to be treated," was another of his guiding principles. Another rule he lived by was, "It's important to realize how much influence a coach can have on his youngsters."

Cody retired to a farm in New Jersey. He died of a heart attack on June 19, 1961, in Mount Laurel, New Jersey at the age of 69. He was inducted into the College Football Hall of Fame as a player in 1970 and the Tennessee Sports Hall of Fame in 1999.

Cody enjoyed a wide reputation as athlete, coach, administrator, and gentleman. Although many things have changed in the last 80 or so years since Cody was at Clemson, some things that he stressed, like the importance of character and respect for others, will never change.

CHAPTER 4
IPTAY SAVES THE DAY

Jess Neely Takes Over Clemson Program

Perhaps one of Clemson's most beloved coaches was Jess Neely. Neely's influence and inspiration is still present today as the IPTAY Scholarship Club was founded during his coaching tenure.

Neely was head coach at Clemson from 1931 through 1939 and spent the next 26 years at Rice University in Houston. Neely coached Clemson to its first bowl game, the 1940 Cotton Bowl, where the Tigers capped a 9–1–0 season by beating Boston College 6–3. Clemson ended the season ranked 12th in the final AP poll, its first top-20 season in history. Boston College was ranked 11th going into the game, and it was Clemson's first win over a top-20 team in its history. The team featured the play of Banks McFadden, Clemson's first Associated Press All-American. Clemson had a 43–35–7 record during Neely's tenure.

Neely coached Rice to four Southwest Conference championships and six bowl appearances, the last being a trip to the Bluebonnet Bowl in 1961. During 40 years of college coaching he compiled a record of 207–176–19. Neely is 26th in major college football history in victories heading into the 2016 season. For his accomplishments, he was inducted into the College Football Hall of Fame.

Neely graduated from Vanderbilt in 1924, after lettering three years in football and serving as captain of the 1922 team. He coached a year of high school football before returning to his alma mater to obtain a law degree, though he never practiced law.

He coached four years at Southwestern College in Clarksville, Tennessee, and then went to the University of Alabama as an assistant coach in 1928. It was there that he met Frank Howard. Neely brought Howard to Clemson as line coach in 1931. Howard replaced him in 1940 and remained as head coach for 30 years. In 1967 Neely returned to his alma mater as athletic director. He officially retired in 1971 but continued to coach golf at Vanderbilt until 1981, when he moved back to Texas.

Jess Neely was Clemson's head football coach from 1931 to 1939 and led the Tigers to their first bowl game and first bowl victory, a 6–3 win in the Cotton Bowl over Frank Leahy's Boston College eleven.

"If I didn't look in the mirror every day, I wouldn't know how old I am," Neely once said. "Working with the boys makes you feel young, I feel that in athletics the boys learn a sense of loyalty and sacrifice and values they don't learn anywhere else. They learn to compete, and that is what life is all about—it's competition. If they make good in football, chances are they'll be successful elsewhere. I like to see that those boys make something of themselves. That's my reward.

"The boys go to college to study and get that degree. Playing football is a side activity. When fellows go to a school first to play football they get an entirely wrong sense of values. And when you start them off with the wrong sense, it isn't difficult for them to go astray."

Neely died at the age of 85 in 1983, but his landmark accomplishments in the 1930s at Clemson contributed significantly to Clemson's outstanding football tradition.

IPTAY—Lifeblood of Clemson Athletics

IPTAY could be described as a mysterious-sounding name that has become synonymous with Clemson athletics since 1934. The name IPTAY came from the phrase, "I pay ten a year." Now there are different levels of contributions that are used to fund scholarships for Clemson's student-athletes.

There were apparently several forerunners to IPTAY at Clemson, but IPTAY is the one that finally clicked and has paid wonderful dividends. The first known aid to Clemson athletics came just before the turn of the century. The Tigers had just closed, according to one article, "the most brilliant football season in the history of athletics at Clemson," trouncing Georgia Tech 41–5 in Greenville on Thanksgiving Day. That was in 1899.

Professor W.M. Riggs, who was later to become Clemson president, had coached this team just as he had the first team in 1896, though this time it was without remuneration. Students decided that the man who brought football to Clemson from Auburn ought to be able to devote his full duties to the academic side and that a full-time coach should be brought in to oversee the football team.

Thus a mass meeting was held December 7, 1899, and the Football Aid Society was formed. At this meeting the conditions and possibilities of the 1900 season were thoroughly discussed, and as a result, the society became a permanent organization with the avowed purpose to render all possible assistance to the football association, a forerunner to the Clemson University Athletic Department.

B.H. Rawl was elected president and W.G. Hill secretary-treasurer of the society. A second meeting was held later, and it was unanimously agreed that a coach—the best that could be obtained—should be engaged, and the society asked its members for subscriptions payable in September 1900.

A total of 132 names appeared on the roll of members and $372.50 was pledged in an hour's time. A ways and means committee was appointed, the object of which was to devise means for raising money. This was done, and money was raised by various endeavors.

Professor Riggs aided the society in bringing in Auburn Coach John W. Heisman, and during the next four years of the Heisman era, Clemson teams had a 19–3–2 record and became one of the South's great football powers. The 1900 team was Clemson's first undefeated squad (6–0).

Although it is not known how long the Football Aid Society stayed in existence, one point seemed to be proved—monetary aid established Clemson as a football giant to be reckoned with—not for scholarships, as IPTAY now does—but in securing a capable coach who put the Tigers on the gridiron map.

As far as can be determined, no organized effort was made to assist athletic teams at Clemson for the next three decades, although there were individual gifts here and there, usually collected at Clemson meetings.

Josh Cody came along in 1927 and had four highly successful seasons (29–11–1) before Jess Neely arrived on the scene in 1931. That season started what has become known as the "Seven Lean Years," and it was during this time that IPTAY was born.

Neely's first season ended 1–6–2. Following the Citadel game at Florence, October 13, 1931, Captain Frank J. Jervey recalled that he, Neely, Joe Davis (former Clemson and Rice coach), and Captain Pete Heffner (boxing coach) were sitting in a car outside the stadium talking following the 6–0 loss at the Cadets' hands. Captain Heffner was a member of the military staff at Clemson, vitally interested in athletics, and assisted with the coaching in his spare time.

Jervey remembered that it was a downcast group in the car. Heffner said in so many words, "What we ought to do is to get the alumni to give Jess some money and help him with the football team."

"How much do you think we should ask from each person?" Jervey inquired. And Neely was asked how much he thought he'd need. Jervey remembers picking the figure of $50 as the amount of the contribution and to form a "50 Club." Neely believed if he could get $10,000 a year he could give the Clemson fans a winning football team.

The group talked some more on the subject on the way back to Clemson and then went their separate ways upon arrival at Clemson. The Tigers finished out the season with a 21–0 loss to South Carolina, a tie with Furman, and losses to Oglethorpe, Virginia Military, and Alabama.

Jervey, who was working in Washington at the time, began corresponding with some of his Clemson friends concerning the "50 Club," and one of those written was Dr. Rupert H. "Rube" Fike, a Clemson Alumnus from the class of 1908, and an Atlanta cancer specialist.

After approximately a year of writing back and forth, certain ones decided to have a meeting in Columbia on the eve of the South Carolina game. So October 19, 1932, found 12 or 13 individuals meeting at the Jefferson Hotel. Clemson had beaten Presbyterian 13–0 and Erskine

19–0, while losing 13–0 to N.C. State and 32–14 to Georgia Tech prior to this gathering.

Some of the group, including Fike, thought maybe the $50 figure was a little too high, but nonetheless, some of those present went about starting the "50 Club." Early records at the athletic department in Clemson show that there were a few contributions of $50, but the total sum came nowhere close to matching the $10,000 Neely had indicated he would need for a winning ballclub. Fike's idea was that if a smaller amount was asked, there would be more money and more members, and he went back to Atlanta with the idea in the back of his mind. The Tigers went on to lose to South Carolina, Georgia, and Furman, getting a win off The Citadel and a 7–7 tie with Davidson to finish 3–5–1.

Dr. Fike, determined to find a way to strengthen Clemson's athletic program, which was as dark as the Depression the nation was in, stuck to his guns for the "smaller amount/more members" idea. And to put across his idea, he enlisted the aid of two other Clemson men living in Atlanta, J.E.M. Mitchell, Class of 1912, and Milton Berry, Class of 1913.

Apparently, over a year passed before the first concrete steps were taken and IPTAY was formed. Meanwhile, the 1933 season had come and gone, giving Neely three straight losing campaigns. The Tigers of that year were 3–6–2, losing to Georgia Tech, South Carolina, Ole Miss, Wofford, Mercer, and Furman; while defeating N.C. State, Wake Forest, and The Citadel; and tying Presbyterian and George Washington. The Tigers had won only seven games in three years under Neely.

Although there are several versions as to just how IPTAY started, a letter written by Dr. Fike to Coach Neely, dated August 21, 1934, seems to pretty well pinpoint the exact date of formation. Dr. Fike said in his opening statement of the letter: "Last night we had a little meeting out at my house and organized the IPTAY Club." He went on to say that those attending the meeting were George Suggs, Gene Cox, E.L. Hutchins, Bill Dukes, J.R. Pennell, George Klugh, Milton Berry, Jack Mitchell, and himself.

The club was to be a secret order, according to an early copy of the constitution, which stated that "anyone who has matriculated at Clemson, has been employed by the college, or is a friend of the college, who can and will subscribe to the purpose of the order by taking the oath of secrecy and paying the initiation and yearly fees, when invited for membership is eligible."

The purpose of the Clemson Order of IPTAY, stated the constitution, "shall be to provide annual financial support to the athletic department at Clemson and to assist in every other way possible to regain for Clemson the high athletic standing which rightfully belongs to her."

Dr. Fike entwined the language of his ritual around the tiger. The Bengal tiger, Persian tiger, and Sumatran tiger would be president, vice president, and secretary, respectively. The Exalted Iryaas would be the head coach at Clemson with "Iryaas" meaning, "I receive yours and acknowledge same." A "lair" would mean a body of the order, and "region" designated a state, province, or foreign country.

Neely recalled in later years that Fike, Mitchell, and Berry approached him sometime before their August meeting at the Fike home and said, "What do you think about this IPTAY?"

"About what?" Neely asked with an amazed look.

Then the enthused Fike, Mitchell, and Berry explained their plan of IPTAY to Neely. The distressed coach was for trying anything that would bring the Tigers out of their gridiron doldrums. Dr. Fike mentions their visit to Clemson in his letter to Neely. Neely's initiation into the order was arranged to be held at Clemson on September 22, 1934, "either before or after the Presbyterian game."

The late Leonard R. Booker once recalled that first initiation. It was held in the office of the late J.H. "Uncle Jake" Woodard, longtime alumni secretary at Clemson. In addition to the three Atlanta stem-winders, present also were Booker, Woodard, Neely, and the late J.C. Littlejohn, Clemson's business manager.

The meeting is believed to be the first initiation of new members into IPTAY. The organizers and these new members then began to preach IPTAY to anyone and everyone, and money began to come in for Neely and his Tigers. As close as can be determined, there were 185 people who were members of IPTAY during that first year of 1934–1935.

Probably none of these people—except Berry, Fike, and Mitchell— ever envisioned what IPTAY would do for athletics at Clemson. Neely recalled on one of his visits back to Clemson after going to Rice that they met a lot of skeptical people while making their rounds asking for money, "and it took about three or four years before we could start helping a lot of boys." The former Rice head coach and athletic director remembered that most of the 1939 Cotton Bowl team was on scholarship, "but some of them had never played high school ball and just came out for football after coming to Clemson."

Frank Howard, who was on the Clemson staff 44 years, 30 as head coach, was in on the same conversation with Neely, and Howard remembers vividly that there were only eight players on the 1950 team that played in the '51 Orange Bowl who came to Clemson without a scholarship.

Although bringing Clemson from its lowest ebb into the Cotton Bowl was one of Neely's highlights, he feels that one even more important was getting the athletic department on a sound financial footing. "When we came to Clemson in 1931," Neely recalled, "there wasn't hardly 20¢ in the treasury, and when I left here [1940], there was over $20,000."

The Tigers had their first winning season with IPTAY in 1934 (5–4–0), the year IPTAY was formed, but it was probably the 1938 season when the net results really began to pay off. That year Clemson waltzed over Presbyterian, Tulane, South Carolina, Wake Forest, George Washington, Kentucky, and Furman, while losing to Tennessee and tying Virginia Military.

89

Following the VMI tie, the Tigers won 19 of their next 20 games with 13 straight being reeled off from the 7–6 loss to Tulane in 1939 to the 13–0 defeat to the same Greenies in 1940. The 1939 team was 8–1–0 in regular-season play and went on to defeat Frank Leahy's Boston College team 6–3 in the 1940 Cotton Bowl.

The men who were out beating the bushes for IPTAY encountered rough going in those early days. On many occasions, a person was interested in giving but lacked funds. Harper Gault, a former president of IPTAY, recalls members giving $10 worth of milk, potatoes, or turnips in exchange for membership.

IPTAY was born for just one purpose—to finance athletic scholarships at Clemson. Today, not only does IPTAY fund athletic scholarships, it also assists in capital projects. About four or five years after its formation, IPTAY dropped its secret ritual and invited everyone to join in support of Clemson athletics. Then in 1954 Dr. Fike asked to be relieved as president after serving 20 years, and a complete revamping of the club took place.

Millions of dollars have been contributed to IPTAY's cause since that meeting in August of 1934 in the quiet surroundings of the Fike home in Atlanta. With these monies, thousands of athletes have received an education that might not have otherwise been possible.

The late Dr. Robert C. Edwards, president of Clemson from 1959 to 1979 and the man who succeeded Dr. Fike as the second president of IPTAY, viewed athletics as a vital segment of campus life. "Athletic teams in all sports, both intercollegiate and intramural," he stated, "are an essential and integral part of Clemson's total educational program. Clemson University has developed a national reputation in athletic competitions. The support of Clemson athletics year after year by IPTAY members has made this achievement possible.

"More recently, Clemson's reputation as an outstanding scientific and technological educational institution is growing at a remarkable pace. IPTAY is contributing to this achievement. Student-athletes at Clemson are currently compiling better academic records than the student body as a whole. We are seeking to develop the same competitive spirit in the classroom that prevails in athletic competition."

At first, only dyed-in-the-wool Clemson fans took an interest and joined IPTAY. But over the last 25 years, parents of students and athletes, as well as people who never attended Clemson, have become a part of IPTAY.

Just what has IPTAY meant to Clemson, to the State of South Carolina, and the many individuals it has helped since 1934? That would be difficult to put into words. But maybe Dr. Riggs had the right idea when he spoke these words on football, and athletics in general, in 1899:

> So long as the game of football helps to make better men of our students, stronger in body, more active in mind—men full of energy, enthusiasm, and an indomitable personal courage; men not easily daunted by obstacles or opposition; who control their tempers and restrain their appetites, who can deal honorably with a vanquished adversary, and can take victory moderately and defeat without bitterness.
>
> And as long as football properly controlled and regulated helps the student in his college duties, instead of hindering him; gives zest and pleasure to college life, make name and fame for the college on account of victories won, not only by skill and prowess of the team on the gridiron, but by their gentlemanly conduct in the streets of the town they play, in the hotels where they quarter, and on the trains.
>
> So long as it helps to bring about a closer bond of sympathy between students and members of the faculty by creating a common interest apart from the routine duties—so long as in all these ways the best interests of his and other colleges are advanced, and the course of education aided in its highest

mission, which is to make the best men out of the material at hand, so long we will say for the game of football, long may it live and prosper.

Although these words were spoken some 35 years before the formation of IPTAY, the ideas expressed by Dr. Riggs are exemplified today in the total education program at Clemson, which Dr. Edwards spoke about.

Dr. Edwards believed that "it is utterly impossible to measure in a material sense all that IPTAY has meant to Clemson in the past years. It would be equally difficult to predict all that IPTAY can and will contribute to Clemson in the years that lie ahead."

Historically, the formation of IPTAY was the first of many infrastructure improvements to the Clemson Athletic Department that have had a positive effect in the wins and losses column.

The chart below documents those changes and corresponding positive results for the Clemson football program within the next four to six years:

Year	Change	Results
1934	Formation of IPTAY	1939 team goes 9–1, first bowl, top-20 season
1942	Building of Memorial Stadium	1948 undefeated season
1953	Join ACC	Three Bowl games in 4 years, 1956–1959
1973	Building of Jervey Center	1977 first bowl bid in 18 years, 1978 No. 6 ranking
1978	South upper deck at stadium	1981 national championship
1983	North upper deck at stadium	ACC titles 1986–1988
1995	McFadden Building opens	2000 team finishes No. 14 in nation

2005	West end zone at stadium	2009 Atlantic title
2009	All football facilities new at stadium	2011 ACC title
2012	New indoor football facility opens	2015 Tigers go 14–1, play for national title

The 1939 Season

Perhaps one of the most significant seasons in Clemson's football history is the 1939 season. This squad played and defeated Boston College 6–3 in the 1940 Cotton Bowl in Dallas, Texas.

So much of the history and heritage of Clemson football documents 1939 as a cornerstone season. Not only was it Clemson's first bowl team, it was Clemson's first team to be ranked and the first to end a season in the national top 20 (No. 12 in the final AP poll).

Clemson opened the year with its annual victory over Presbyterian, then suffered its only loss, a 7–6 squeaker to Tulane in New Orleans. The Tigers would win their next seven to finish 8–1 and would accept their first bowl bid.

Oddly enough, that one loss to the Green Wave saw Banks McFadden first rise to national prominence. Many observers say that is where McFadden made the All-America team on his punting exhibition, especially on his quick-kicks from the single-wing tailback position. He averaged over 43 yards a kick in 12 punts that afternoon and had six punts of at least 50 yards, still a single-game record today.

Starting out with a 1–1 record after two games, few would even hazard a guess that Clemson would play in its first bowl game at the end of the season. Few also figured that coach Jess Neely would move on to Rice at the end of the season, the school he would remain at for the next 27 seasons.

Neely fought adversity and the Great Depression with slow and well-thought-out solutions. How many coaches today could win 36 games in

Banks McFadden was named the nation's most versatile athlete for 1939–1940. He is the only Clemson athlete to earn All-America honors in football and basketball.

six seasons with only 14 of 56 games played at home? Only once did Clemson play as many as four games at home during Neely's stay and only twice were there even three home games in a year. (Thirteen of the 56 games were played on neutral sites.) Even this '39 team only played two games at home—its opening 18–0 win over Presbyterian and then a 20–7 victory over Wake Forest in week 7.

With the exception of the Tulane loss, the Tigers were only behind twice the entire season and were tied once, though it didn't last long. Players went both ways, and only gave up 45 points in the 10 games, including the Cotton Bowl.

In the third game, the Tigers defeated N.C. State 25–6 in Charlotte with the Pack's lone score coming in the final quarter. Clemson played Navy at Annapolis, then went back to the nation's capital the next Saturday and downed George Washington 13–6.

There were many stars on this team. McFadden and Joe Blalock were both All-Americans and joined George Fritts and Shad Bryant on the All-Southern Conference team. That quartet, along with Walter Cox and Bob "Red" Sharpe were members of the all-state squad. Payne, Tom Moorer, and Carl Black were the only three to start all 10 games.

They suddenly found themselves—a group of players from small-town environments—playing big-time football. Neely rewarded the team for its efforts by taking all 51 players to Dallas for the game. The long trip was made by train. Of the 11 starters on the team, 10 were from the state of South Carolina.

While in Dallas for the bowl game, talk was rampant that Neely would leave Clemson for the head-coaching job at Rice. Bill Sullivan was the publicity man for Frank Leahy and Boston College, and he said that he was in the hotel room in Dallas when Neely told a small group that he would definitely take the Rice offer.

Frank Howard, who was Neely's line coach, spoke up and said, "Well, I'm not going with you." And according to Sullivan, Neely replied, "I hadn't planned to ask you."

When Howard was confronted with this, he denied it and said that J.C. Littlejohn, Clemson's business manager, had promised him the Clemson head-coaching job if Neely left. Sullivan, incidentally, is the same Sullivan who used to own the New England Patriots and Sullivan Stadium at Foxboro, Massachusetts.

1940 Cotton Bowl

It was a cool day in Dallas, Texas, on January 1, 1940. The high temperature was 49 degrees.

"That McFadden put a lot of these gray hairs on my head," Jess Neely told *Boston Post* reporter Gerry Hern in an article prior to the Cotton Bowl. "I don't discourage him any. He's a smart tailback; and if he feels he has worked the team into a bad spot, I like to see him get reckless. We've scored a few touchdowns on plays I've never seen before."

Neely never had an issue allowing McFadden to improvise. If a player came back to the huddle and told McFadden that a certain play might work, the All-American would instruct his teammate to see if the defensive player made the same mistake twice. If he did, McFadden would expose him on the next play call.

"Every now and then they would make [a play] up on the field," Neely said. "If I don't recognize a play, I'm sure Boston coach Frank Leahy won't."

Jess Neely's last Clemson team won eight games in the regular season with just one loss to Tulane. The 8–1 Tigers were rewarded with an invitation to play Boston College in the fourth Cotton Bowl, but Clemson first had to get permission from the Southern Conference, which they immediately granted. The 1939 season not only resulted in Clemson's first bowl appearance, but also the Tigers' first first-team All-American, Banks McFadden.

On the last play of the first quarter, Bru Trexler punted to BC's Charlie O'Rourke, who fielded the punt on the Clemson 40 and returned it to the 13. Two running plays lost 10 yards, but on third down Frank Davis gained six. Alex Lukachik then kicked a 34-yard field goal to put the Eagles up 3–0.

Clemson's scoring drive began when McFadden returned an Eagles punt to the 33. Charlie Timmons rushed for 15 yards in two plays, and two plays after that, McFadden hit Wister Jackson with a 16-yard pass to the Eagle 20. Timmons ran the final 20 yards in three carries, but Shad Bryant missed the extra point.

Later in the period, a 51-yard punt by McFadden pushed Boston College back to its own 20. The Eagles fumbled on first down, and Clemson's George Fritts recovered at the 24. The Tigers could do nothing with the gift, however, as Joe Blalock fumbled after a short pass.

Banks McFadden is shown with
the 1940 Cotton Bowl Trophy.

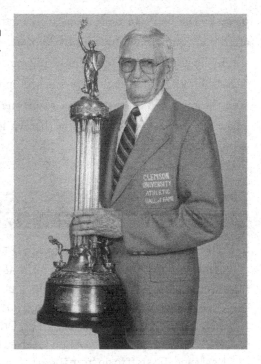

The game turned into a defensive struggle in the second half, although Boston College did penetrate deep into Clemson territory on two occasions. The Eagles took the opening kickoff to the Clemson 19, but a holding penalty and an incomplete pass ended the threat, and BC was forced to punt. Late in the game, the Eagles drove to the Clemson 11, but Bryant and McFadden each broke up two passes and Clemson took over on downs.

McFadden effectively bottled up the Eagles other than those drives with his punting. His 44-yard average on nine kicks, including boots for 51 and 55 yards in the second half, prevented Boston College from getting good field position, and the Clemson defense made the 6–3 score stand.

Timmons led Clemson with 115 yards on 27 carries. Defensively, McFadden went sideline-to-sideline knocking down Charlie O'Rourke's passes, as he had four deflections in the game. The Eagles finished the afternoon completing only four of 23 passes, with one interception. As a whole, Boston College netted only 102 yards of total offense. "Clemson is every bit as good as they were cracked up to be," Leahy told reporters after the game. "We lost to a great team, one of the best I have ever seen. I have the satisfaction of knowing that while we were beaten, the game wasn't lost on a fluke."

CLEMSON'S VERSION OF THE 12TH MAN

Clemson has a version of its own 12th man story when it comes to football, very similar to Texas A&M's. Clemson's version involves a boxer who played some football at Clemson as well.

Clemson boxing star Warren Wilson was participating in the Sugar Bowl Boxing Tournament in New Orleans in late December of 1939. The Tigers' heavyweight received a telegram from Coach Neely and the staff to go from there to Dallas, Texas, where the Tigers were going to play in the Cotton Bowl on January 1, 1940. The telegram said, "WARREN COME TO DALLAS. BOSTON COLLEGE IS BIG IN THE LINE AND WE MAY NEED YOU."

Although not on the 1939 varsity football roster, but having played football for Clemson earlier, he took a train to Dallas and was ready to play in the Cotton Bowl if Clemson needed him. It is not known if he played in the game, but he was ready to do his part if the Tigers did need him to play.

Former world heavyweight champion and boxing great Jack Dempsey once wrote Wilson and said that Wilson would be the next heavyweight champion of the world, as no one hit harder than he did. Wilson trained to be a heavyweight prize fighter, but because of World War II and an accident he was involved in prior to the war, his dream was never realized.

Joe Blalock, Two-Time Football All-American

Joe Blalock was a three-sport athlete at Clemson, but Walter Cox believes his one-time teammate "could have been a five-sport man had he had the time. He played football, baseball, and basketball, but he would have been a heck of a track man or a boxer," Cox surmised.

The Charleston native "was the best football player we had at Clemson at the time [1940]," recalls Howard. "I was a young football coach and hadn't had any experience. But Joe was a versatile player in that he was a good pass receiver, he could come around from his right end position and pass [left-handed], and sometimes he wouldn't pass the ball, but would keep it and run on an end around."

McFadden remembers a game against Furman, in which the Tigers were trailing 3–0 at halftime. "Joe threw me a touchdown pass in the end zone, and I dropped it. I was so wide open that I looked like a player who came out at 2:00 o'clock when practice had been called for 3:00." But McFadden did score a touchdown later in the game, and the Tigers won 14–3. Clemson received a bid to play Boston College in the Cotton Bowl after this victory.

Howard was quick to correct anyone who would mention that Blalock was "a good football player." "I remember that he was a great football player—not a good one—but a great one."

McFadden played on the 1939 team with Blalock, then was in pro ball with the old Brooklyn Dodgers for one year before returning to Clemson. By then (1941), Blalock was a senior, but McFadden was coaching the secondary and really had no opportunity to tutor him as an offensive player.

"He is one of the most outstanding athletes Clemson ever had," McFadden said. "Back when I played, you didn't start sophomores. But we had both Blalock and George Fritts [an interior lineman] my senior year starting as sophomores. Joe was the easy-flowing type...it didn't seem for him to take any effort in doing anything. He could do all of the

Joe Blalock was Clemson's first two-time All-American. He was a sophomore starter on the 1940 Cotton Bowl team.

things kind of effortlessly. I had to work like a dog to get things out of myself. Joe was exceptional. He could have played most any position on the team, except interior line, and he might have been able to play that. And Joe was not the flashy type. He was easy-going, quiet, always had a little smile, and always had something nice to say about people. Boy, what a wingback he would have made on the old single-wing formation."

Blalock helped vault the Tigers into national prominence during the 1940 season with an effort that started him on the way to his All-America rating. Clemson and Wake Forest were both undefeated (3–0) when 15,000 crowded into Riggs Field for the Southern Conference showdown. The first quarter ended scoreless, but the Tigers put 13 points on the board in each of next three quarters for a surprising 39–0 triumph.

"Joe [Blalock] proved himself. And nothing ordinary, understand," one description in a newspaper said. First, he blocked a punt to put his team in scoring position. On the following play, he came back from end to pitch a touchdown pass. A little later he ran for a touchdown on an end around, and wound up the day by intercepting a pass and reeling off a 45-yard return for a touchdown. It is the only time on record a Clemson player has run for a touchdown, passed for a touchdown, and returned an interception for a score in a single game.

But the quiet, unassuming Blalock thought nothing about it. He seized the opportunity every chance he had to help his team to greater heights, be it on the gridiron, basketball court, pitcher's mound, or batter's box. His work, not his words, spoke for him. That's one reason he became Clemson's first two-time All-America football player.

Banks McFadden, "The Great"

Banks McFadden is regarded as the greatest all-around athlete in Clemson sports history. McFadden, also known as "Bonnie Banks" or "The Great" was a standout at Clemson in football, basketball, and track, earning three letters in each sport from 1936 to 1940. He earned All-America honors in both basketball (1938–1939) and football (1939) and was named the nation's most versatile athlete in 1939.

On the basketball court, McFadden led Clemson to the 1939 Southern Conference Tournament Championship, the only postseason tournament title in Clemson basketball history. The Tigers center was Clemson's top scorer each season and finished his career with a then Clemson record 810 points.

In track, McFadden won three events in the state track meet in one afternoon, setting state records in all three of them. Earlier in the same year he placed first in five events in a dual meet, scoring 25 points while the opposing team's total score was 28 points. His senior year he also pitched in one game for the Clemson baseball team.

On the gridiron in 1939, McFadden was a triple threat, leading the Tigers to a 9–1 record and Clemson's first-ever bowl bid. With McFadden batting down four passes in the second half, and averaging 44 yards on 11 punts, the Tigers defeated a Frank Leahy–coached Boston College team 6–3 in the 1940 Cotton Bowl.

"I had seen safety men play center field in a football game and cover a lot of defensive territory, but that was the only time I saw it done from a half-back position," Howard said in *The History of Clemson Football*. "McFadden put absolutely everything he had into that effort—ability, speed, heart, endurance, determination, and a sixth sense of where the ball was going."

McFadden held the Clemson single-season punting record (a 43.5-yard average in 1939) for 40 years, and his 22 punts of at least 50 yards in 1939 still stands as a Clemson single-season record.

At the conclusion of his career, he was a first-round draft choice of the Brooklyn Dodgers of the NFL, the fourth selection of the draft, and still tied as the highest draft choice in Clemson history. He played one year in the NFL with the Dodgers and ranked second in the NFL in yards-per-rush before returning to Clemson.

In 1959 McFadden became the first Clemson football player inducted into the College Football Hall of Fame.

After coaching Clemson's defensive backs under second-year head Coach Frank Howard in 1941, McFadden joined the Army Air Corps and spent four years in North Africa and Italy. He was discharged as a colonel. McFadden came back to Clemson after his service and was again the secondary coach, this time for four seasons (1946–1949), and then took over as head freshman football coach for five years before returning

Banks McFadden was a true triple-threat player for the Tigers from 1937 to 1939.

to coach defensive backs in 1955, a spot he held until Howard retired following the 1969 season.

Besides his football coaching years, McFadden also served as varsity track coach, freshman basketball coach, and for 10 seasons (1946–1956) Clemson's head basketball coach. From 1947 to 1952, Clemson improved its conference victory total each year, the first coach in the history of college basketball to realize a conference victory improvement five consecutive years. The streak was culminated with an 11–4 Southern Conference record in 1951–52, still the Clemson record for conference wins in a season through 2016.

After Howard resigned as head football coach in 1969, McFadden took over the university's intramural department, which he directed for 15 years. McFadden came to Clemson a skinny 6'3", 165 pounds. Frank Howard, who was an assistant coach under Jess Neely when McFadden arrived in 1936, said of him, "If McFadden drank a can of tomato juice, they could have used him as a thermometer."

"I can remember the first time I saw him on the practice field," Howard recalled. "He looked like one of those whooping cranes. I thought sure as the devil that Coach Neely had made a mistake by giving this boy a scholarship. But he proved me wrong."

McFadden was granted a long list of honors throughout his career. In 1966 he was presented with Clemson University's Distinguished Alumni Award. He was a charter member of the Clemson Athletic Hall of Fame and the South Carolina Athletic Hall of Fame. In 1987 both his uniforms, No. 23 in basketball and No. 66 in football, were retired by Clemson University, the only Tigers athlete to have two jerseys so honored. In 1994 he was inducted as a charter member of the Clemson Ring of Honor at Clemson Memorial Stadium. In 1995 the Banks McFadden Building at Jervey Athletic Center was dedicated in his honor.

Of all of the honors he received as an athlete, he said the 1939 football team MVP award was his highest honor. "To me, when your teammates vote you something, then you feel pretty good. That award meant more than anything else."

HOWARD DIDN'T CALL McFADDEN "THE GREAT" FOR NOTHING

Frank Howard was not only the head football coach for 30 years at Clemson, he was the head track coach from 1931 to 1940. During this time McFadden was one of his star pupils.

On May 4, 1940, at the state track and field meet in Clinton, South Carolina, McFadden was participating in the long jump. University of South Carolina's Dick Little had defeated McFadden the previous two years, and McFadden wanted badly to avoid a similar fate. Nevertheless, Little broke the state record on his first jump, and McFadden wasn't close on his. McFadden got closer on his second attempt, but he felt something was still wrong and had serious doubts about beating Little's leap at this meet. Walking away from the pit, McFadden told Howard about his problem.

"I told him I didn't know if I was over-striding or under-striding, or what was wrong, but I just didn't feel confortable," McFadden said. "Coach told me, 'Boy, come on down here with me.'" They walked back to the pit, and Howard took out a tape measure and set one end at the takeoff board and stretched the tape into the landing area. Howard told him, "Here's 22 feet. So that you will have a target, I will put this towel right here. What I want you to do is just clear this towel, and you'll be all right." McFadden said, "Thanks, coach, I appreciate that."

When McFadden turned his back to go back up the runway, Howard took the opportunity and moved the towel further down the pit another foot. "I was in the right frame of mind," said

McFadden. "I reared back and took off. I aimed for the towel and I missed it, I was just short. I was disappointed. I saw Coach Howard there, and he saw that I was disappointed. I said, 'Coach, what did I do wrong?' About that time, they announced that I had broken the state record and beat Little's mark. Coach Howard looked at me and said, 'You didn't think I was going to leave that towel at 22 feet, did you?'"

Coach Howard said after telling this story, "Now that's great coaching!"

Clemson won the state meet that year as McFadden not only won the long jump but also won both hurdle events, and for good measure finished third in the shot put for 18.5 of the Tigers' 58 total points.

Howard had introduced McFadden to hurdles. "I had never run the hurdles before and knew nothing about it," said McFadden. "Coach Howard threw me the book on hurdling techniques and said, 'Read it, I'm just the football line coach.' Coach Howard was a man who really knew how to handle people. I had never jumped that far in my life. I have to believe he thought I was a pretty good athlete, and he tried to get something out of me that I wasn't getting out of myself."

CHAPTER 5
CLEMSON'S
MILITARY HERITAGE

The Price of Freedom

Freedom is not free. It's a very powerful and significant statement. The price of this freedom is paid by the sacrifice, and sometimes, the lives of brave men and women.

Clemson's football stadium was named Memorial Stadium as a tribute to the Clemson students who made the ultimate sacrifice in service to the United States. An additional memorial named the Scroll of Honor, completed this past spring, is located just across the street on the east side of the stadium. It is a permanent epitaph to those who have laid down their lives to preserve the freedom we enjoy today.

A famous American general once wrote to his wife, "What a cruel thing is war: to separate and destroy families and friends, and mar the purest joys and happiness God has granted us in this world; to fill our hearts with hatred instead of love for our neighbors, and to devastate the fair face of this beautiful world." War, no matter how fought or when, always has devastating consequences. At Clemson, almost 500 students and graduates have been killed in this nation's wars and in peacetime operations. All the way back to World War I until the present, the Clemson family has lost members who served so bravely and courageously.

Clemson has a long, rich military tradition of answering the call when needed. In the early years, the board of trustees decided that Clemson would use a system of military discipline modeled after Mississippi State as did most land-grant colleges of the time. Students were required to wear uniforms that they had to buy. The board of trustees asked the War Department for the detail of an officer to act as commandant, responsible for the lives of cadets outside of the classroom.

Clemson can claim many proud moments in military history. In 1917 the entire senior class sent President Woodrow Wilson a telegram, volunteering its services to the United States' World War I effort. During World War II, Clemson supplied more Army officers than any other institution except West Point and Texas A&M; Clemson also had the largest infantry ROTC in the country.

In 1955 the Corps of Cadets was officially abolished, and the student body became civilian. ROTC was compulsory for the freshman and sophomore years until 1969–1970, when it became voluntary.

The Clemson students and graduates who lost their lives while serving our country are listed at the Scroll of Honor outside the east end of Memorial Stadium, their names etched in stone and laid respectfully and neatly at the foot of a mound.

A closer look at the ones who served and lost their lives in the line of duty would find many former Tigers athletes. One such brave soldier was Jimmie Dyess. Dyess was on the Clemson football team in the late 1920s and holds the distinction of being the only person in the United States to have won the Congressional Medal of Honor and the Carnegie Medal. The third of four children, he was born on January 11, 1909, in Augusta, Georgia. Arriving at Clemson in 1927 at 6'1", 190 pounds, he was the starting end on the freshman football team and made the varsity squad as a lineman during his sophomore and junior years.

On July 13, 1928, in the summer between his freshman and sophomore years, Dyess was vacationing with his family at a beach just north of Charleston on Sullivan's Island when a storm rolled in, bringing high winds and waves. He came upon a group of onlookers, as apparently one woman, Miss Barbara Muller, was attempting to rescue another, Mrs. Roscoe Holley, who had been swept out to sea. Several other unsuccessful attempts had been made by some of the onlookers on the beach. Miss Muller made one last effort to save Mrs. Holley. Upon realizing the situation, Dyess immediately went into the sea after the two women, who had been carried out as far as 200 yards. Dyess was not an experienced swimmer or used to such rough currents. After several minutes of near doom, Dyess helped the two women to shore, after which he gave further assistance in aiding the resuscitation.

An article in an Augusta newspaper chronicled the incident, citing that "onlookers give high praise to Miss Muller for a display of bravery and self-sacrifice seldom equaled and never surpassed, and added that but for the strength and cool-headedness of Jimmie Dyess, both girls would undoubtedly have been lost."

Dyess received the Carnegie Medal for his heroism on that day, an award that is given to heroic Americans and Canadians who, at risk to their own lives, save or attempt to save the life of another. It is "America's highest award for heroism by civilians," and it was presented to Dyess in 1929. Dyess always gave credit to Miss Muller, who also earned the Carnegie Medal, for diving in first after Mrs. Holley.

Dyess was a letterman on Clemson's 1929 team that finished with an 8–3 record. But toward the end of that year, his junior season, he suffered a serious knee injury that would prevent him from playing his senior season, so he shifted his focus to the rifle team, where he was the captain and an accomplished marksman.

The Augusta native, nicknamed "Big Red," was a Marine Corps reservist called to active duty in 1940. On February 1, 1944, he led his men in the Fourth Marine Division during battle at Green Beach on Roi-Namur Island—one of the Marshall Islands. At the end of the first day of combat, he discovered that there were marines caught beyond enemy lines who were facing heavy pressure. It was almost dark, but Dyess organized a small rescue force, and they broke through enemy lines and braved heavy gunfire to rescue the stranded men.

Closing in on the remaining Japanese military on the second day, Dyess maneuvered troops and tanks inland. Around 10:45 PM on February 2, Dyess was struck by a bullet in the head, killing him instantly as he was leading his men. Dyess left behind a 32-year-old wife and eight-year-old daughter.

Because of his bravery and his service beyond the call of duty, Dyess was awarded the Congressional Medal of Honor posthumously.

Aubrey Rion—A True Hero

Aubrey Rion had an early connection to Clemson even before the school was founded. Aubrey's great grandfather, Colonel James H. Rion, went to school with John C. Calhoun's children in Pendleton, South Carolina, at the Pendleton Male Academy. The colonel's mother was the housekeeper at Fort Hill, the home of John C. Calhoun. He developed a close relationship with the Calhoun family, including Calhoun's daughter, Anna Maria Calhoun Clemson and her husband, Thomas Green Clemson. The town of Rion, South Carolina, is named for Colonel Rion, who became a prominent lawyer.

Colonel Rion was Thomas Green Clemson's lawyer, financial advisor, and close friend. Rion was the author of Clemson's original will, which gave the Fort Hill estate and money to start the school that is Clemson University today. Rion passed away in 1886 of a heart attack.

Colonel Rion's wife, Catherine, is said to have advised Clemson on the estate's usage and helped plan some of the early buildings and their location on the Clemson College campus. It is believed that she was an architect and also enjoyed gardening and landscape design and had a lot of experience in this area.

Aubrey Rion was an all-star athlete at Columbia High School. He and his cousin, Holbrook Rion, won the state championship in the 220-yard low hurdles five times. Aubrey was also a star football player for his high school team. His cousin Holbrook went to the University of South Carolina, and Aubrey chose Clemson.

"My father, Holbrook, thought the world of Aubrey," said Tuck Rion, a second cousin to Aubrey. "Aubrey had and still has a lot of influence on our family. We talk about him and his accomplishments quite often. He was someone you can look up to and respect. We are very proud of him. I even named my son after Aubrey."

"He was a wonderful brother," said Martha Alvey, Aubrey Rion's sister. He was an excellent student and athlete growing up. Our other brother Wallace was an excellent student as well. Aubrey loved athletics and excelled at them. You couldn't have asked for two better brothers. I was very close to Aubrey and was very proud of him."

"There is no doubt about it, Aubrey loved Clemson," said Alvey. "When he first started at Clemson he wanted to be a doctor. He was preparing for that field and was going to medical school after Clemson, but World War II changed all that. He used to take me to the Clemson dances, and I would meet his friends and they would be in their Clemson uniforms. He met his wife, Janette, at one of the dances they used to have. He was a good dancer and was very popular with the ladies. He was very special."

"He was the best brother, friend, son, and husband there was," said Rion's sister, Mary Wittenberg. "Anyone who knew him always considered him their favorite. He was good to everyone. His death devastated our family."

One of the football teams that helped put Clemson on the national radar was the 1939 team. At that time, the Tigers were experiencing a special year. The school won the Southern Conference basketball and swimming championships on the same day on March 4. Both events were unexpected, as neither team was favored. It was one of the greatest days in Clemson athletic history.

World War II began five months later. The Clemson cadets probably had in their minds that they may have to serve later. But at that time, they were focused on school and working hard to obtain a degree. It was a special time at Clemson as the athletic teams were doing so well. It was toward the end of the Great Depression, and the Clemson campus was growing. It was an exciting time, but still an anxious time as the events of the world were so uncertain.

In the fall, it was the football team's time to grab the headlines. The 1939 team was a bright spot for the student body and alumni as Clemson went through the season with an 8–1 record. The Cotton Bowl issued a bid to the Tigers, which they gladly accepted. This was a big-time bowl inviting Clemson to the limelight of the New Year. It was a first for Clemson and the state.

Many of the Clemson players were from the state of South Carolina, including Rion. He was a junior that season and was a backup tailback to the legendary Banks McFadden. He was in great company with stars like Joe Blalock, Bob Sharpe, Walter Cox, Shad Bryant, Charlie Timmons, and Joe Payne. Rion averaged 4.0 yards per carry and scored two touchdowns that season, one against South Carolina and the other against Southwestern.

In his senior season, Frank Howard became the coach of the Tigers. In that season, the Tigers won the Southern Conference championship with an undefeated league record. In probably the best game of his career, Rion scored two touchdowns in the N.C. State game in 1940 at Memorial Stadium in Charlotte, North Carolina. He led the team in scoring that year with 28 points and averaged 3.5 yards a carry. Rion scored the winning touchdown against Furman on November 23, 1940, that gave Clemson the Southern Conference title with a 13–7 victory.

Rion was a three-sport athlete at Clemson. In addition to football, he was a boxer for the Tigers and a member of the Tigers track team, running the 100- and 220-yard dashes. On February 15, 1941, Rion graduated early from Clemson with a degree in general science. He is a member of the prestigious Tiger Brotherhood (an honorary fraternity unique to Clemson), the Columbia-Clemson Club, Block C Club, and the Sigma Tau Epsilon fraternity.

Like many others, Rion was living the American Dream. He graduated from Clemson, was a star athlete, and met his future wife at a dance that was held at Clemson. Everything was looking up for Rion, and his future seemed bright. He got a job at Bennettsville High School in South Carolina as a teacher and coach. He married Janette Stevenson on July 16, 1941, in Georgetown, South Carolina.

Then, on December 7, 1941, the Japanese bombed Pearl Harbor and the United States was drawn into World War II. Rion volunteered for service on June 30, 1942, less than two years after his final appearance on the Clemson gridiron and only six months after Pearl Harbor. Rion was stationed at Fort Benning, Georgia, for infantry training. He was an instructor at the infantry school for one year and was transferred to the parachute infantry in 1944.

He volunteered to go overseas in October 1944 because many of his men that he taught were shipping off to Europe. As a member of the 501st Parachute Infantry Regiment of the 101st Airborne Division, he saw action in Holland in November of that year. On June 6, 1944, the Allies landed on the beaches of Normandy, beginning the offensive to push the Germans out of western Europe and put an end to World War II. Another big event for Rion was the birth of his son Aubrey Jr. on June 17.

Early on the morning of December 16, the Germans launched their last major offensive as an attempt to reach the American and Allied supply depots and ports. It would become known as the infamous Battle of the Bulge. The next day, the 101st Airborne and Rion's regiment were ordered to the Belgian crossroads of Bastogne, a key road junction in the path of the Germans' attack. The Allies refused to surrender to the Germans and held off Gerd Von Rundstedt's attack until help came. Rion's 501st Regiment was the first to come in contact with the Germans. The 501st fought bravely and did not lose any ground. By Christmas the weather had cleared, which allowed air strikes, and General George Patton's Third Army reached the tired and embattled 101st Airborne Division.

Rion did not live to see the victory as he was killed by a sniper's bullet on December 20. He was one of 580 paratroopers killed, wounded, or captured from the 501st Regiment. Rion saw one of his men wounded and went to his aid. He picked up the wounded soldier and tried to carry him to safety, and that is when he was shot by the German sniper.

Winning this battle was the beginning of the end for the Germans. Aubrey Rion, a first lieutenant, was awarded the Purple Heart. He was survived by his wife, Janette, and son, Aubrey, and is buried at the Luxembourg American Cemetery not far from General George Patton's grave.

Clemson During the War Years

In the United States, World War II brought the American people together, perhaps the closest they have ever been, in an effort to win the war. To help the war effort, morale was so important on the front lines and back home in the United States.

To keep the morale up at home, President Franklin Roosevelt encouraged Americans to continue their customs and their unique way of life. Major league baseball was at the top of his agenda in the continuation of this American way of life. During this era, people were keeping track of Joe DiMaggio's hitting streak and the powerhouse New York Yankees. College football was another thread in the fabric of the American way of life that was important in keeping up the morale of the people.

During the years 1941 to 1945, times were hard for many colleges trying to field a football team—many colleges disbanded football, and some never came back. Most schools had players drafted right off the practice field. In 1943 Notre Dame quarterback Angelo Bertelli played just six games because he received a midseason call from Uncle Sam. Bertelli still won the Heisman Trophy and received word of the honor while stationed at a base in South Carolina.

In 1946, after the war, service men returned to campuses across the country to finish their studies and athletic eligibility, giving the college football world a swollen pool of athletic talent it had never seen before.

"There were very few football teams during this time," said former Clemson head coach Frank Howard. "Travel was hard, money was tight, everything was hard. A boy would enroll one semester and be gone the next. Once the war was over with we had some good football teams with the return of our boys."

One example of a player enrolling and coming back was Frank Gillespie. Gillespie played football, basketball, and baseball during his Clemson career. He also served on the student council and was student body president. As if he were not busy enough, he earned two degrees, in electrical engineering and textiles. "When I came back to Clemson after missing time for the war, I noticed my throwing arm was not as good. But other than that I was still the same in other activities. The professors were willing to help and work with you. I had two good friends I studied with, and this helped me a great deal. I didn't have much time for socializing. I didn't notice much difference at Clemson before and after the war. Coach Howard did not change either, he was still the same great coach."

Probably the one story that exemplified this era and the uncertainty of the times was that of Marion "Butch" Butler. Butler entered Clemson in 1940 and became one of the best tailbacks ever to play at Clemson. However, once World War II started, it was uncertain from one day to the next if he would be wearing the orange and purple of Clemson or the green fatigues of Uncle Sam's Army.

One of America's greatest resources during World War II was the ingenuity of its people. The ingenuity of Coach Frank Howard helped Clemson keep its all-star tailback. Coach Howard paid Butler to help with odd jobs around the athletic department before school started, something that was legal back then. Besides coaching football, Howard also played matchmaker from time to time.

"There were only three dateable girls on our whole campus," said Coach Howard. "Butch came and said to me, 'I don't like this place at all—there's nothing to do.'" Howard introduced him to Rox Rentz, who lived next door to Howard. Later they dated and eventually married. "It almost ruined me," he recalled. "I didn't have but two dateable girls left then. The whole football team almost quit."

After a successful year as Clemson's starting tailback in 1942, Butler was stationed at Fort Jackson in 1943 as any army private. But Howard arranged with his company commander (a Clemson graduate) for Butler to receive weekend passes so he could play football on Saturdays. Although he was not formally enrolled as a student at Clemson, this did not matter—a minute detail in that day and age compared to the events of World War II. (NCAA eligibility rules were lax back then because of the war.)

In the fall of 1945, Butch was still in the service, and Howard needed a tailback. Howard visited the commanding general at Fort Jackson and arranged for Butler to receive a 60-day pass. So Butler, his wife Rox, and their new baby arrived at Clemson just in time for the 1945 season. Butler was instrumental that year in Clemson wins over Tulane (47–20), Georgia Tech (21–7), and in a 0–0 tie with South Carolina. Still he was not enrolled as a student. Butler was probably the greatest unenrolled tailback in collegiate football history. Butler led the team in passing in 1942, 1943, and 1945, and led the Tigers in rushing in 1942.

However, Butch later graduated in 1946.

Dr. Bill Hunter, a local Clemson physician, recalls his experiences during World War II and playing football at Clemson:

> I played [in 1942], and after the football season everyone enlisted. I missed the 1943 to 1945 seasons. I was in the Marine Corps and flew with the Black Sheep Squadron. In 1942 at Clemson, we had a small squad composed of teenagers. This was the first team that played in Memorial Stadium and ran down the hill. I started at right guard that season when I was only 18 years old.
>
> While I was in the service, Coach Howard would write me, and I would get his letters on the carriers out in the Pacific Ocean. He would stress to us, "stay in shape." The war ended

in August 1945, but I was still on an airplane carrier in the Pacific. I played again in 1946 and 1947. However, we suffered a lot of injuries both of these years. Tulane was the Florida State back in those days, and I remember they beat us badly. When we arrived back in Clemson at the train station, the Clemson corps of cadets and townspeople met us at the train station and escorted us back to the campus. Situations like that will turn your blood orange.

The noticeable change at Clemson after I returned from World War II was the veterans did not have to participate in the military drills. The married students lived in prefabricated housing. This was a big help to us veterans.

When I was at Clemson before I went to war, I told Coach Howard I weighed 185 pounds when I actually weighed 170 pounds. I confessed to him after I left campus and was on the ship. When I came back after the war, I really weighed 185 pounds.

One of the reasons Clemson faired so well in football later in the 1940s and early 1950s was that Clemson did not drop football during the war years and "kept things going as best as possible," according to Howard.

CHAPTER 6
THE BASHFUL BARON
OF BARLOW BEND

Frank Howard the Legend

An era ended at Clemson University on June 30, 1974, when Frank Howard officially retired from the payroll. But instead of playing golf or fishing every day as many do after retirement, Howard never truly left Clemson, as he came to his office seven days a week in the Jervey Athletic Center.

Clemson's most animated figure retired from coaching on December 10, 1969, after 39 years on the Clemson coaching staff, 30 as head coach. He was also athletic director during this time and kept this position until February 4, 1971, when he was named assistant to the vice president of student affairs at the university. He held that post until the mandatory retirement age of 65 rolled around in 1974.

"I had to do it [retire from football] sooner or later," he liked to joke. "The reports would get out every year that I was retiring, and it would ruin my recruiting. The only way we're going to build this place up is to get a coach in here who isn't retiring every year."

At his press conference when he announced his retirement, he said, "I'm retiring because of health reasons…the alumni got sick of me."

Shortly after his retirement when he reached the age of 65, the Clemson board of trustees named the playing surface of Memorial Stadium (Death Valley) as "Frank Howard Field" in honor of his long service to the university. It was only the third time that a building or installation had been named for a living person by the trustees.

Howard was a charter member in both the South Carolina Athletic Hall of Fame and the Clemson Athletic Hall of Fame. During his career he was elected to the NATA (National Athletic Trainers Association) Hall of Fame, the NACDA (National Association of Collegiate Directors of Athletics) Hall of Fame, Helms Athletic Hall of Fame, State of Alabama Hall of Fame, Orange Bowl Hall of Honor, National Football Foundation Hall of Fame, Mobile (AL) Athletic Hall of Fame, Mobile High (Murphy) Hall of Fame, and the Gator Bowl Hall of Fame.

Frank Howard spent 39 years on the Tigers football coaching staff, 30 as head coach, and was also Clemson's athletic director until 1971.

Howard was presented the Order of the Palmetto, the highest honor that the governor of the state can bestow to an individual. Clemson University also recognized Howard once more with the presentation of the Clemson Medallion, which is the highest public honor bestowed by the university to a living person who exemplifies the dedication and foresight of its founders.

Clemson's "Legend" stepped onto the rolling hills of Clemson in August 1931 fresh from the varsity football ranks at the University of Alabama, where he was a starter on Coach Wallace Wade's 1930 team that drubbed Washington State 24–0 in the Rose Bowl. Howard was known as the "Little Giant" of the Tide's "Herd of Red Elephants."

The bald veteran came to his first coaching post under Jess Nealy as a line tutor. "At least that was my title," Howard recalled. "Actually, I also coached track, was ticket manager, recruited players, and had charge of the football equipment. In my spare time I cut the grass, lined tennis courts, and operated the canteen while the regular man was out to lunch."

Howard was not only track coach from 1931 to 1939, but served as baseball coach in 1943, and his 12–3 record that year is still the best percentage for a season in Clemson history. Howard held the line-coaching post until Neely went to Rice University as head coach in 1940 following Clemson's 6–3 victory over Boston College in the 1940 Cotton Bowl. When the Clemson Athletic Council met to name a successor to Neely, Professor Sam Rhodes, a council member, nominated Howard to be the new head coach. Howard, standing in the back of the room listening to the discussion after being interviewed by the council, said, "I second the nomination." He was given the job and a one-year contract, which he lost after about three months. He never had another contract his entire career.

Altogether, he served Clemson 43 years. When he retired as head coach following the 1969 season, he was the nation's dean of coaches, having been a head football coach at a major institution longer than anyone else in the United States.

Howard had the reputation of being a jokester, hillbilly, and country bumpkin. A thick Alabama drawl helped the effect. In reality, Howard was one of the nation's most successful coaches. When he retired, he was one of five active coaches with 150 or more victories.

While line coach during the 1939 season, Howard helped Clemson beat an undefeated Boston College team coached by Frank Leahy in the Cotton Bowl. (Leahy is still the second-winningest coach in college history on a percentage basis, trailing only Knute Rockne.) Clemson's 1948 mark of 10–0 carried the Tigers to the fourth annual Gator Bow, and two years later a 9–0–1 record sent Clemson to Miami's 17th annual Orange Bowl.

The Country Gentlemen were champions in their first three bowl ventures. Boston College fell 6–3, Missouri was nipped in the Gator 24–23 (Howard said this was the best football game he ever witnessed), and Miami felt the Tigers' claws, losing 15–14. The total point spread in these three bowl wins was five points. Howard said with a smile, "We humiliated all three of 'em."

The seventh annual Gator Bowl beckoned the Tigers again in January 1952, and by being conference champions in 1956, Clemson played in the 23rd annual Orange Bowl and again in 1957. Miami downed Clemson 14–0 in their second Gator Bowl trip, and Colorado led Clemson 20–0, then trailed 21–20, before finally defeating the Tigers 27–21 on Clemson's second trip to Miami. The Tigers then played in the 25th annual Sugar Bowl in 1959 and held No. 1–ranked Louisiana State to a standstill before losing 7–0.

The invitation to play in the first Bluebonnet Bowl in Houston in December 1959 was the eighth bowl that Howard had been a part of either as a player (one at Alabama), assistant coach (one), or a head coach (six). It was the seventh bowl trip for a Clemson team and the sixth in 12 years.

Howard said that Clemson's 23–7 triumph over seventh-ranked Texas Christian in the Bluebonnet was the best performance he ever witnessed by a Clemson team. By playing in that Bluebonnet Bowl,

Clemson became the first team to play in two bowls in the same calendar year. The Tigers played LSU January 1, 1959, in the Sugar Bowl and the Horned Frogs in the Bluebonnet December 19, 1959. The Tigers' victory over TCU was their fourth success in seven postseason appearances. In all seven, Clemson was the established underdog.

In his 30 years as a head coach, Howard went 165–118–12. In addition to heading up the Clemson football program, Howard also had the job of directing the school's entire athletic program, and at the same time, raising all of the required scholarship funds. The athletic department was always on a sound financial footing under the guidance of Howard.

In 1959 the Tigers presented Howard with an 8–2 season, which led to the Sugar Bowl invitation. One of these 1959 wins was the 100th of Howard's coaching career. That came against Jim Tatum of North Carolina, a coach whom Howard had never beaten. And the Tigers had to come from behind three times to win 26–21.

Howard was named Southern Conference Coach of the Year in 1948. In 1958 he was named Atlantic Coast Conference Coach of the Year and was accorded that honor again in 1966. Howard, who coached nowhere else but Clemson, won ACC championships six times (1956, 1958, 1959, 1965, 1966, and 1967) in the first 15 years of the conference. In 1966 Howard recorded his 150th collegiate victory when the Tigers defeated Maryland 14–10.

Howard was born at Barlow Bend, Alabama (three wagon greasin's from Mobile), March 25, 1909. He spent his early days on the farm playing mostly cow pasture baseball because there were not enough boys around the community to form a football team. Howard said he left Barlow Bend walking barefooted on a barbwire fence with a wildcat under each arm.

He graduated from Murphy (now Mobile) High School in Mobile, where he played football, baseball, and basketball and served as president of both the junior and senior classes. After graduating from Murphy

High, Howard entered the University of Alabama in the fall of 1927 on an academic scholarship provided by the *Birmingham News*. He played guard as a reserve his sophomore year. During his junior year he started every game but two, when an ankle injury sidelined him. His senior year he was again a regular. Howard was president of the freshman class at Alabama, a member of Blue Key, and president of the "A" Club.

After coming to Clemson, Howard married the former Anna Tribble of Anderson, South Carolina, on August 23, 1933. They were the parents of a daughter, Alice, and a son, Jimmy.

For over five decades, Howard was in great demand both as a banquet speaker and a clinic lecturer. Few states escaped his homespun oratory, which brought the house down on many occasions. Many felt his digs, especially if they had been to the podium before Howard. Many stories were told on Howard, but for every one poked toward him, he could fire two back. People found that it was best not to throw too many darts in Howard's direction, especially if he was given the opportunity to have the microphone again.

Most stories told on Howard are true, and some, classified as fiction, have been told so many times that even Howard believed they were true. Here are a few:

In the 1940s Howard was told of a big, strapping, young lineman in Charleston who was interested playing football at Clemson. It was the middle of the summer, and Howard was convinced by a loyal IPTAY member in Charleston that he needed to check out this young prospect. So Howard got in his car for the eight-hour, dusty drive to the port city. Upon arrival, Howard brushed himself off and went to the front door of the prospect's home. After knocking on the door, he was greeted by a high school–aged boy who was about 5′10″ and 170 pounds.

Howard asked if the young man he'd come to see was home. The boy replied, "I'm him." Howard quickly realized his IPTAY contact hadn't done a very good job scouting—even in the 1940s linemen were much bigger than 5'10", 170. Without missing a beat, Howard then said, "Would you like to buy a set of encyclopedias?"

He already had a set, he said. Howard bid him farewell, turned around, got in his car, and drove the eight hours back to Clemson.

Howard recalled another time when he received a letter from a coach in Virginia, telling him about a 155-pound tackle he had. Trying to make his point, this coach told Howard that this player was sure to grow and fill out. He explained that the boy's great great grandfather came over on the *Mayflower*, one of his uncles was a former governor of Virginia, another uncle had been a Supreme Court justice, and that he didn't see how he could go wrong in giving this player a Clemson scholarship.

"I wrote this coach back real quick," Howard recalled. "I told him that I was looking for a boy to play football...I didn't need one for breeding purposes."

Howard said that he always tried to get on the right side of the player's momma. "I found that the momma is the one behind most of the decisions made at home. I remember one time I did such a good job on selling Clemson to this boy's momma that she came to Clemson, and he went to South Carolina."

Maybe the greatest duo to ever travel the banquet circuit was Douglas Clyde "Peahead" Walker and Frank Howard. They were like pro wrestlers—they'd tear each other apart in front of a live audience, then ride in the same car to the next engagement.

Howard and some of his coaches were invited to go to Europe in the summer of 1958 to conduct football clinics for the armed forces. This led Walker to write Howard a letter on how to conduct himself while out of the country, passing on some tips "from my vast storehouse of international *savoir faire*." Among the things Walker offered to Howard: "Don't talk politics. They're having enough trouble over there without getting involved with someone from South Carolina with an Alabama accent.

Dress the part. Buy some new clothes and wear coats that match the pants. Egg on the tie is not in style."

On another occasion, Howard had Walker arrested prior to a game at Clemson. On Friday afternoon as the Wake Forest team was coming into the stadium, Howard shouted, "There he is! He's the fugitive!" A state policeman who was in on the gag immediately handcuffed Walker to a telephone pole as Howard walked away laughing. But the next day Walker experienced further problems. As the team entered the stadium, a security guard stopped Walker. He did not have his sideline pass, and the guard was adamant about not letting him in. Walker yelled to his team captain, Pat Preston, to identify him. "I've never seen him before in my life," said Preston, who had been enticed to take part in the prank by Howard. Finally, Walker got loose and was allowed into the stadium.

"Peahead was so cheap, he usually sold his sideline pass for $2," said Howard. Reportedly, Preston did a world-record number of sprints when the team returned to Winston-Salem.

Howard also had a friendly, almost brotherly relationship with Bear Bryant. As an Alabama alumnus, and senior to Bryant in the head-coaching fraternity by a few years, Howard could put the Bear in his place from time to time as only an older brother can.

One year he visited Bryant in his office and saw a red phone on his desk. "What is that for?" asked Howard.

"It speaks direct to God," replied Bryant.

"You mean I can call God?"

"Sure can," said Bryant. "It will only cost you $20."

The next year Bryant returned the visit to Howard's office. Howard had an orange phone on his desk. "What's that orange phone for?" asked Bryant.

"That's a special phone direct to God," said Howard.

"How much would it cost me to call God from here?"

HOWARD DISCIPLINES A TENNIS PLAYER

Gordon Herbert was a former United States marine and had survived the famous Hill 81 Battle in Vietnam.

"After those experiences, one could say he had the right to be a free spirit," said former tennis teammate Jim Poling. "During his Clemson days, he was one of the first really long-haired students any of us had seen. However, he could sure play tennis."

One day after Herbert had finished getting his ankles taped up in the training room, he ran into athletic director and head football coach Frank Howard.

The two got into a heated discussion about the length of his hair. It ended with Coach Howard chasing Gordon out of Fike Field House and out to the tennis courts with a pair of scissors. Howard was bound and determined that he was going to give a hair cut that day. About 50 people enjoyed the spectacle with the rotund Howard running after Herbert. Coach Howard was only wearing his boxer shorts!

"It was a scene that I will never forget," said Poling.

"It doesn't cost a thing," said Howard. "Around here, that's a local call."

One day when he was coaching, Howard was returning from Greenville to the Clemson campus. At that particular time, one had to travel first to Easley, then to Liberty, next to Norris, and on to Central before finally arriving in Clemson.

Norris had a one-man police force, and there's no telling how many Clemson students, staff members, and professors had been flagged by this one person. One could never guess what his routine was, but from town-limit sign to town-limit sign, it was best to travel about 34 mph.

On this particular day Howard wasn't paying much attention to his speedometer and was pulled over by this Norris policeman. Figuring he was only eight miles from home, Howard struck up a friendly conversation to try and get out of the ticket. But it seemed that the more Howard talked, the more the policeman wrote. Finally, Howard said, "I'm the head football coach over here at Clemson."

And the officer replied, "Yeah, I know. And I'm the head catcher here at Norris."

Howard was always ready to talk about his players, whether they were still in uniform or already out on their own. He got ragged quite a bit by his Coffee Club members at the Clemson Holiday Inn for not having as many NFL players as some of his counterparts.

"The most satisfaction I have is seeing some ole guard or tackle or halfback become a lawyer, or a doctor, or a successful businessman and a good citizen. It's worth more than a hundred touchdowns. And that's the truth, if I ever told it."

One Monday morning while downing their coffee, members of the group framed up on Howard again concerning the pro games of the day before, where several ex-ACC players had had decent days, but former Clemson players were not mentioned prominently.

"Yeah, but my players are going to be making a lot more in the long run than those pro players," Howard boasted. "I got boys out there who are presidents, engineers, college professors, diplomats, college presidents, and believe it or not, I even have four or five who are preachers."

About that time, as luck would have it, one of his ex-players who had become a preacher, Joe Bowen, walked into the dining room.

"Reverend Bowen, come over here for a minute, please, sir," Howard said reverently. "Reverend Bowen, did you ever play football for me?" he asked.

"Why, yes," Bowen answered without batting an eye. "I heard the Lord's name used a lot more on the practice field than I ever did in the seminary."

In 1977 Howard entered the Anderson Memorial Hospital to have a few tests run because he hadn't been feeling too well lately, as he put it. As it turned out, Howard had to have his gall bladder removed. He said the thing exploded, and they had to pick it out with a pair of tweezers. During this ordeal, his blood pressure went almost to zero, and only the quick action of a Clemson graduate nurse pulled him through, although it was touch and go for several days.

After the crisis was over, he was taken out of intensive care. Bob Bradley, who was in Omaha with the Clemson baseball team for the College World Series, went down to Western Union and sent the following telegram to Howard: "THE CLEMSON BASEBALL TEAM, BY A VOTE OF 10 TO 9, WISHES YOU A SPEEDY RECOVERY." After the baseball team returned from the CWS, Howard tried to find out who the "nine so-and-sos were who voted against me."

Howard told his son Jimmy that, after coming through all of the complications, he thought he had died.

Jimmy asked, "Did you see Jesus?"

Howard said, "No."

Jimmy then asked his dad, "Did you see the devil?"

Howard said, "No, but I must have been in hell because I saw [former Wake Forest Coach] Peahead Walker."

"When I die, I want to be buried up there on that hill [Cemetery Hill] behind the stadium," Howard would say. "I want to be there so I can hear all them people cheering my Tigers on Saturday and where I can smell that chewing tobacco in every corner of the stadium. Then I won't have to go to Heaven. I'll already be there."

Howard died on January 26, 1996, the same day on the calendar as his friend Bear Bryant, who had died 13 years earlier. He left behind a legacy that will probably never be equaled in the annals at Clemson. His honesty, humor and down-to-earth sense of humor will be remembered for other generations to pass on. And, as he wished, he is buried behind Death Valley, where he can hear the roar of the crowd cheering for his Tigers on Saturdays in the fall.

CARY COX, TWO-WAY PLAYER

One of the most bizarre situations of the Clemson–South Carolina football series or any rivalry of this consequence took place in the 1940s when a player served as captain of both squads during his playing career.

Cary Cox was a member of the 1942 Clemson football squad that beat South Carolina. Cox signed up for the V-12 Program in 1943 and was placed at the South Carolina campus. The V-12 Navy College Training Program was designed to supplement the force of commissioned officers in the United States Navy during World War II. Between July 1, 1943, and June 30, 1946, more than 125,000 participants were enrolled in 131 colleges and universities in the United States.

The Naval instructors at South Carolina ordered him to play on the Gamecocks football team, and he was named captain for the Big Thursday game against Clemson. Cox was reluctant to play against Clemson, but the Gamecocks head coach, Lieutenant James P. Moran, told him, "Cox, I cant promise you'll get a Navy commission if you play Thursday, but I can promise you this: that you won't get one if you don't play." Cox and the Gamecocks defeated Clemson 33–6 that year.

He returned to Clemson after the war and played for the Tigers in 1946 and 1947, becoming a captain during the 1947 season, before graduating in 1948. He served as an assistant football coach at Clemson in 1949 under Frank Howard, and then went on to pursue a career in business and finance.

Building Death Valley

The 1939 season was one of Clemson's greatest. That squad played in the 1940 Cotton Bowl under head coach Jess Neely. Before the game, there were rumors that Jess Neely would leave Clemson and go to Rice and be their head coach and athletic director.

It was thought that Clemson would use the building of a new stadium as a bargaining chip and would help convince Neely to stay at Clemson. Officials at Clemson and Neely were thought to have discussed this situation on the way out to Dallas for the bowl game. But Neely accepted the Rice offer.

Neely gave new coach Frank Howard some advice in a helpful way. "Don't ever let them talk you into building a big stadium," he said. "Put about 10,000 seats behind the YMCA. That's all you'll ever need."

Instead of following Coach Neely's advice, however, Clemson officials decided to build the new stadium in a valley on the western part of campus. It was announced on September 17, 1941, that the $104,000 stadium construction would soon begin. Clemson civil engineering students surveyed the land and drew up plans for the grandstands, which were built in concrete along the red clay walls of the natural bowl. Credit for the design of the stadium goes to Carl Lee of Charlotte, North Carolina, a Clemson graduate of 1908, and professor H.E. Glenn of the Clemson engineering faculty.

The site that was selected would take some clearing—there were many trees. The crews went to work—clearing, cutting, pouring, and forming. When the original part of the stadium was built in the early '40s, scholarship athletes, including many football players, did much of the work. Two members of the football team, A.N. Cameron and Hugh Webb, did the first staking out of the stadium. Webb returned to Clemson years later to be an architecture professor, and Cameron went on to become a civil engineer in Louisiana.

The building of the stadium proceeded with a few problems. One day during the clearing of the land, one young football player proudly announced that he was not allergic to poison oak. He then commenced to attack the poison oak with a swing blade, throwing the plants to and fro. The next day, the boy was swollen twice his size and had to be put in the hospital.

Howard recalled hitting a snag during the laying of the sod. "About 40 people and I laid sod on the field," he says. "After three weeks, on July 15, we had only gotten halfway through. I told them that it had taken us three weeks to get that far, and I would give them three more weeks' pay for however long it took [to finish]. I also told them we would have 50 gallons of ice cream when we got through. After that, it took them three days to do the rest of the field. Then we sat down in the middle of the field and ate up that whole 50 gallons."

"Now that's motivation!" said Howard.

Finally, on September 19, 1942, Clemson Memorial Stadium, with a 20,000-seat capacity, opened with the Tigers thrashing Presbyterian College 32–13. Coach Howard said that on the day of the first game in the new stadium, "The gates were hung at 1:00 PM, and we played at 2:00 PM."

Although named Memorial Stadium to honor those Clemson students who have lost their lives in the nation's wars, the nickname "Death Valley" is a helpful reminder and serves as a warning to Tigers opponents that it's a difficult place to play.

The Origin of the Name Death Valley at Clemson

Running down the hill and touching Howard's Rock are stalwart traditions that allow Clemson to be unique in the college football world.

Another original, but imitated tradition, is Memorial Stadium's nickname, "Death Valley." The nickname has its origins at Clemson just after World War II, before the stadium was even five years old, many years before LSU claims to have started using the moniker.

The name Death Valley originated in the 1940s and stemmed from the Clemson–Presbyterian College series. For 29 straight seasons (1930–1958), Clemson opened the season with the Blue Hose. All of these games but one were played in Clemson, and that was in 1940, Coach Howard's first season as head coach.

In 1943, with many college players away in World War II, there was naturally a scarcity of players. Many who played in 1943 were freshmen, and in that season, Presbyterian surprised the Tigers with a 13–12 victory in Tigertown. In 1944 the Tigers got revenge over the Blue Hose and won 34–0. In 1945 the Tigers must have still been angry about losing in 1943 and defeated Presbyterian 76–0.

In the spring of 1946, and in the preseason practices before the season began, Presbyterian was preparing to play the Tigers. According to former Presbyterian player and later head coach, Cally Gault, the trip to Clemson was very special. Gault was head coach of the Clinton, South Carolina, school from 1962 to 1984. "We talked about the upcoming Clemson game quite often when I was a player, as it was a tradition to open the season with them," said Gault. "After we were beaten so badly in 1945, Presbyterian coach Lonnie McMillian and us players referred to the Clemson trip as going to 'Death Valley.' I'm not sure when the press picked up on it, but I'm sure it was real soon."

A relative of Coach McMillian stated that on the way to the 1932 Olympics in Los Angeles that McMillian stopped in Death Valley, California. This leads to the belief that he was well qualified to compare the temperatures in Death Valley, California, and in Clemson.

Gault recalled:

> I remember during the 1945 season that somebody out in California sent a newspaper clipping about a team in California

that Presbyterian College should meet, as both teams were struggling. They suggested in their letter that these two winless teams meet in Death Valley, California, and they should call it the "Futility Bowl."

Coach Lonnie McMillian [Presbyterian College, 1941–1953] was a good coach. In 1943, he was one of the first, if not the first, to run the T formation in the South. I guess you could say he was ahead of his time. He had a good sense of humor about him too.

I remember both the 1945 and 1946 Presbyterian-Clemson games. I was 16 years old as a freshman, and playing in Death Valley was special. I do remember this more than anything—it was hot, and I mean real hot at Clemson! You haven't felt hot until you played in Death Valley in early September!

Coach Howard picked up on the new nickname of his stadium and started using it in the media, and it became really popular when he started using it.

McMillian also used the now-famous term in the media to describe the newly built stadium.

To say that Death Valley has been good to the Clemson football fortunes is an understatement. Clemson has won over 73 percent of its games in 73 years in one of the shrines of college football.

Bobby Gage—All Around Great

Bobby Gage was one of the finest all-around football players in Clemson history. He played in the one-platoon era, and he really had an effect on both sides of the ball.

He would change the course of games with his punt and kickoff returns. A close look at his statistics in 1948 reveals a season in which he had a 100-yard rushing game (104 yards on 12 attempts) versus Furman, a 172-yard passing game against Mississippi State, a two-interception game on defense also against the Bulldogs, and a 100-yard punt-return game (101 yards on three returns) against N.C. State. His 90-yard punt return in that N.C. State game proved to be the game-winner and is still the second-longest punt return in Death Valley.

Gage was the true triple-threat football player of the 1940s. He ended his career with 35 touchdowns, 24 from TD throws, eight on rushes, one via punt return, one by kickoff return, and one reception.

For his accomplishments in 1948, Gage was named a first-team All-American. He was a first-round draft choice of the Pittsburgh Steelers after the season. "In my junior and senior years, there was some substitution, but not much. A coach wanted to keep the best 11 out on the field. I remember in the Auburn game, I set a school record of 374 yards total offense (141 rushing, 233 passing), and I punted the ball seven times. I also returned punts and kickoffs, as well as playing defensive back. I was a little tired after that game. With the two-platoon system like today, the game may have more scoring and offense, but it still boils down to which team blocks and tackles the best."

"Gage was another of my players who was fun to be around," said head coach Frank Howard. "We called him 'School Boy.' We had a naked reverse in our offense. In the single-wing offense on this particular play, the ball would be centered to the fullback. He would give it to the tailback. The tailback would stick the ball behind him and hide it. Then the fullback would fake a handoff to the wingback coming around. The guards would pull out and even a tackle would pull. They would all be leading the wingback around the other way. That would leave the tailback out there by himself with the ball. I was talking to Bobby along the sideline when the other team had the ball and told him, 'School Boy, that end is not playing right. Don't try that naked reverse play, it won't work.' The next time we got the ball, Gage went back out on the field, and the very first play he called was that naked reverse. And, sure enough, everybody on the defense started chasing the flow of the play and bought the fake. School Boy hesitated a minute, then started coming around the other way. He was headed right toward our bench. When he went by me, he held the ball out at arm's length and said, 'I told you this play would work.' Then he ran down the sideline about 50 yards for a touchdown."

COUNTERFEIT TICKETS

One of the oddest occurrences of the Clemson–South Carolina football series occurred in 1946, in Columbia, South Carolina. This particular year about 10,000 counterfeit tickets were printed and sold.

"I remember our team got there about the time the big crash took place," said Clemson head coach Frank Howard. "My players got through all right, but a ticket-taker stopped me and said I couldn't get in. I told him, if I didn't get in there, I'm certain that there would not be a game that day."

An estimated 10,000 people crashed the gates that day, and there were so many people that they spilled out onto the field. There was barely enough room to play the game. The game was stopped several times to clear the field. Coach Howard remembered a woman in a big hat stood in front of him during the game, and he had to ask her what was happening on the field.

"It was almost impossible to do any coaching," said Howard. "I'd look around to yell for a substitute and there would be 50 people between me and my bench. People were all over the playing field, and when the teams would get at one end of the field, the other end zone would fill up with people. Most of the people on ground level that day just sat about talking to old friends, because you certainly couldn't see anything. Two of these vendors came up and tried to sell me some of their wares during the game. I heard one fellow say, leaving the game, 'That was the best game I never saw.'"

Fred Cone—
The Greatest of All Recruiting Tales

It is perhaps the most unusual story concerning an athlete's journey to Clemson in school history. Fred Cone was visiting his sister in Biloxi, Mississippi, far from his hometown, a small place called Pineapple, Alabama. Unbeknownst to head coach Frank Howard, Cone's sister lived next door to his sister, Hazel, in Biloxi. On years when Clemson would play Tulane in New Orleans, Howard would send Hazel a pair of tickets. "One year she asked for two more tickets," Howard remembered, "and said she'd like to take her next-door neighbor to the game as well."

That was in 1946, Cone's senior year in high school. Howard remembers that after Cone graduated, Hazel wrote him and said, "Brother, I have you a good football player, but he's never played football."

Howard recalled that he had told the Clemson registrar to save him 40 beds in the barracks and that he would turn in that many names on September 1. "When Hazel wrote me about Fred Cone, I had 39 names on that list. So I just wrote 'Fred Cone' in as the 40th name, and that was that," Howard recalled. "And that's how I got probably one of the best, if not the best, football player I ever had." Howard should have made his sister recruiting coordinator.

Cone graduated from Moore Academy in Pineapple and came to Clemson in 1947 as a freshman, but first-year players were not eligible to play then. It was probably best for Cone, because he had not played high school football. He needed a year to get acclimated. When Cone became eligible for the varsity team in '48, the football program took on a different air.

In the second game of 1948 against N.C. State, Cone had the first of his eight 100-yard career rushing games, leading Clemson to an important victory. He was Clemson's top rusher (635 yards and seven touchdowns) that season, a regular season that saw Clemson complete a perfect

Fred Cone was considered by Frank Howard as "the best player I ever coached."

10–0 record and receive an invitation to the Gator Bowl in Jacksonville, Florida, against Missouri.

Clemson won the thriller 24–23. Cone rushed for 72 yards and scored twice in the first quarter, but it was his effort on a fourth-down play late in the contest that was the difference in the game. Of all the thrills that Howard had as a player at Alabama and as a coach at Clemson, Cone is involved in the play that stood out in his mind the most.

Against Missouri in the Gator Bowl, Clemson held a one-point lead and faced a fourth-and-3 at the Mizzou 45. It was either gamble for a first down or punt and give Missouri another chance to score. As Howard would later say, "We hadn't stopped them all day, so I took my chance with a running play." Cone hit a stone wall at left tackle, but kept digging and slid off a little more to the outside, found a little wiggling room, and mustered six yards and a first down at the Missouri 39. Clemson retained possession those few remaining minutes and ran out the clock.

Despite a down year for the Tigers in 1949, Cone gained more yards (703) rushing and scored more touchdowns (eight) than in his sophomore year.

In 1950 the Tigers enjoyed another undefeated season; the only scar was a 14–14 tie with South Carolina. Cone had his third 100-yard rushing game in four contests and scored twice against the Gamecocks, but South Carolina's Steve Wadiak was unstoppable that day, outgaining the entire Clemson team with 256 yards rushing. However, Cone played most of the game with a busted lip after taking a shot to the face by a Gamecocks defender. In those days, there were no facemasks on helmets, and just before halftime, he was hit on the right side of his mouth as he went to cut on a running play.

At halftime the team doctor sewed him up without the help of any Novocain, stitching his lip with just a needle while Frank Howard was talking to the team. "It wasn't too painful because I was too excited about the game," Cone said. "In this game, you just didn't feel pain."

The 1948 and 1950 seasons marked the only time in Clemson football history that there have been two undefeated seasons over a period of three years. Cone and Ray Mathews were the only common denominators in the starting lineup on those two teams.

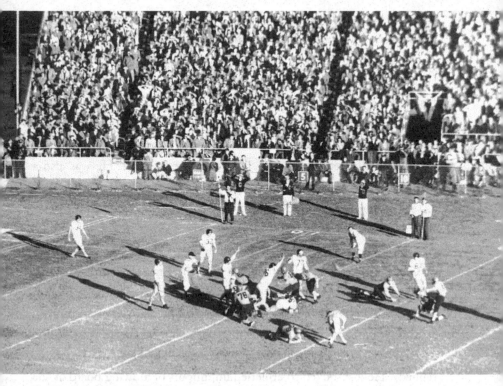

The Tigers won the 1949 Gator Bowl by a 24–23 score over Missouri. Jack Miller's 32-yard field goal in the fourth quarter proved to be the winning margin.

In 1950 Clemson scored 50 points in three different games, but Cone saved his best until the last regular-season game against Auburn. Rumor had it that if Clemson scored over a certain number of points on Auburn that the Orange Bowl bid was in its pocket. The Tigers from South Carolina took the Tigers from Alabama 41–0. Cone gained 163 yards and scored three touchdowns on the ground, with his one reception a 28-yard touchdown.

Icing on the cake this time came against Miami in the Orange Bowl. Sterling Smith's tackle of Fred Smith in the end zone for a safety late in the fourth quarter brought a 15–14 victory Clemson's way. Cone gained

81 yards on the ground, scored once, punted four times, and returned one kickoff. It was a great climax for Cone's career.

His number of carries (184), rushing yards (845), and touchdowns (15) were all school season records at the time. Also, he became Clemson's first 2,000-yard rusher (2,183), and his career touchdowns (31, to match his uniform number) were also a school best, as were his 189 points scored.

A seven-year career with the Green Bay Packers was so impressive that he was inducted into their Hall of Fame in 1974. He was also a member of the Dallas Cowboys in their first year of existence in 1960. Later he returned to Clemson as its chief football recruiter for 10 years beginning in 1961.

Accolades have come Cone's way over the years. He is a member of Clemson's Athletic Hall of Fame and the State of South Carolina Athletic Hall of Fame. He is also a member of Clemson's Ring of Honor.

After Cone completed his Clemson career, Howard was still stumped as to how his sister could predict that her neighbor's relative would be such an outstanding football player. When asked by Howard, she simply replied, "He just looked so athletic jumping off of a diving board at the local swimming pool," Hazel said, without skipping a beat.

1948—11–0 and No. 11 in the Nation

The 1948 team was one of the most talented in Clemson history, especially when you consider it was a unit with just 37 players on the travel squad. Eight players on this club are in the Clemson Hall of Fame. The team was a perfect 11–0, including a school record seven wins away from home (tied by the 2015 Clemson team), and a No. 11 final AP ranking.

Clemson was one of just three undefeated, untied teams and had the most wins in the nation that year. Michigan and Notre Dame were also undefeated, but neither team played in a bowl due to university policy. It was a club that was dominating on defense (allowing just 76 points), and had a precision single-wing offense that performed in the clutch. Six of the 11 wins were recorded by a touchdown or less, more close wins than any team in Clemson history. It might have been the greatest squad in school history in terms of special teams.

The perfect season of 1948 was as much a surprise to Clemson fans as the perfect season of 1981. Both years the Tigers were coming off mediocre campaigns. In 1947 Clemson was just 4–5 and had to win the last three games to manage that.

"Entering the 1948 season, we didn't think we would be as good a team as the previous year because Henry Walker decided not to come back," recalled Phil Prince, captain of the 1948 Tigers. "He had been our leading receiver the previous year and would have been one of the top players in 1948. He had already earned one degree from Virginia and then got another from Clemson in the spring of 1948. He was offered a job in the textile industry and decided to take it. He went on to become president of the company."

Many teams in recent Clemson history have had a formula that featured talented youth and wise veteran players. According to Prince, that was one of the reasons for the success of the 1948 Tigers. "We had an interesting mixture of seniors and sophomores. The difference in the 1948 team compared to 1947 was the sophomore class. That group of sophomores was the greatest group of athletes Clemson had had in one class up to that point. At the same time, we had some experienced players in the senior class. It just seemed that the leadership of the seniors jelled with the athletic talent of that sophomore class."

Fred Cone, a sophomore in 1948 who is among just four players in the Clemson Ring of Honor, agrees with Prince. "We had a lot of great athletes on that team. Bobby Gage—he could run, he could pass, he did everything. He called the plays, he ran the team, he gave everyone confidence. Frank Gillespie, Phil Prince, Gene Moore—they were all great

The 1948 team was undefeated with an 11–0 record. The squad ran the single-wing offense, seen above, to perfection.

team leaders who set an example for the sophomores. We were lucky to have such a group of leaders.

"We also had an outstanding coaching staff. Coach Howard was our leader, but the assistants were very good. I remember 'Goat' McMillan drilling us on how to hide the ball when we were practicing the spin for the single-wing offense. He taught us all the tricks of hiding the ball from the defense."

Prince summarized another important team characteristic. "Vince Lombardi once said, 'To be a successful team, you have to love each other.' We were always there for each other. To go undefeated and untied, we had to stay together. We had a lot of cliff-hangers in that season, and we had to stay together to pull them out. We didn't have any quit in that team."

The 1949 Gator Bowl is still considered one of the most exciting games in the bowl's history. "From a spectator's standpoint, I still think it is the most exciting game I ever saw a Clemson team play," Howard said. "We couldn't stop them, and they couldn't stop us. That's the reason we went for it on fourth down late in the game. I was afraid to let them have the ball back. I guess we were fortunate, but we had some good players, and they came through for us."

For Clemson, it jump-started an era that saw the football program go to six bowl games in 12 years, including two trips to the Orange Bowl and one to the Sugar Bowl.

"I don't think I have ever had more satisfaction out of one season than I did in 1948," Howard said.

The Legendary Dumb-Dumb Wyndham

When Dumb-Dumb Wyndham first came to Clemson, everybody called him Friendly. "I didn't know at first why they called him Friendly, because he was the most unfriendly boy on the team," said Howard. "But I later found out that Friendly was actually his given middle name." So how did he end up with the unfortunate nickname "Dumb-Dumb"?

Howard explained: "He got confused on a play I called at practice, so I finally straightened him out. I told him, 'Boy, you're so dumb you ought not be one, you ought to be twins.' After that, all his teammates didn't call him 'Dumb' but 'Dumb-Dumb' because of my remark about twins."

But Wyndham's play was anything but dumb, as Howard recalled:

> I remember we were playing [No. 17] Missouri in the second game of the 1950 season. It was hot that day. I remember

kicking off after we scored a touchdown. It was a high but short kick. They had a big tackle, he was 6'6" and weighed almost 290 pounds, and that was big in those days. That big tackle had his hands up to catch the kick off. The second the ball touched his hands, Dumb-Dumb hit him right in the stomach and knocked him cold.

They recovered the ball and went on offense. The right halfback ran with it. Dumb-Dumb tackled him and knocked him out. The fullback ran with it on the next play, and Dumb-Dumb knocked him out. Then the left halfback ran with it, and he knocked him out. The Missouri captain went up to the referee and asked him to "get that wild so-and-so out of this game, before he kills every one of us."

In the 1949 Gator Bowl game against Missouri, Harold Entsminger was the Missouri quarterback. He pitched the ball to one of his halfbacks. Entsminger was leading the sweep coming around the end. Dumb-Dumb was playing linebacker and literally ran over the quarterback to get at the ball carrier, and he knocked both of them out. "Dumb-Dumb was a killer," said Howard.

Howard told another story about Dumb-Dumb:

We were going up to play Boston College. I was showing a Boston College film to Dumb-Dumb. The year before, this fellow from Boston College had made a lot of good runs against us. So I told Dumb-Dumb, "We got to stop that boy this Saturday." He said, "Coach, the third time I hit him, he'll be out of the game for keeps." I didn't pay much attention to that. I thought it was a boy talking big.

We kicked off to Boston to start the game. That boy caught the ball and started up the field. Dumb-Dumb hit him so hard the kid's shoes came off. He threw the football down on the ground, staggered off the field and never came back in the rest of the game.

I asked Dumb-Dumb coming back on the plane how he knew he was going to knock that boy out of the game. He said, "Coach, I told you it would be after the third time I tackled him just to protect myself. But I really figured the first time I hit him he would come out of there."

Dumb Dumb was a real terror. He was a great one.

Howard told another story of how Dumb-Dumb inadvertently recruited a player to Clemson:

Dumb-Dumb was the reason I got one of my best players from Greenwood, South Carolina. His name was Harvey White.

Harvey's father was the sheriff in Greenwood. Some of his prisoners got out one night, and he called for the bloodhounds to track them down. Dumb-Dumb was a South Carolina law agent. He was the one who brought the bloodhounds to Greenwood. The dogs got to running and barking when they picked up the scent of the prisoners. Dumb-Dumb was right behind them, running with the dogs.

Mr. White later told me that when those prisoners saw that fellow chasing those dogs, they surrendered. They said they weren't scared of the dogs, but they didn't want that wild fellow behind the dogs to get a hold of them. The sheriff later told me that Dumb-Dumb was one of the main reasons he sent his son up to Clemson.

Frank Gillespie—Three-Sport Star

Frank Gillespie was the model student-athlete during his career at Clemson. He was an excellent student, double majoring in electrical engineering and textile engineering. As if that weren't enough, he was a starter on three teams—football, basketball, and baseball. He was also student-body president. And in the 1947–1948 season, he won the McKelvin Award as the Athlete of the Year in the Southern Conference.

Coach Howard remembers Gillespie when he came to Clemson on a visit. "When I was younger, I'd put on the pads and work out with the players some," said Howard. "I remember a boy I tried out, which was legal in those days. His name was Frank Gillespie. He was from Beckley, West Virginia. I hadn't heard much about him, but he wanted to come to Clemson. I said, 'Come on down, and I'll work you out.' I put on the pads with him. I lined up in front of him and told him to charge into me. *Whomp! Bam!* I said, 'That's enough, son.'

"'Coach, I thought we were going to work out,' he said.

"'We have. Welcome to Clemson.' I signed him on the spot. He went on to be one of the finest we've ever had. He was a great leader and athlete and could do pretty much whatever he wanted."

CHAPTER 7
THE FABULOUS
'50s AND '60s

1950 Season and 1951 Orange Bowl

In 1950 head coach Frank Howard was not anticipating great things at the season's outset. The 1949 season had been a disappointment with a 4–4–2 record. But this decade, the 1950s, would be different. Clemson would have the 15th-best winning percentage in college football in that decade, and the 1950 season certainly got the Tigers off on the right foot.

As fate would have it, all the tough games on Clemson's 1950 schedule were on the road. Boston College and Wake Forest had scored a combined 75 points at Clemson in 1949 and, along with South Carolina, Missouri, and Auburn, would host the Tigers this time around.

In early September workouts, it was obvious that senior backs Fred Cone, Ray Mathews, and Jackie Calvert had been working out together in the summer to perfect the deceptive features of Clemson's single-wing offense. Mathews, who had tried his hand at tailback in 1949, was now settled at wingback where he had excelled in 1948. Cone was in his third year as the spinning fullback, and Calvert, a multitalented substitute for two years, was sparkling at the key tailback position. Coach Howard was impressed. He began calling them his "dream backfield." As for the men up front, they were tagged his "nightmare line."

This derogatory heading didn't last long. By dividing his linemen into offensive and defensive units, Howard employed two-platoon football at Clemson for the first time on a full-time basis. In the middle of the line, on defense, guards Sterling Smith and Barclay Crawford and tackles Billy Grigsby and Bob Patton concentrated on stopping the opposition.

This left the blocking assignments to offensive starters Pete Manos, Dan DiMucci, Dick Gillespie, and Jack Mooneyhan. And freed of centering the ball and blocking duties by center Jack Brunson and blocking back Dick Hendley, linebackers Don Wade and Dumb-Dumb Wyndham provided the leadership on defense that had been missing in 1949.

These changes and others, such as adding ex-Furman coach Bob Smith to the staff and Billy Hair's emergence as a great offensive force, really helped the team. Coach Russ Cohen's molded sophomore baseball speedster Knobby Knoebel, 155-pounder Peter Cook, and veteran reserve back Gil Rushton into a quality defensive backfield. Coach Bob Jones' starters at end, Glenn Smith and Bob Hudson on offense and the contrasting giant Dreher Gaskin and 170-pounder Jim Calvert on defense, paved the way for a huge Tigers turnaround in 1950.

The season opener against Presbyterian College was a 55–0 romp for the Tigers. With Calvert excelling at tailback in the manner of 1948 All-American Bobby Gage, the offense actually produced three 100-yard rushers—Calvert, Mathews, and Cone—for the first time ever.

What was expected to be the real test, at No. 17–ranked Missouri the second week, proved more of the same. The three members of the dream backfield once again accounted for over 100 yards rushing each, and the nightmare line, aided by fine secondary play, shut down the home team for a 34–0 Clemson victory. It was the first time a Dan Faurot–coached team had been blanked since 1946—a span of 35 games. It is still tied for the largest victory margin over a top-25 team in school history (with the 2014 Russell Athletic Bowl versus Oklahoma.

No one was more in awe of what had happened than Coach Howard. He figured on the way home that he had potentially a top-10 team, one comparable to the 1939 and 1948 bowl teams—if he played his cards right and got some good bounces of the football. There was no trouble the next week, as visiting N.C. State fell with relative ease, 27–0. But coming up after a weekend off was archrival South Carolina, to be followed by nationally ranked Wake Forest. They had both defeated Clemson by two-touchdown margins in 1949.

As expected, both came to play. A partially blocked field goal in the final minute of play salvaged a hard-earned 14–14 tie against Carolina, and a Clemson block of a Wake Forest extra-point attempt in the final seconds of play preserved a 13–12 Tigers win. In the case of the Gamecocks, they just outplayed Clemson. Still, when a female fan suggested to Coach Howard that he must be happy to have held on for a tie, he quipped, "Lady, a tie ball game is like kissing your sister!"

The closeness of the Wake Forest game was caused in large part by the absence of All–Southern Conference players Ray Mathews and Fred Cone following rib injuries suffered in the first quarter. Remarkably, Clemson held on to win despite coughing up the ball five times deep in their own territory via four fumbles and a blocked punt. Cone would miss the next two games against Duquesne and Boston College, returning against Furman and Auburn. Mathews did not reappear until the Auburn game. Even so, the Tigers ran rampant over their final four foes by a combined 186–36 margin.

Clemson (8–0–1), ranked 10th in the nation, met Miami (9–0–1) in the Orange Bowl on January 1, 1951, and won in dramatic fashion, 15–14, after blowing an early second-half 13–0 lead. This time it was not final-minute blocked kicks as at Carolina and Wake Forest, it was a safety in the Miami end zone, caused by defensive guard Sterling Smith.

Clemson would field five bowl teams in the '50s—1950 Orange, 1951 Gator, 1956 Orange, 1958 Sugar, and 1959 Bluebonnet. And in the two seasons when the Tigers posted 7–3 records (1955 and 1957), they may have been better than some of those teams that went "bowling" in those days of limited bowls.

Coach Howard liked to refer to the players on most of his top-rated teams as "small-town boys playing big-city football." The 1950 team had its full share of country boys. However, perhaps more important to him was taking largely unknown and unwanted boys and molding them into a team that opened the eyes of football fans in Boston and St. Louis and Miami.

Twelve members of the 1950 team are in the Clemson Hall of Fame: offensive backs Calvert, Cone, Mathews, Hair, and Hendley; offensive ends Smith and Hudson; defensive end Gaskin; linebackers Wyndham and Wade; defensive guard Tom Barton; and defensive back Knoebel. Also, the entire full-time coaching staff of 1950 resides in the Hall of Fame. No other Clemson team has been so honored.

COACH HOWARD AND BEHIND-THE-SCENES POLITICS

"I got mixed up in behind-the-scenes politics only once in my life," said Frank Howard. "The waiting for the results was a bit nerve-racking." A few days before the 1951 Orange Bowl, in Miami, blocking back Don Wade, end Glenn Smith, and fullback Fred Cone missed curfew. Howard was there waiting on the trio.

Howard gave them a verbal tongue-lashing that would not soon be forgotten. "I'm sending you back to Clemson—tomorrow," announced Howard. Then he turned to assistant coach Walter Cox and told him to pick up three bus tickets back to Clemson.

The trio begged and pleaded and promised that it would never happen again. At first, Howard would not listen. Then he agreed to put it to a vote among the players, and their decision would be final. After they had seen Coach Cox leave for the bus station, and after the players headed to the rooms, Howard told assistant coach Bob Jones about what had happened.

He told Coach Jones, "Make sure—make double-sure—that the team votes the right way." The vote took place, and the results were unanimous. The vote went against Coach Howard, and the players were allowed to stay and play in the bowl.

Although he made a point, Coach Howard was never happier about losing a vote!

1951 Orange Bowl

The Tigers completed an undefeated season in 1950 and Clemson's 8–0–1 mark and second-place finish in the Southern Conference earned them a bid to play Miami, which was also undefeated at 9–0–1, in the 17th Orange Bowl. This marked the second undefeated season for the Tigers in three years, as the 1948 team finished with an 11–0 record. It is also believed that the 1951 Orange Bowl marked the first-ever appearance of the Clemson Tigers mascot.

After a scoreless first quarter, Clemson got on track with a 45-yard pass from Billy Hair to Bob Hudson that put the Tigers at the Miami 1. Fred Cone capped the 76-yard drive on third down with a sweep for the score, and Charles Radcliff tacked on the extra point.

Clemson mounted a six-play, 70-yard drive in the third quarter for its second touchdown. Hair threw a 31-yard pass to Ray Mathews, who, as the papers said, "made a circus catch with two men on his back," to move the Tigers to the Miami 28. Hair tossed a pass to Glenn Smith at the Miami 7, and Smith scrambled in for the score. Radcliff's extra point try was blocked.

Miami caught fire two minutes later when Jack Del Bello intercepted a pass in the Clemson end zone and returned it to the 40, and then a 10-yard penalty was assessed against the Tigers for unnecessary roughness. On the next play, Frank Smith ran a reverse for 45 yards to move the Hurricanes to the Clemson 5. Harry Mallios took a pitch from quarterback Bob Schneidenbach in for the score, and Gordon Watson added the conversion.

Miami went 95 yards in five plays for its second score in the third quarter. Ed Lutes caught a pass at midfield and rambled down to the Clemson 17 before he was stopped. On fourth down, Jack Hackett threw to Frank Smith for the score, and Watson's point put Miami in the lead for the first time, 14–13.

Mallios' 80-yard punt return was called back, and two clipping infractions and one unnecessary roughness penalty put Miami in a deep hole with six minutes left in the game. Frank Smith took a pitch from Hackett, but before Smith could get out of the end zone, Sterling Smith, a defensive guard for Clemson, tripped him up for a safety, and Clemson took the lead 15–14. Don Wade ended the last Miami threat with an interception, his second of the game, and Clemson ran out the clock for the win.

"I charged across the line and I grabbed the Miami runner and held on for dear life until he was down," said Sterling Smith. "It was the most memorable tackle in my career."

Sterling Smith tackled Miami's Frank Smith in the end zone for a safety with six minutes left in what proved to be the winning margin of a 15–14 Clemson victory.

Fred Cone, Sterling Smith, and Frank Howard celebrate in the locker room after the Tigers defeated 15th-ranked Miami in the 1951 Orange Bowl.

Don King—The Great Act of Sportsmanship

More than 60 years ago, Clemson running back Don King brought notoriety to Clemson by winning the nationally renowned and prestigious Swede Nelson Award by a simple act of kindness and respect for an injured opponent.

At the time, this was a coveted award that was presented by the Boston Touchdown Club and was given to the college football player who demonstrated sportsmanship during the year. It remains one of the oldest awards in the nation given to a collegiate player. After Wake Forest's Kenny Duckett won the award in 1981, it became a regional award and is now only presented to players from the New England area.

In 1953 winning this award was big news for the Clemson football program.

On October 31, 1953, Clemson was playing Wake Forest in Tigertown. In the third quarter, Wake Forest had the ball at midfield, trailing Clemson 12–0 when Demon Deacons quarterback Sonny George failed to get up after being tackled. Coaches, trainers, and teammates surrounded George for at least 15 minutes. Ultimately, King left his Clemson teammates, who were waiting for action to resume, and went over to talk to the Wake Forest players and officials. Then George got up and resumed play. At the time, rules stated that if a player left the field because of injury he would have to sit out the remainder of the quarter, and Wake simply did not have a reliable substitute.

"It was not until Monday morning when Tigers starting linemen Mark Kane and Clyde White stopped by my office that I found out what happened," said Brent Breedin, Clemson's sports information director at the time. Kane and White explained that Don learned that George would be playing with an injured knee, so he told the rest of the team, "When you tackle their quarterback Sonny George—tackle him high and not low," reminding them of his situation. King had had knee injuries himself in several games the past two years.

Kane and White went on to say that King explained to his teammates that he is the only quarterback that Wake Forest had and that they didn't want him to have a permanent injury. King had already missed the Miami game and much of the South Carolina game because of the same injured knee. So Don told them again, "If you tackle him the rest of the game, hit him high."

"I decided to share this incident with the Boston Gridiron Club," said Breedin. "They obviously liked it, coupled with the good relationship Clemson and Coach Howard had with many of the people in Boston via the Boston College rivalry that began in the 1940 Cotton Bowl, and King was their choice for the award."

In addition to King demonstrating class and sportsmanship, he was an outstanding football player. The native of Anderson, South Carolina, played for the Tigers and Coach Howard from 1952 to 1955 as a quarterback and safety. He established a Clemson freshman single-game rushing record in 1952 that still stands today. On November 4, 1952, he rushed for 234 yards in a tie game at Fordham, the last time Clemson played a football game in New York City. Fordham entered the game leading the nation in rushing defense. King played the tailback position in this game because of injuries to Clemson's regular running backs. It was the only game King played tailback in his Clemson career. It is still the third-most rushing yards in a single game by any Clemson back and a record for a Clemson player in a road game.

King led the Tigers in passing for four straight years and in rushing in 1953. He was the first Clemson player to lead the Tigers in passing four consecutive years. It is an accomplishment that has been equaled only by Nealon Greene (1994–1997) and Charlie Whitehurst (2002–2005).

The 1992 Clemson Hall of Fame inductee was a second-team All-ACC quarterback in 1953 and 1954, his sophomore and junior seasons, respectively. King passed away on February 14, 2013, at the age of 79.

This act of sportsmanship in the Wake Forest game that Halloween afternoon not only won King a prestigious national award, but he also won the respect of his teammates, coaches, and foes, as well as the admiration of countless others.

Formation of the ACC

The formation of the Atlantic Coast Conference in 1953 gave Clemson a chance to prosper and be more competitive on the national stage.

One of the reasons a new league was formed was there were 17 teams in the Southern Conference. Many of the larger schools thought it was simply too many. Another reason was that, at the time, the Southern Conference had a ban on bowl games. After the 1951 regular season, Maryland and Clemson both defied the conference ban and went to bowl games anyway. Maryland went to the Sugar Bowl and won the national championship, and Clemson went to the Gator Bowl.

The Southern Conference put Clemson and Maryland on probation for one year. They could play each other, but were forbidden to play other Southern Conference teams unless it was state law that two teams should play. Legislators in South Carolina immediately made it state law for one year that Clemson and South Carolina play football during the 1952 season.

The new conference was formed, and an agreement was reached to start the new league at the Clemson House in Clemson, at the Southern Conference Winter Meetings on December 12–13, 1952. Representatives from 17 schools were in attendance. The schools withdrawing from the Southern Conference met and conducted business and made plans. It was decided that the conference would not be formed or announced in Clemson, and it would be initiated at the Southern Conference Spring Meetings in Greensboro, North Carolina, on May 8–9, 1953.

With the Spring Meetings at Sedgefield Country Club, a new era in Clemson athletics began. Tagged "the Seceding Seven" by the media, Clemson, South Carolina, North Carolina, N.C. State, Duke, Wake Forest, and Maryland made plans for a new league of big schools only and formally withdrew from the Southern Conference.

The ultimate goal of the new seven-team conference was to build intra-conference rivalries among all member teams in all sports. On June 14, 1953, there was a meeting of the seven schools in Raleigh, North Carolina, to form definite plans. "I am hoping that we will be able to work out all of the common problems and form this new compact organization, give it an appropriate name, and start to work on what I consider will be one of the best if not the best conference in the United

States," said Clemson head coach Frank Howard. "The new conference should work out to everyone's benefit. For the past 20 years, we have been trying to schedule athletic contests with some of the schools but haven't had too much success. Since we all belong to the same conference, we will have six football games scheduled ever year and will be at liberty to schedule three or more nonconference games each season. In this manner a true conference champion can be decided. I feel sure that schools in the new conference will feel more kindly toward each other, as they will have more in common. An organization like this is what our alumni and friends wanted. We are going to have to work hard in this new league, and IPTAY will have to raise more money and get more members for us to be successful."

IPTAY did grow and more members joined. It is one of the most successful scholarship clubs in the nation. In the ACC there are now 15 members, 14 that play football.

Doctor Lee Milford—Pioneer of the ACC

Dr. Lee W. Milford Sr. was one of Clemson's most influential and highly regarded leaders in the late 1920s through the 1950s.

Dr. Milford came to Clemson on January 1, 1926, and was hired as the school's medical doctor. In this role, he was the physician for the student body and the various Tigers sport teams. The 1917 Emory graduate also was the Clemson town doctor. It's hard to imagine how many people he helped during his practice.

In addition to his medical duties, he had the responsiblity of being the chairman of the Athletic Council at Clemson and a faculty representative to the Southern Conference for 26 years. He was a three-time Southern Conference president and was instrumental in the organization of a booking office for conference football and basketball officials.

During his Clemson career, the Tigers went to their first bowl game, Banks McFadden was a two-sport All-American, Frank Howard was hired as head football coach and athletic director, and the ACC was formed. In the early 1950s, Milford was a leader in the organization of the ACC and was one of four people to write the conference's constitution and by-laws. Head Football Coach Frank Howard credits him with countless game-winning decisions made over injured players and helping with their recovery.

Dr. Milford was well respected in the medical profession. He was the founder of the Southern College Health Association and served as the president of the organization for eight years. He also served as vice president of the National Health Association. He was a member of the American Medical Association, the American Academy of General practice, the Southern Medical Association, the Southern Surgical Congress, and the South Carolina Medical Association. He retired from Clemson in 1956 after a 30-year career. When he retired, he held the title of director of student health services.

Dr. Milford's son, Lee Jr., played basketball and tennis for Clemson before he graduated in 1943. Like his father, he became a doctor and graduated with a medical degree from Emory in 1946. Dr. Lee Milford Jr. was recognized as one of the world's best hand surgeons and a pioneer in that field. He authored a book titled *The Hand*, which went through multiple printings and was published in four languages.

Lee Jr.'s son, Dick, was a tennis standout for head coach Chuck Kriese from 1977 to 1980, making him the third generation to be part of Clemson athletics. Dick was one of Kriese's first recruits. He was a four-year starter and won 61 singles and 69 doubles matches in his career. He was also a member of the 1980 ACC championship team.

Dr. Milford Sr. died on Saturday, January 5, 1980, at the age of 88. He had a long, distinctive career of helping others and serving Clemson.

Charlie Bussey, Clemson's First
Academic All-American

To Charlie Bussey, Clemson has always been and always will be a special place. Having played football at Clemson and later serving as director of the Tiger Letterwinners Association (now the Block C Club), he appreciated Clemson and the people that have shaped the school to make it what it is today.

His relationship with Clemson started in 1953 when Bob Smith recruited him as a T formation quarterback. Clemson was switching to the T formation that fall, and it was vital to recruit players who ran this offense in high school and knew how to execute it.

"I visited Clemson, and I think I am typical of what happens to many athletes and many students," said Bussey. "If you come on campus and take a look at what Clemson has to offer, that is the selling point. If you meet the Clemson people, see the campus, and tour the facilities, you are hooked. That's what happened to me."

Once Bussey arrived as a freshman in the fall of 1953, he says, "We scrimmaged the varsity every day, helping them get used to the T formation. We had a freshman game with Georgia Tech one Friday night, and they had a lot of talent. We lost 14–12, but we knew we had a good ballclub. After that game, we made a pact with one another that we would do what it took to win the ACC championship before we left Clemson. Back then the winner of the ACC would go to the Orange Bowl, and that gave us more incentive."

In Bussey's senior season, the class of 1956's dream came true as the Tigers won the Atlantic Coast Conference championship and received an invitation to the Orange Bowl for a game with Colorado.

Clemson fell behind and was losing 20–0 going into the locker room at halftime. Head coach Frank Howard was so discouraged with his team that he said, if they can't play any better than that, he would resign as head coach of the Clemson Tigers. "Coach Howard gave us

162

a fiery pep talk at halftime and deservedly so. We came back and went ahead 21–20 in the fourth quarter. However, Colorado scored a touchdown in the middle of the fourth quarter to go ahead and eventually won the game 27–21."

Speaking of memorable games, one that sticks out in Bussey's mind is the South Carolina game in 1955. "One of my favorite games was the Big Thursday game against South Carolina my junior year. Don King, our starting quarterback, got hurt, and I got a chance to start. We put in some new plays that season. We were watching Oklahoma on television one afternoon, and they used a misdirection play, and it went for a long gain." It didn't take the Tigers long to try this new wrinkle.

"We were up 7–0 against South Carolina. It was a second-and-7 situation, and I called "1-24x," which was the misdirection play that we saw Oklahoma use and had just installed. We were near midfield, and Joel Wells went down to the Gamecocks' 2-yard line after a 46-yard run. We won the game 28–14. That play, "1-24x," was good for at least 20 to 25 yards every time we ran it for the next two years. Wells was a big, fast running back, and he was a great teammate." Bussey intercepted a pass and was 2-for-2 on point-after conversions against South Carolina that day. He also threw a 55-yard pass to Willie Smith for Clemson's first touchdown.

As he was on so many players, Coach Howard was a big influence on Bussey, and they had a close relationship that lasted many years. "Coach Howard and I had a father-son type relationship. When he switched to the T formation, it was a gutsy move. Everyday I would go to his office and sit down, and he would draw plays on a yellow legal pad. I learned a lot from him, and I think he found it helpful, bouncing ideas off of me. We had this father-son type of relationship until his death. He had a great football mind, and he had a big influence on me. He once said in an article about me that I may not be the fastest player, the best passer, or the best runner, but I could win the game. In other words, I was an average player, but I would give above-average effort. I always appreciated his confidence in me. He was very special to me."

When Bussey graduated from Clemson, he served in the Air Force as an instructor pilot, and his business career included positions with Laurens Glass, Louis Batson Company, and Palmetto Chemicals. Bussey was also the athletic director at Louisiana Tech University, in Ruston, Louisiana, from 1981 to 1983.

After retiring from business in Greenville, South Carolina, in the late 1990s, Bussey and his wife, Joyce, moved to Clemson. Bussey became the director of the Tiger Letterwinners Association soon after his move to Clemson and worked in this position for 14 years until 2012. During this time he worked to unify Tigers letterwinners together regardless of age or sport and stressed that everyone is needed and welcome in this organization.

Over the years, Bussey was the president of IPTAY and was a member of the IPTAY board of directors. Bussey had three daughters, all of whom went to Clemson and two of whom were homecoming queens. A third, Laurie, worked in the Sports Information Office He also had seven grandchildren.

Bussey had many honors from Clemson while he was a student. He was the captain of the 1956 ACC-champion Tigers. He was the school's first Academic All-American and was named first-team All-ACC. In addition, he was a member of Tiger Brotherhood, Blue Key, and graduated with academic honors as well as an Outstanding Military Graduate (AFROTC).

Bussey passed away in 2015. When he died, Clemson head football coach Dabo Swinney said, "When you talk about a model student-athlete, and a model representative of Clemson University, that was Charlie Bussey. He was our first academic All-American, a successful businessman, president of IPTAY, then served as director of the Tiger Letterwinners Association when I came to Clemson. I enjoyed our many conversations about Clemson football and former players. Charlie Bussey has always been there for our football program and for me personally. We will miss him," said Swinney.

1958 Team—Sugar Bowl–Bound, Blue-Clad Tigers

Frank Howard's 1958 Clemson football team does not hold a lot of school records. There are teams with more yards rushing, more yards passing, more points scored, and the same goes for defensive highwater marks. For the season, this ACC championship team ranked 12th in the final AP poll, yet outscored the opposition by just 31 points.

But the 1958 team does have one important distinction. Four times that season Clemson overcame a deficit in the final period to gain victory. Three times this team came back from a deficit to gain victory over North Carolina, and they did it twice against Virginia. The touchdown that gave the Tigers a 12–7 victory at Vanderbilt was registered with nine seconds to spare, and the ACC championship was clinched with a 13–6 win over N.C. State.

What was this team's secret to success? One need only look to the example set by team captain Bill Thomas. This club put the team first in every manner. Thomas even delayed his wedding until after the season in accordance with Coach Howard's wishes. "We didn't play very well against Colorado in the 1957 Orange Bowl," recalled Thomas, who was a sophomore in 1956. "A lot of the players had gotten married that year and brought their wives to Miami for the bowl game. We went down 20–0 in the first half, and Coach Howard thought the players' minds weren't on the football game. He said he didn't want me to get married until after the bowl game. I wanted to get married in December and have a honeymoon in New Orleans at the Sugar Bowl, but Coach Howard said no."

That is just one example of the self-sacrifice and the team-first attitude of the 1958 Tigers. It was a true team, the deepest of Frank Howard's career. Clemson won the ACC title, but had just one first-team All-ACC player and no All-Americans. This team had talent, but it was balanced. Eight players off the 1958 Tigers made it to the NFL, including five who played at least five years and two who were first-round draft choices (Lou Cordileone and Harvey White). Harold Olson, a tackle, went on to make All-Pro in the AFL.

The statistics from that season document the incredible level of balance. Clemson led the ACC in rushing with 225 yards a game, yet no one had over 500 yards, and only one player, quarterback Harvey White, had a 100-yard rushing game. Eight different players had at least 100 rushing yards for the year. The team completed 69 passes for the season, but to 15 different players. No receiver had over 60 yards in any game, never mind a 100-yard game. Twelve different players returned kickoffs, and another dozen returned a punt. Three different quarterbacks ran the attack, and seven different players had interceptions.

"Coach Howard played two full teams and sometimes three," said Thomas. "That depth was the big reason we were able to dominate the fourth period and win games in the final quarter."

Clemson opened the season with a victory over Virginia at Death Valley. This was a special opening day because Memorial Stadium had been enlarged over the summer to hold 40,000 fans. There was a new press box, a new scoreboard, and the team ran down the hill on a rug for the first time.

Clemson dominated the action, gaining 384 yards on the ground and winning the total-offense battle, 438–300. In addition, Clemson intercepted four passes, appropriately, by four different players, but gave up 174 passing yards on 13 completions, a high total for those days. Lowndes Shingler scored on a one-yard run with 14 minutes left, and the Tigers defense held Virginia in the final moments.

After the game, Howard said he was disappointed with his pass defense, something that was apparent to a lot of people, even his wife, Anna. "I tried to get my wife interested in football for 15 years," said Howard in a newspaper account the week after the game. "Then our son Jimmy started playing, and she went to all his games. When I saw her after the game, she asked me what I was going to do about that pass defense. I've created a backseat driver."

Game two was against North Carolina, and it might have been the biggest game of the season. A record 40,000 fans jammed Death Valley on a 93-degree day. Concessions ran out of soft drinks and ice in the third period. It was so hot that the North Carolina team warmed up in just T-shirts and didn't put their pads on until just before gametime.

This was a day when team depth would be the difference. Howard had nine different players rush the ball, and Harvey White and Shingler split the quarterback duties. Mrs. Howard was satisfied with the pass defense on this day, as North Carolina gained just 145 yards in the air. Clemson, on the other hand, had its most efficient day of the year, hitting 9 of 14 passes for 110 yards.

The game went back and forth with many clutch plays. Clemson scored early on a blocked punt. North Carolina attempted a quick kick by Don Coker, but Jim Payne raced through the line to block the attempt. Jim Padgett got to the ball first and raced 28 yards for a touchdown.

One of the biggest plays took place right before halftime when George Usry scored a touchdown on a one-yard run on the last play of the half. Clemson was sending its kicking unit on to the field to try for the PAT, but when North Carolina's Jim Tatum argued over the allowance of the late score, the Tar Heels were hit with a delay of game penalty, moving the ball to the one-yard-line. Howard then tried to go for two, but the attempt failed, and the score was tied at the half. That is one of the few times that getting a penalty indirectly helped the penalized team on the scoreboard.

The second half went back and forth until the Tigers drove 80 yards for the go-ahead score. With 2:52 remaining in the game, George Usry scored from a yard out to put Clemson up 26–21, and that would remain the final score.

This was a landmark day for Howard. First, he finally defeated fellow future Hall of Fame coach Jim Tatum after five straight losses. Second, it was the 100th head-coaching victory for Howard, still the only Clemson coach with 100 wins (he would end his career with 165). After the game, he was presented the game ball and proudly stated it was going to be placed prominently on his mantle at home next to a picture of Fred Cone, who was a key player for Howard in the late 1940s.

"I think the smartest thing I did today was substitute every five minutes," said Howard. "I knew depth was going to be a factor in this heat." Howard also singled out the play of Jim McCandless, a fine player who would go on to the pros. McCandless was playing for the first time after breaking his neck in a swimming accident two years previously.

While game three won't go into the books as a game decided by seven points or less, it was decided by just one touchdown. Clemson scored just one touchdown and then made a two-point conversion to gain an 8–0 triumph over Maryland in College Park. This was Clemson's first victory over Maryland since the formation of the ACC. White connected with Wyatt Cox on a 50-yard scoring pass in the third quarter, then George Usry scored the two-point play.

There were a lot of two-point conversion attempts in this season. The 1958 season was the first year of the two-point play in college football. Coaches at that time, including Frank Howard, thought it would be easy to score from the three. Clemson scored 25 touchdowns that season and went for two 20 times, converting eight times.

While Clemson did not have a star system in 1958, the Vanderbilt game produced the single best performance of the year by a Tiger. Harvey White gained 105 yards rushing in just 14 carries, and completed 8 of 12 passes for 60 yards. In addition, White scored both of Clemson's touchdowns in the final period of a thrilling 12–7 victory in Nashville.

Clemson trailed 7–0 going into the fourth quarter, thanks to five turnovers over the game's first 45 minutes. But White and Rudy Hayes, who had 99 yards rushing on the night, led Clemson back. Trailing 7–6 with just 6:30 left in the game, White took the Tigers on a breathtaking drive that included a fourth-down conversion at the Vanderbilt 10 with 53 seconds left. Finally, with nine seconds remaining, White burst over the goal line from three yards out. This remains the latest fourth-quarter, game-winning touchdown in Clemson history. For his heroics, White was named Associated Press National Back of the Week.

"With Harvey White you knew he was going to get the job done," recalled Thomas. "He could take a team down the field in the clutch." The scores of the games to this point backed up Thomas' statement. It was the third victory by exactly five points for the Tigers in the first four games, and all four games were won by a touchdown or less.

Clemson hit a midseason slump, however, losing to South Carolina, beating Wake Forest, and then losing at Georgia Tech. The Wake Forest game was a 14–12 Clemson victory. One of the highlights was a touchdown by Johnnie Mac Goff. He scored what proved to be the winning touchdown in the fourth quarter.

His score gave Clemson a 14–6 lead. But Wake Forest came back behind the passing of future NFL star Norman Snead. He scored a touchdown on a five-yard run that culminated an 88-yard drive with just four minutes left. But, on the touchdown play, Snead was injured, and reserve Charlie Carpenter had to come off the bench cold to try for the two-point play. His pass was incomplete, and Clemson had another close victory.

Clemson closed the regular season with three consecutive victories. A 13-6 victory in Raleigh clinched the ACC Championship. Bill Mathis, who later became the first former Clemson player to win a Super

Bowl Championship ring with Joe Namath and the New York Jets, was the top rusher against the Pack with 13-75. Usry and Bobby Morgan scored the touchdowns, as again Clemson scored both of its touchdowns in the fourth period.

After the team's most convincing victory of the season, a 34–12 win over Boston College, Clemson clinched a Sugar Bowl bid with a 36–19 win over Furman. Clemson was outscored 19–6 in the second half by Furman, and Clemson players and coaches were worried that they had blown the Sugar Bowl bid in the process. Immediately after the game, Coach Howard went to his office and called the bowl committee to get a reaction. The committee offered Clemson the bid. Howard went into the dressing room to inform the team, "We got it." The Tigers were matched with undefeated and No. 1–ranked LSU and 34-year-old coach Paul Dietzel.

Clemson's invitation was met with disdain by many in the national media. "A lot of people thought SMU should have been LSU's opponent," said Thomas. "We were not shown much respect, but we came to play."

The Tigers put in many hours of practice at home and in Biloxi, Mississippi, in preparation for Billy Cannon, the 1958 Heisman Trophy winner. Coach Howard kept all the articles that ridiculed the Clemson program and showed them to the players prior to the game in an effort to fire up his team.

Another point of interest was that Clemson would take the rug the Tigers used to run down the hill with them to the Sugar Bowl. The rug weighed 527 pounds. At the time it was called the "World's Largest College Banner."

Since both team's jerseys were light-colored, and because everyone in America had black-and-white televisions, something had to be done about the players' attire. LSU wore a gold uniform, and Clemson, as the visiting team, was going to wear white. NBC-TV executives wanted one

Clemson wore blue jerseys when the Tigers played LSU in the 1959 Sugar Bowl, then wore the same "Sugar Blues" in a win over South Carolina (above) in 1962.

team to wear a darker jersey so the viewers would be able to distinguish the team on the field. Clemson decided to wear a dark blue jersey for this game.

Clemson gave LSU its toughest game of the season. LSU's high-powered offense gained just 182 yards of total offense and only nine first downs. The LSU Tigers had to score on a halfback-option pass in the third quarter after a Clemson fumble at its own 11 to take a 7–0 lead.

Clemson drove 17 plays from its own 17 to the LSU 28 late in the game, but a fourth-down pass from White to George Usry went incomplete, and LSU held on to win the game 7–0. Clemson had shown America that they deserved to be in the Sugar Bowl. Never had a

Clemson team gained so much respect from a loss. "I wish we could line up and play LSU again...today," said Thomas.

It was this type of spirit, which still lives on today, that made the 1958 Clemson team one of Clemson's most successful and respected teams in history.

1963 Clemson-Georgia, "The Hail Game"

The most unusual weather occurrence in Clemson football history took place on October 12, 1963. A beautiful day had shaped up for the Clemson-Georgia game at Death Valley—it was sunny and 84 degrees at kickoff. However, by the time the Georgia band took the field at halftime, the skies grew dark, and halfway through the Georgia band's show, hail and heavy rain suddenly bombarded the field, bouncing off tubas and taking its toll on the drums, many of which were immediately torn. Fans were seen running, taking refuge underneath the north and south stands.

The Georgia band made a hasty retreat to the shelter of the west end zone seats. A group of Clemson students, including many Tiger band members, offered the 125 rain-soaked Redcoat band members, shelter in nearby dormitories for drying out and some fresh clothes.

The torrential hailstorm hit at 2:50 PM and caused temperatures to plummet from 84 to 57 degrees in 45 minutes. Almost an inch of hail came down in a 20-minute period, and the game was delayed.

Clemson head coach Frank Howard and Georgia head coach Johnny Griffith met under the stands and delayed the start of the second half for 30 minutes. The field looked like a sheet of ice. Clemson's grounds crew cleared the field as much as possible.

The Tigers dealt with the conditions better during the second half and tied the score 7–7 in the third quarter, which ended up being the final score. Clemson also blocked two Georgia field-goal attempts to preserve the tie on this memorable day.

The Day Kennedy Died

Two buses transporting 60 Clemson football players, along with 20 coaches, administrators, and student managers pulled out of the parking lot at Fike Field House just after noon on November 22, 1963. It would be a three-hour ride to Batesburg, South Carolina, the road headquarters for the Tigers during the era when Clemson played South Carolina in Columbia.

Head athletic trainer Fred Hoover and line coach Bob Smith were riding together in the front seat of the first bus. "We went through a lot of little towns to get to Batesburg," said Hoover, then in his sixth season of a 40-year career. "It was a much longer ride in those days, because I-26 had not been built yet. We were riding through Saluda, and as we passed the post office, Bob noticed that the American flag in front of the building was at half-staff. We thought that was odd, because it took a major event for that to happen."

Something major had in fact taken place. At 12:30 PM (Central Time), President John F. Kennedy had been shot at Dealey Plaza in Dallas, Texas, while riding in an open-car motorcade. He was pronounced dead at Parkland Hospital at 1:00 PM, and 33 minutes later, a press conference was held to tell the world.

"We obviously didn't have cell phones in those days, and I don't even know if the bus had a radio," said Hoover. The team continued its trip and arrived at the hotel in Batesburg at 3:00 PM. "None of us knew of the assassination until we got off the bus and someone from the hotel staff told us."

Similar to the events of September 11, 2001, it took a while for the gravity of the situation to sink in within the sports world. (Clemson and most other college football teams practiced on the afternoon of September 11, 2001, after the Twin Towers were attacked, and games for the next weekend were not postponed until the next day.)

"We didn't know if the game would go on or not," recalled Hoover, who still helps out at Clemson home football games as a liaison between the football office and Tigers opponents. "We had a practice scheduled at a local high school, so we went ahead and did the workout." However, it was not much of a practice.

"We were up for the game, but after our boys heard of the president's death, things started to happen," said Coach Howard in an interview with Jake Penland of the *State* the next day. "There were busted signals with two boys running together...things like that. They didn't have their mind on football."

When the team returned from practice to the hotel, the game had not been cancelled. In fact, Clemson president Robert C. Edwards and South Carolina president Thomas F. Jones had released a joint statement saying the game would go on as scheduled. Some in the media later speculated that the game was not postponed immediately because CBS was planning to televise the Saturday afternoon contest on a regional basis. It was to be just the second regular-season game televised in Clemson history, and it was to be shown on 50 CBS affiliates in 11 states. Each school was to be paid $53,000 for the appearance. Some believed CBS had an influence on the two university presidents.

So the Clemson team had dinner at the hotel and monitored television coverage provided by Walter Cronkite on CBS. The television coverage was dramatic, and speculation had the country wondering if the United States was going to be attacked by a foreign country. Remember, we were just 18 years removed from World War II, and the Cuban Missile Crisis had taken place the previous year (October 16–28, 1962).

N.C. State and Wake Forest were actually scheduled to play a game Friday night, and that game went on. But as the evening continued, more and more schools announced postponements or cancellations. At 9:30 PM, Howard received a call from Dr. Edwards, who informed him the game would be postponed until the following Thursday, Thanksgiving Day.

At 10:00 PM, Clemson and South Carolina released a joint statement:

> The Clemson vs. South Carolina football game scheduled for November 23, 1963, has been postponed due to the death of President John F. Kennedy. We regret any inconvenience that may be caused to individual fans, but we feel this action is in accord with the solemnity of the hour.

Coach Howard called the players together, and one of the players suggested the team return to Clemson that night and practice on Saturday. Howard agreed, and the team was back on the road to Clemson by 10:30 PM.

The teams played in relative obscurity the following Thursday on Thanksgiving Day, as the game was not televised on CBS. A Detroit Lions game had priority. The Tigers defeated the Dan Reeves–led Gamecocks by a score of 24–20 thanks in part to a touchdown by Howard's son, Jimmy.

Similar to the way sports helped heal the country after September 11, 2001, the games helped put the nation on the path to healing in 1963.

Bruce McClure—A Tough Decision

Over 50 years ago, Bruce McClure and his teammates faced TCU. The Horned Frogs came to Tigertown very highly touted in 1965, and it was going to take a great Clemson performance to knock off TCU in this particular meeting. For Clemson lineman Bruce McClure, it was the most memorable game of his life.

It wasn't the hype of the football game that McClure remembers, nor was it the fact that a member of the old Southwest Conference was coming to town for the first time. Instead, it was the events surrounding this late October weekend that forced him to make the hardest decision in his young life.

McClure, a native of Charlotte, North Carolina, came to Clemson from Myers Park High School. Coach Whitey Jordan recruited him in high school. Clemson found out about McClure from Hap Carr, also a Myers Park graduate and a football player and baseball manager at Clemson. He told the Clemson coaches about McClure, and the staff was very much impressed.

"Coach Jordan gave me a scholarship in the fall of 1961," said McClure, "and when I started I was on the 12th team. I worked my way up and ended up on the first unit on the freshman team."

McClure was in his fifth year at Clemson in 1965, having redshirted the 1962 season due to a knee injury. McClure said that on the Friday morning before the TCU game, he got a message in his dorm that Coach Howard wanted to see him, and fast. McClure said he was wondering why in the world Howard wanted to see him, and the thought entered his mind, *I wonder what I've done?*

McClure explained why Coach Howard had summoned him:

> I went as fast as I could to his office in Fike Field House. His secretary announced that I was there. He told me to come in, and I sat down. He simply said, "Boy your momma is dead." I was shocked. I knew she had been sick with leukemia, but I thought there was more time. She had been coming to the games. At that time, they were coming out with new innovations in treatment, and we were very encouraged. But during surgery, she had a brain hemorrhage and died. I was numb, I didn't know what to say. Coach Howard went on to say, "We need you to play tomorrow, but we also understand if you don't. But we need you." By the time I left his office, I knew I would play in the game. I told him I would play, but I was going to Charlotte that night and spend time with my family.

I was shocked and hurt, and other thoughts were going through my mind. I was the oldest brother; I had to take care of my family. I had to go and tell my brother, who at that time was a freshman at Clemson. I ran into Dean Walter Cox, and he was a big help to me. I knew I had to get home. I drove up to Charlotte with my brother, and it was the longest drive I have ever made in my life. I drove back to Clemson with a family friend early Saturday morning, and we got back to campus around 2:00 AM, and I went to my dorm room. I didn't sleep but maybe two hours.

I kept thinking, *I just talked to Mom.* And she had said go back to school on a previous visit. I wanted to stay home and make sure she was all right just days before. She told me whether she lived or died, that I had my own life to live. You will get in trouble if you stay at Charlotte and you'll get behind on your studies. One thought that kept going through my mind was that she told me to fulfill my commitments under any circumstances. I loved my parents, and they had made many sacrifices for the family. I was going to fulfill my commitment to Clemson and my teammates.

I got up on game day and met the team for the pregame meal. Coach Howard, Coach Wade, and Coach Jordan all came and talked to me. I went to the fieldhouse to get dressed for the game. I went in the dressing room, and trainers Herman McGee and Fred Hoover were very helpful. I remember both of them talking to me. The rest of the team pretty much let me have my time to myself.

In the press box, McClure's name was not included on the depth chart for the TCU game, as Clemson's longtime sports information director Bob Bradley explained, "We didn't put his name on the depth chart because we didn't figure he would play, given the circumstances."

"I didn't start, but I got in late in the first half," McClure said. "I started thinking about football. At the half, Coach Howard asked if I was doing okay. He talked about my situation and me during the half-time talk. I played most of the second half. It was Homecoming, and I had a sponsor—there was so much going through my mind. All that was so difficult, but I knew somehow everything would work out. Back in those days, you played both ways on offense and defense. I played really hard, and we defeated TCU 3–0." According to the *Charlotte Observer*, "McClure figured strongly in Clemson's 3–0 victory over the Horned Frogs."

During the final seconds of the game, Clemson was running out the clock. Quarterback Thomas Ray ran a sneak to kill the clock. When the mass of Texas Christian players climbed off him and the final seconds were counting down, he scrambled to his feet and dashed to the Tigers player dressed in uniform No. 68 on the field, Bruce McClure. Ray thrust the ball into McClure's hands. It was the game ball.

"Take this," Ray said. "We won this one for you."

McClure said after the game to the media, "It would have been Mom's wish that I play. She wanted me to live up to my commitments. That's the only thing that enabled me to do it."

N.C. State—The Shoes

The Clemson–N.C. State series has always been an interesting one. The two schools are land-grant institutions with similar curriculums. Both fan bases share a passion for sports, and both schools saw the need to play at neutral sites to build interest not only for their respective football teams, but also for the school. In the series, Clemson has an 11–1–1 record when the two schools play at a neutrual site. The Wolfpack from N.C. State is also one of Clemson's oldest foes.

Clemson and N.C. State met for the first time in football in 1899, in Rock Hill, South Carolina. The Tigers dominated the game. As a matter of fact, the game was shortened due to the fact that many of the Wolfpack players were getting injured and they didn't have enough players to finish the game. The Tigers won 24–0.

Clemson won a home game with N.C. State in 1902, 11–5. The 1903 and the 1906 games were played in Columbia, South Carolina, as part of the South Carolina State Fair in mid-October. After a home-and-home series, the two teams played the 1928 and 1929 games in Florence, South Carolina, as part of the Pee Dee Fair. Around 5,000 fans were in attendance at each game. The contest was part of the Clemson–N.C. State Day festivities at the fair. Fireworks were also shot at halftime of the game. The press box was filled to capacity, as this was a big game in the Southern Conference race.

The 1930 and 1931 games were played in Charlotte, North Carolina, at Central High School. It's near the site of current Memorial Stadium in downtown Charlotte. The 1930 game had an additional attraction as it was broadcast on Charlotte radio station WBT. News reports said that wiring was installed at the stadium days ahead of the game so that the game could be broadcast. This may have been Clemson's first football game ever to be aired over radio.

From 1939 to 1944 Clemson played six games in Charlotte at Memorial Stadium. People also know this as the stadium where the Shrine Bowl used to be played, and it is also the current home to the major league lacrosse team, the Charlotte Hounds.

It was a festive time for Clemson and N.C. State in Charlotte. The Clemson cadets were in attendance, and they had a parade down the streets of Charlotte where the cadets and the Senior Platoon, Clemson's precision drill team, performed. This afforded Clemson an opportunity to win friends and publicity in the Queen City.

On November 18, 1967, it probably was the shoes that enabled Clemson to upset 10th-ranked N.C. State 14–6 in Clemson's first ever win over a top-10 team in Death Valley.

Coming into this Atlantic Coast Conference classic, the Wolfpack was enjoying a fabulous year, defeating their first eight opponents. After defeating Virginia in Charlottesville in the eighth game, only two opponents remained, Penn State and Clemson, both on the road. Before the Nittany Lions game, there was talk that N.C. State had the Sugar Bowl bid wrapped up, provided there was at least a split in the last two games. The Wolfpack lost to Penn State 13–8, making the Clemson–N.C. State game even more crucial for the Wolfpack's New Year's Day bowl hopes.

The Wolfpack had become nationally famous in 1967 because of their tenacity and the distinctive white shoes worn by the defensive unit. At this time, every team in the nation, along with N.C. State's offensive unit, wore black shoes.

N.C. State started wearing the white shoes on defense when left cornerback Bill Morrow noticed a member of the Kansas City Chiefs wearing white shoes. Morrow, who scored the first touchdown for N.C. State in the new Carter-Finley Stadium when he intercepted a pass in 1966, went to co-captain Art McMahon with the idea. Linebacker and future Wolfpack head coach (2000–2006) Chuck Amato said he would paint his shoes white, and the idea spread through the Wolfpack defense. State was ranked No. 1 in the ACC in defense coming into the Clemson game and was a sure bet to beat a 4–4 Tigers team.

In the week before the game, a few of the Clemson players wanted to paint their shoes orange to counteract the perceived intangible advantage of N.C. State's white shoes. "I remember a lot of players got together, and we decided to paint our shoes orange," recalled former Clemson tailback Buddy Gore. "Our trainer, Herman McGee, rounded up the orange paint needed for our idea, and we went to the dorm that week and painted our game shoes orange. I have no idea where he got the orange paint.

Coach Howard did not know what we were doing until that Saturday morning. I think he liked our plan." Gore was one of Clemson's greatest backs ever, and in 1967 he was named the ACC's Player of the Year.

Assistant coach Don Wade was also involved in the scheme. "We got the paint from eight or nine different places. It was tough to find orange paint that would be suitable for shoes," he said.

N.C. State jumped ahead 6–0 as Gerald Warren hit two second-quarter field goals from 37 and 47 yards out with his back to a gusty 22 mph wind. Gore scored what proved to be the winning touchdown for the Tigers early in the third quarter. With a third-and-11 situation facing the Tigers on N.C. State's 27, Clemson was obviously facing a throwing situation.

"N.C. State was in a defense that would provide double coverage on the wideouts and forced the linebackers to cover the man coming out of the backfield," remembers Gore. "I was not the primary receiver by any means. After all, I only caught seven passes my entire career. I was in the flats around the 12-yard line, and I was open after beating the linebacker, Chuck Amato. The cornerback and the safety were with our wide receivers. I will never forget when I was open in the flats. I looked at our quarterback Jimmy Addison, and he stared right back at me and threw me the ball, and I went in for the touchdown."

Dennis Byrd, N.C State's All-America defensive tackle had written Gore a letter that gave him extra incentive to do well. "Before the game, Byrd wrote me a letter that said I wouldn't score," Gore said. "Every time he tackled me during the game, he would say, 'Gore, you stink.' After I caught that touchdown pass, I was coming out of the end zone, and he was standing right there. I remember it like it was yesterday. I asked him, 'How do I smell now?'"

The touchdown occurred when Clemson's Phil Rogers went to the post and took the cornerback with him. Gore and his 4.5-second 40-yard-dash speed had Amato covering him, and he had him beat by several steps.

"I went into the flat and turned up the sideline," he recalled. "The next thing I knew the ball was coming toward me."

After the Tigers scored, N.C. State was forced to punt. The Tigers took the ball and marched 43 yards for a touchdown. Rogers caught a 27-yard pass from Addison to set up the Tigers' second touchdown. Jacky Jackson scored from seven yards out around right end with 7:45 left in the third quarter, giving Clemson a 14–6 lead.

N.C. State drove to the Clemson 29-yard line with three minutes left to go in the game. But quarterback Jim Donnan's pass, intended for right end Harry Martell, was intercepted by Richie Luzzi in the end zone. Donnan would later become head coach at Marshall (1990–1995) and Georgia (1996–2000). He also played for the Wolfpack tennis team.

Clemson went on to win the game 14–6, ensuring the Tigers at least a tie for the ACC crown. The Tigers defeated South Carolina the next Saturday 23–12, to clinch the championship outright and finish with a 6–0 mark in the ACC. N.C. State went on to defeat Georgia 14–7 in the Liberty Bowl.

"How many tackles did those orange shoes make, coach?" a sportswriter asked Coach Howard after the game. "None," Howard replied in a word. "But I tell you, there is something about football that makes boys believe in something that will help them. When they believe they can do something, they usually do it."

"I will never forget when we ran down the hill and the fans saw us in those orange shoes," said Gore. "There was silence for about three or four seconds, and then you heard the loudest roar when they realized we were all wearing orange shoes. When I go back to Clemson, and I see the Tigers run down the hill, I think about that loud roar we received that day quite often."

On that particular day for the Tigers, it must have been the shoes!

Herman McGee, Everyone's Friend

Although he never scored a touchdown or pitched a strike for Clemson, for scores of Clemson student-athletes and coaches he was just as important. This key person in the Clemson athletic department was Herman McGee. McGee was the long-tenured athletic trainer/ equipment manager, counselor, confidant, and everybody's pal who served Clemson for 46 years, more than any other Athletic Department employee.

Frank Howard once said about McGee during his retirement years, "When former athletes come back to visit, I'm not the first person they look for. They want to know, 'Where's Herman?'"

Football great Joel Wells echoed this in a 1976 interview. "Anytime I go back to Clemson, I check and see if Coach Howard is around and then I check and see if Herman's around, too. I just wouldn't feel that I'd been back to Clemson if I didn't see them."

McGee meant a great deal to many student-athletes at Clemson. From massaging a bruise, taping an ankle, or talking to a student-athlete and sharing words of encouragement, McGee was there, giving his wholehearted effort to help the Tigers attain success.

Herman first started working for Clemson in an unofficial capacity when he was just a youth. Jess Neely was the athletic director and head football coach, and Howard was one of his assistants. Bert Johnson, Herman's stepfather, worked at Clemson and also served as a grounds-keeper for the athletic department. Each afternoon a group of young kids helped him work on the fields.

"They'd cut grass and picked up rocks, and we paid them off in old baseballs, footballs, and sweatshirts," Howard said. "Herman was always in the crowd, and he would catch your eye because the little fellow worked so hard, a lot harder than the others. I guess I first met Herman when he was six years old. When his stepfather died, I had become the athletic director and head coach, and I gave Herman his job. He was 16 years old when we officially put him to work." Except for a stint in the Army during World War II, he proudly worked for Clemson his entire career.

Little did McGee know that in March 1934 when they put him on the payroll at the age of 16 that he had found a home. At that time the athletic department was operating out of a small cramped area in the basement of Godfrey Hall (an old textile building). "We had an infrared light and a hot plate that heated water in a big galvanized tub where we kept our hot towels," McGee said. "About every second or third towel you'd take out you'd get the full force of 110 volts where that tub was touching that hot plate."

"We just taped the ones who really needed it," said McGee. "If they could walk, we sent them on out to the practice field." Back in those days the practice field and the playing field were at Historic Riggs Field. McGee remembers the mode of transportation in the late '30s and early '40s. "It was either by bus or by train. I remember the first flying trip I went on. People saw us off in Anderson and wished us well. But it wasn't too long until we were back on the ground in Anderson with a dead engine. While most people thought we were at our destination, we were sitting at the Calhoun Hotel [in downtown Anderson] eating and waiting for another plane to arrive."

McGee once said in an interview that he helped take 18 sections of bleachers down to Columbia for the Big Thursday game with South Carolina each year for the Clemson fans to use. McGee was part of the growth of Clemson athletics. He recalled when the athletic department moved into the front part of Fike Field House. A year later the first game was played in Memorial Stadium. He said those were big events for Clemson.

The native of Pendleton, South Carolina, was always out there on the field when Clemson athletes were on the field in practice or at games. But his work wasn't always done when the games or practices were over.

When student-athletes had athletic problems, school problems, or personal problems, many called Herman during the night and had conversations with him. "Through the years, our athletes have told Herman things, have shared problems with him that they wouldn't be about to share with anybody else," Howard said. He was just about as good at helping solve problems and making people feel better mentally as he was in curing their physical ailments. What was his secret? A dose of sympathy and understanding. His door and heart were always open.

"If anybody loved Clemson, then Herman loved them," said former Tigers baseball coach Bill Wilhelm. McGee was also the trainer for Tigers baseball throughout much of his career. There were just two things he refused to do—to name his favorite sport and his favorite athlete. "I like whatever sport is in season. I love everyone who played or coached here at Clemson," McGee once said.

He did say in an interview that the play that stands out in his mind the most was in the 1951 Orange Bowl. Against Miami, the Tigers' Sterling Smith tackled Frank Smith of the Hurricanes for a safety giving the Tigers a 15–14 victory. "I'll never forget that one," said McGee.

He was inducted into the Clemson Athletic Hall of Fame in 1976, the first African American to be inducted. In June 1965 McGee was recognized by the National Athletic Trainers Association for "twenty-five or more years of meritorious services in the field of athletic training."

McGee died suddenly on March 9, 1980, at the age of 62.

"I never heard anyone say anything bad about Herman," said Wilhelm. "That's a pretty high tribute to a man." The impact that McGee had on Clemson and the student-athletes he helped will never be registered on a scoreboard, in a record book, or on a stat sheet, but more important than that, the countless Tigers coaches and athletes he touched are winners for having known him.

CHAPTER 8
RETURN TO NATIONAL
PROMINENCE

The Tiger Paw

The Tiger Paw might be the most widely recognized school symbol in the nation. It is something unique to Clemson, and Tigers fans are very proud of the logo. It's been Clemson's logo since 1970, and it is as much a part of Clemson as some of the legendary heroes who brought fame to the school during its athletic history.

Dr. Robert C. Edwards, then Clemson's president, decided in 1969 that he would like "to upgrade the image of the university" and hired Henderson Advertising Company in Greenville, South Carolina, to work on this idea. Company president Jimmy Henderson, a Clemson graduate in 1944, had an idea of what Edwards was thinking. Henderson put together a team to work on the "Clemson Project." The team was composed of vice president Fred Walker, account supervisor Paul Seabrook and creative designer and artist John Antonio. Among the possible changes being discussed were new uniforms and a new logo that would not replace the Tiger, but complement it.

After about six weeks of thinking out loud on several angles, Henderson presented what was first called a "tiger track" as the new logo. Henderson's people wrote to every school in the nation that had "Tigers" as its nickname, asking for a picture of its mascot. After most of them had responded, the conclusion was reached that a tiger is a tiger, regardless if it was a Persian, Bengal, or Sumatran. Several other ideas were kicked around, one being the impression of a tiger's foot or paw. In order to get the real thing, Henderson wrote the Field Museum of Natural History in Chicago asking for a plaster-of-paris cast of the imprint of a tiger's paw. The imprint was changed to a print, tilted about 10 degrees to the right and presented to the Clemson committee working with Henderson.

Antonio is given credit with coming up with the idea. "I think we have a winner," he reported to his group. A few more days of work, and the final project was ready to be presented. Now the task was to sell the idea to the Clemson committee.

A meeting was scheduled with the Clemson committee around the first of July, 1970. From Henderson Advertising, Fred Walker, Paul Seabrook, and John Antonio attended. From Clemson, athletic director Frank Howard, assistant athletic director Bill McClellan, head football coach Hootie Ingram, head basketball coach Tates Locke, and several assistant coaches for basketball and football were there, as well as dean of students Walter Cox and executive director of IPTAY Gene Willimon. Antonio made the presentation using examples he had put together with the paw on stationery, T-shirts, sweaters, auto tags, etc. He also had paintings of the paw on the football field and the basketball court.

Frank Howard did not seem to be impressed and asked where the other presentation was. Then Antonio opened a box and took out an orange football helmet with a white Tiger Paw on both sides. Howard's attitude changed immediately, and soon the Paw was approved. Another test that helped win approval took place when logos from different schools were held up several feet away. Many could not recognize the logos from a distance, but when Antonio's brainstorm was held up, it was immediately recognized as the new Clemson Tiger Paw, without any hesitation. Further approval came from Dr. Edwards and the board of trustees.

Now the news had to be spread about the Tiger Paw. Hootie Ingram, Tates Locke, All-ACC tailback Ray Yauger, and Wright Bryan, the university's vice president for development, made a one-day whirl-wind trip to six cities on Tuesday, July 21, 1970—Florence, Columbia, Charleston, Greenville, Charlotte, and Atlanta. They made the excursion in around nine hours via private plane. The purpose of the trip was to introduce the two new head coaches, Ingram and Locke, to the general public and to show off the new Tiger Paw. According to the news release, the six-city tour was "an opportunity to hear how the Clemson Tiger is alive in a ferocious way, stalking the campus with a new version of the traditional Clemson spirit."

At each stop, they held a press conference. Bryan told the people at each press conference, "At any university, from time to time there needs to be some symbol that keeps the whole thing together, and the Clemson University hierarchy believes the paw is the answer."

"Symbols like the Tiger Paw won't help us win football games," Ingram said at one of the stops, "but we hope it will retain the enthusiasm Clemson people are known for around the country."

Assistant sports information director and later promotion director Jerry Arp had been hired at Clemson two days earlier. He is credited with emphasizing to Tigers fans to wear orange, and he also was a big factor in making the Tiger Paw famous during its infancy.

John Antonio died May 30, 2013, at the age of 83, but over the years he definitely saw how his idea had grown to become an integral part of Clemson University, especially its athletic teams. Today, Tiger Paws are found everywhere in Clemson and around the country on every imaginable surface and merchandise. They are even on the roads leading into Clemson.

Running Down the Hill

In an interview with All-America quarterback Deshaun Watson during the 2015 football season, he was asked about the gameday atmosphere at Clemson. He said, "It is second to none as far as I am concerned. It all starts with running down the hill. It just sets the tone for the entire day."

Clemson's celebrated entrance has been one of the iconic images of college football, not just Clemson football. How many times have you turned on *ESPN College GameDay* and seen it as part of an opening montage?

ABC devoted six minutes to the spectacle at the opening of the 2013 Georgia game. It had 1.7 million views on YouTube in its first six months.

The history of Clemson's famous entrance is well documented, and the names Frank Howard, Gene Willimon, and Hootie Ingram have been prominently attached to the story. But one former Clemson player and one former Clemson coach deserve much of the credit for the tradition as it exits today.

Ben Anderson aspired to play for Clemson when he was in junior high school and actually wrote a letter to Frank Howard, telling him that he would one day play for the Tigers. As a senior at Strom Thurmond High School in Johnston, South Carolina, Anderson helped his team to its first state championship in 1968. But at 6'0" and 170 pounds, he was not offered a scholarship by any Division I school.

Anderson came to Clemson as a student in 1969 and walked onto the football team. He impressed the coaches immediately and started all 33 games in his Clemson career (freshmen were ineligible), one of the few walk-ons in Clemson football history to start every game in his career. A defensive back, Anderson finished his career with nine interceptions, fifth best in Clemson history when he graduated. His total included a pair of interceptions at South Carolina in 1971.

Prior to his final game as a senior in 1972, Anderson, a three-time Academic All-ACC selection and second-team Academic All-American, led a small group of seniors to head coach Hootie Ingram's office the week of the South Carolina game. One of the players who attended the meeting was teammate Bobby Johnson, who went on to a long coaching career and became a member of the College Football Playoff Committee in 2015. "It was Ben Anderson who said we should run down the hill for our final game," said Johnson. "I went along to the meeting as support, but this was all Ben's idea. He had it all planned out. It was like he was trying his first law case in front of a judge." Coach Ingram liked the idea and then worked with Anderson on the plan to bring the team around the stadium on busses to the top of the hill just before kickoff.

Clemson had not run down the hill since 1969. Prior to the 1970 season, Clemson's locker room moved from Fike Field House to the west end zone of the stadium, so there was no longer a need to run down the hill to get to the field. When Clemson had run down the hill from 1942 to 1969, it was not quite as celebrated, because the team made their entrance for pregame warmups, over an hour prior to the game. The pregame tradition did not occur just minutes before kickoff until that 1972 South Carolina game, and that important aspect of the tradition was Anderson's idea. Clemson went on to beat South Carolina 7–6 that rainy afternoon.

The following fall, for the season opener against the Citadel, the Tigers were led on the field by new coach Red Parker. For that September 8, 1973, against his old school, Parker and the Tigers did not run down the hill. Clemson won by just a 14–12 score, and the atmosphere was flat. "When I went to Clemson, attendance was way down," said Parker, who coached at Clemson from 1973 to 1976. "It was just a period of time when the enthusiasm was not the way it is now."

That following Monday morning, Parker went to athletic director Bill McLellan and said they needed to do something to get the spirit and enthusiasm back in Death Valley. "I thought about a lot of things I had heard about Clemson before I went there," Parker said. "One of the things that struck me as being a goldmine of potential was the Tigers running down the hill in the east end zone prior to the game. I saw that as a spirit uplifter. When I came to Clemson, I was astounded that running down the hill was dropped because of that new locker room."

McLellan gave Parker his blessing to bring back the ritual, and for the second home game of the 1973 season against Texas A&M, Clemson went back to running down the hill. The tradition has not stopped since.

"In my opinion, running down the hill is one of the greatest motivators in all of college football," said Parker. "In fact, when I was at Clemson, we believed if we could get the prospects there on a Saturday afternoon when the Tigers ran down the hill, we had a chance to recruit them. And we brought in a lot of them."

Ben Anderson and Red Parker both helped to revive and reinvigorate the ritual of the Tigers running down the hill, one of the most iconic traditions in college football. Anderson died at the age of 63 on May 16, 2015, after a five-year battle with lung cancer. Bobby Johnson, his close friend for 46 years, gave a memorable eulogy at Anderson's funeral in Tillman Hall. Parker passed away on January 4, 2016, just seven days before Clemson played for the national championship against Alabama.

Don Kelley's Greatest Game

Ever do anything perfectly? For Don Kelley, the effort he gave at the 1970 Clemson vs. Maryland game may not have been perfection, but it was just about as good as it gets. It was an effort that set an example for future Clemson football players who brought Clemson to national acclaim by the end of the decade.

On that cold, rainy Halloween Day in College Park, Maryland, Clemson posted a 24–11 win over the Terps due in large part to Kelley. Consider that he had four punt returns for 167 yards and a touchdown. He had an interception return, which set up another touchdown. For good measure, he also recovered a fumble. His four punt returns for 167 yards earned Kelley the Atlantic Coast Conference record for most punt-return yards—a mark that stood until 2006. But he still has the yards-per-punt-return record at 41.8.

Kelley said the Tigers had a feeling they would be able to do some good things in the punting game. Maryland's punter was the son of the legendary NFL quarterback Otto Graham. "He kicked the ball a long way, but he kicked it low and we thought we would be able to return some," Kelley said. The day began quickly for Kelley as he took a punt back 58 yards to the Maryland 6-yard-line in the first quarter. "I actually thought I had scored," recounted Kelley. "The officials said I stepped out of bounds on the 6." We bet Kelley wished there had been replay in those days.

The Tigers were not able to capitalize on Kelley's efforts as a fumble on third down was recovered by the Terps at their own 2-yard line. Kelley had two other punt returns in the second quarter, but they only netted 24 yards. Maryland held a slim 3–0 halftime lead with both teams struggling on offense. The third quarter was much the same, with neither team scoring, setting the stage for a wild fourth quarter. Kelley began the fireworks in the fourth when he returned a Maryland punt 85 yards for a touchdown, giving the Tigers their first lead, 10–3.

"We had a wall set up to the right," said Kelley. "But after I got the punt, there was no way I could get to the wall, so I just put on the brakes and went left. It was almost like all the Maryland players went to the right side, and I just went up the left side. I made a few guys miss and went all the way this time."

First year head coach Hootie Ingram gave Kelley a breather after the punt return as Maryland took the kickoff and began their next possession. When Kelley was ready, he went back into the game in the secondary and produced more magic. "On my first play back in the game, I intercepted a pass and ran it back to the 2-yard line where they knocked me out of bounds," said Kelley of his 56-yard return. On the first play after the interception, Clemson's Dick Bukowsky went the final two yards to increase Clemson's lead to 17–3.

Clemson's final touchdown came via interception, as Jewel McLauren picked off a Maryland pass and went 68 yards for the final Tigers points. Clemson had tallied three fourth-quarter touchdowns thanks to the help of two interceptions and Kelly's punt return.

The Maryland game was the capper of three impressive weeks for the Greenville native. Kelley began the hot streak with a 67-yard punt return for a touchdown against Wake Forest. The next week against Duke in

Death Valley, Kelley intercepted a Leo Hart pass and returned it 102 yards for a touchdown. The final part of the three-game stretch was the Maryland game on Halloween at College Park. No Clemson player has had such a run before or since, when it comes to return yards.

"The touchdown against Duke was the only touchdown I scored in Death Valley," Kelley said. "The next year I moved back to my normal position of wide receiver and never scored a touchdown at Clemson. I did all my scoring on the road except for that interception."

The 102-yard effort (100 officially) against the Blue Devils still stands as the longest interception return in Clemson history. As for the Maryland game, his 223 yards of punt and interception returns are the gold standard for Clemson. "It really is amazing that this is still the record for Clemson on returns," said Kelley. "When you think of all the great players who have played, it is amazing that one of them has not had a better day than my game at Maryland."

Kelley finished 1970 sixth in the nation in punt-return yardage with an average of 16.2 yards. Years later people still remember that performance. "A friend of mine is a pilot and flew into the airport in Columbia a few years ago. He saw a plane there with a Maryland sticker on it that had just landed. My friend started talking to the pilot of that plane and discovered the guy had played football at Maryland. My friend told him he had a friend named Don Kelley who played football at Clemson. The Maryland pilot said, 'I played football at Maryland against that guy, and he just went crazy against us one day in 1970. He was the best return man I have ever seen.'"

Kelley is now a dentist in his native Greenville. He and his wife have four children, all of whom graduated from Clemson. Two of his three son-in-laws are also Clemson grads. When reflecting on the Maryland game, Kelley added one more fact that made the day his best ever. "It was Halloween, and that was my Mom's birthday," he said. "That really made that game and that day a special one for me."

The 800 Rule

While many of the subjects in this chapter deal with accomplishments on the field by notable Clemson teams and individuals, this particular entry is about a court ruling. It might be the most important factor in Clemson's return to national prominence in the 1970s.

Prior to the 1964 season, ACC presidents decided to adopt a rule whereby all incoming scholarship and walk-on student-athletes in football and basketball (there were very few women's varsity sports then, none at Clemson) had to post at least an 800 combined verbal and math score on the SAT. Two years later, the presidents voted to have the 800 Rule in effect for all sports.

No other conference in the nation had such a rule. Minimum admission requirements for all other schools required that the student-athlete "predict" a 1.6 grade-point average as a freshman. (A formula was implemented that took the SAT score and the class rank to predict the GPA.)

The 800 Rule reduced the recruiting pool for all ACC institutions. Many high school seniors who wanted to go to ACC schools could not because they didn't have the SAT score, but their résumé predicted at least a 1.6 GPA. Thus, many in the Southeast went to SEC schools.

There were some examples of high school football players who grew up in Clemson, but could not get a scholarship to Clemson because they didn't have the 800. They went to Georgia or Florida or Tennessee instead. The most famous example took place in basketball. Pete Maravich grew up in Clemson, but moved to Raleigh for high school when his dad, Press, became the head coach at N.C. State. Press wanted to coach his gifted son, still the greatest scorer in the history of college basketball. When it became apparent that he was not going to have the 800 for the SAT, Press took the head-coaching job at LSU. Think what he could have done in the ACC and what that would have done for the Wolfpack basketball program from 1967 to 1970.

Just look at the following ACC football statistics for the years 1964–1972 (when the rule was enforced):

- ACC schools were a combined 8–58 against nonconference schools ranked in the top 20 of the AP poll.
- ACC schools were 11–58 against SEC schools.
- The ACC *champion* during those years was a combined 11–31 in nonconference competition the year they won the title.
- ACC teams were 97–193 in all nonconference games in those nine years.
- Only four ACC teams were ranked in the final AP or UPI top 20 polls in those nine seasons, none in the top 10.
- ACC teams won just four bowl games in the nine years.

With the results listed above, some of the ACC member institutions thought it was time to change the 800 rule. But motions were deadlocked at 4–4. Finally, after the 1970–1971 academic year, South Carolina voted to leave the ACC. There were many reasons listed for their decision, but certainly a main one was the 800 rule. Ironically, the rule soon changed as a result of a lawsuit brought about by South Carolina's biggest ACC rival at he time, Clemson.

During their senior years in high school, Clemson prospects Henry Allen, a linebacker from Manning, South Carolina, and Willie Anderson, a defensive lineman from Mayesville, South Carolina, signed letters of intent with Clemson before they had learned of their final SAT scores. By the end of their senior seasons, it was determined they had not reached the 800 threshold and were thus ineligible to be members of the Clemson football team.

A lawsuit had already been filed by two Clemson students who wished to join Clemson varsity teams. Joey Beach was a Clemson student who wanted to join the swimming team, and James Vickery wanted to join the football team. Neither had the 800 SAT school, but were already Clemson students.

Allen and Anderson joined the suit, making it a class-action suit.

After months of deliberation, Judge Robert Hemphill made a ruling on August 7, 1972. He basically said the 800 rule was arbitrary and invoked a standard for athletes that did not apply to other students at the ACC schools. He said the league had no right to invoke the rule. Eleven days later, the ACC voted to drop the 800 rule and adopt the NCAA's 1.6 rule, thus ending the eligibility advantage other conferences had over the ACC.

Allen became a part time player for Clemson in 1973. Anderson had a much more significant career. As a senior in 1974, he was a first-team All-ACC middle guard and team co-captain. He and Bennie Cunningham were the top players on a 7–4 team that beat Georgia, Georgia Tech, and South Carolina in the same season for the first time in history. Anderson's performance against South Carolina, his last game as a Clemson Tiger, was inspiring and noteworthy as he recorded 21 tackles, still the only game a Clemson defensive lineman has had 20 tackles in a single game. He was named the National Defensive Player of the Week by *Sports Illustrated*.

Charley Pell

"**I** just closed my eyes and my mind traveled back 20 years. These were the same words I had heard 25 years ago from this great man. He was our coach, our leader."

With those words, former Clemson All-American Joe Bostic took a crowd of more than 600 mourners on a journey. They were gathered at the First Baptist Church in Gadsden, Alabama, for the funeral of former Clemson head football coach Charley Pell, who had passed away on May 28, 2001. Those gathered were former teammates, coaches, players, and friends. They were all there because they loved this man and respected what he had brought to their lives.

Bostic was speaking of an electric moment just two months earlier. Coach Pell was in Clemson for the annual spring football game, and he knew his days were limited. Cancer was taking its toll. He had visited with his former players from the 1977 and 1978 teams on Friday night and now he was addressing Tommy Bowden's current Tigers. Coach Pell, speaking in the soft tones left him by his draining strength, told the 2001 Tigers of what it means to be a team. He told them that each man must play his part, however large it may seem to be. He told them they must play together, they must play with one heartbeat.

The words brought Bostic back to his playing days.

Charles Byron Pell came to Clemson in December of 1975. He had left the Virginia Tech program and was brought in to be Clemson's defensive coordinator. He was the only change on coach Red Parker's 1976 staff. He took the defensive assistants and laid out a summer game plan heading toward the opening of the 1976 season. Those defensive assistants saw a change immediately. Summer afternoons on the golf course were over. Coach Pell always said if you were a good golfer, you weren't a good football coach.

The 1976 season was frustrating. Vince Fusco kicked a 56-yard field goal on the last play of the game for Duke to tie the Tigers at 18–18 on homecoming. Too many penalties were crucial in a loss at Tennessee. Things jelled for the last game, though, a huge 28–9 win over South Carolina in the rain at Tigertown. It was not enough, however, and Parker was fired at season's end.

Pell was promoted to head coach on December 1, 1976. Everyone involved knew there was a new sheriff in town and there was no doubt who that was. Things were gong to be done one way and one way only— the right way! Coach Pell made sure everyone was on the same page. As he used to say, "We are going to move with one heartbeat."

Charley Pell and Danny Ford (squatting) combined for seven ACC titles from 1977 to 1989.

The Pell approach paid dividends in the second game of the 1977 season when the Tigers upset defending SEC champion Georgia 7–6. Clemson had not won there since 1914. Noted *Atlanta Constitution* columnist Lewis Grizzard described Coach Pell's reaction to the win at Georgia in this way: "The coach sat on the floor and cried. He is 36 years old. But he sat on the floor and cried. He didn't sob. He cried like a man cries when he sits back down in the pew after giving his only daughter in marriage."

We look back now and see names like Steve Fuller, Jerry Butler, Joe and Jeff Bostic, Steve Kenney, Dwight Clark, Randy Scott, and Jim Stuckey. It's easy to see how Clemson won with that group of players. However, in early 1977 the mindset was completely different. Clemson hadn't had a big winner in so long, and a berth in the Gator Bowl looked about as attainable as going to the Super Bowl. Remember that change in attitude.

Next came wins at Georgia Tech and Virginia Tech and then triumphs in the ACC against Virginia, Duke, and N.C. State. All of a sudden the Tigers were on a roll. Clemson's first bowl bid since 1959 seemed certain. All of a sudden football was fun!

The Tigers had a 17–7 lead over fifth-ranked Notre Dame in their final home game before Joe Montana led a fourth-quarter comeback and the Irish prevailed 21–17. They would win the rest of their games and be crowned national champions. But Clemson had taken the Irish to the brink, and the Tigers program gained great national acclaim for that performance.

A victory at South Carolina in the season finale clinched a Gator Bowl berth against defending national champion Pittsburgh. The South Carolina game turned out to be an epic. The Tigers took a 24–0 lead midway in the third quarter only to have the Gamecocks put on a 27-point blitz. Their last touchdown gave South Carolina a 27–24 lead with just over two minutes to play.

Poise, pride, and leadership were never more in evidence as Steve Fuller took the Tigers the length of the field, capped off by Jerry Butler's game-winning catch with 49 seconds left. The storybook season culminated with the awarding of the bid after the game.

Much has happened since that year. Pell took Clemson to a 10–1 record and No. 6 national ranking in 1978. But, at the conclusion of the season, he decided to move on to head up the Florida football program. He thought he had a better chance of winning the national championship there.

Ironically, Clemson won the national championship just three years later with many of the players he had recruited leading the way. Coach Pell had some success at Florida, but some transgressions involving NCAA rules led to his demise. The phone never rang after he left Florida, and it brought great challenges to his life.

Late in life he became a Christian and lived his last four years in peace. Not even the lung cancer, which was the final blow, could take away the peace he felt.

Pell came back to Clemson for one last journey. Ron West, the offensive-line coach of the Tigers at the time, Jeff Bostic, Joe Bostic, and a few others listened in that crowded home locker room in April of 2001 as Coach Pell spoke.

Joe Bostic just closed his eyes and let his mind race back to 1977. It was a moving experience. "There are coaches for times and places," said Bostic. "He was the man for us. He came here and made us a team. He made us believe in ourselves. We were good players, but we just did not know it. Most of all, he made us men."

Steve Fuller

In many ways, Steve Fuller's career is the most important in Clemson history because it jumpstarted the rebirth of Clemson football in the 1970s, and those accomplishments have had a direct effect on what has been accomplished in recent years under Dabo Swinney's direction.

College football in the 1970s was a different game, and that was especially the case under Clemson mentors Charley Pell and Danny Ford. It was a much more ground-oriented offense across the nation, not just Clemson.

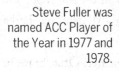

Steve Fuller was named ACC Player of the Year in 1977 and 1978.

Most of the records Fuller set 38 years ago have been eclipsed thanks to the proliferation of the spread offense. In that 1978 season Fuller, a third-team All-American, threw 187 passes in 12 games. In 2015 Deshaun Watson threw 491 passes and completed 333. For his career Fuller averaged just 12.9 passes a game compared to Watson's 27 per game through the 2015 season.

One record Fuller still holds is most selections as ACC Most Valuable Player (Watson could tie that mark in 2016). He won the award in 1977 and 1978 when he took a program that had not been to a bowl game or ranked in the top 20 in 18 years to consecutive bowl games and consecutive top-20 rankings, including a then program-best No. 6 final ranking in 1978.

Fuller is the only quarterback in Clemson history to be named Academic All-America and on-the-field All-America in the same season. In 1978 he was the first-team Academic All-America quarterback and was a third-team Associated Press All-American on the field. He was sixth in the voting for the Heisman Trophy. Only Watson has had a higher finish at No. 3 in 2015.

Fuller was a terrific leader. When the Tigers defeated Ohio State in the 1978 Gator Bowl in Fuller's final game, Danny Ford was coaching his first game as a head coach at age 30. Ford will be the first to tell you that Fuller's command of the offense and team leadership made his job a lot easier that night as the Tigers beat Woody Hayes and the Buckeyes 17–15.

At the conclusion of his career, Fuller was awarded one of the 11 National Football Foundation Scholarships. For the 1978–1979 academic year, he was the recipient of the Jim Weaver Award, which goes to the top ACC scholar-athlete across all sports. In those days there was just one recipient.

Coming out of high school, Fuller was first in his class of 826 students at Spartanburg High School. He graduated from Clemson with a 3.9 GPA. When he was drafted in the first round of the 1979 draft by the Kansas City Chiefs, an NFL scout told Clemson coaches Fuller had the highest Wonderlic Test score among all the players drafted.

Fuller achieved at the NFL level as well. A starter with the Chiefs, he went on to win a Super Bowl ring with the 1985 Chicago Bears. Today Fuller lives in Hilton Head, South Carolina, where he has been very successful in the real estate industry.

Deshaun Watson has an appreciation for Clemson football tradition and the uniform number he wears (Fuller's No. 4). He certainly has a great predecessor to emulate.

Jerry Butler

The image of a Jerry Butler stretching in the Columbia, South Carolina, night sky to catch a pass in the end zone to score the winning touchdown against South Carolina in the 1977 classic is one of the

Jerry Butler was a first-team All-American and the No. 5 selection of the 1979 NFL Draft.

most iconic moments in Clemson football history. "I was excited, but I wasn't shocked that I could catch it," said Butler about what is now know as "The Catch I."

In the 1977 game against the Gamecocks, Clemson had built a 24–0 lead and was dominating the game. The Gamecocks came charging back and took a 27–24 advantage with 1:48 left. "After we won at Georgia early in the year, Coach Pell started giving us cigars after every win," said Butler. "I looked at their bench after they scored. Some of the players had pulled up their jerseys to show off T-shirts that said, 'No Cigars Today.' I was very irritated."

Then "the Butler did it" on Clemson's next possession. "I ran a corner route." he said. "I came out of my cut and saw that Steve [Fuller] had been rushed, and had to break containment. I knew he would get rid of the ball and wouldn't take a sack."

Fuller apparently fired a pass just to get rid of it.

"I saw the ball out of the corner of my eye," Butler said. "I went for it and made a leaping grab [moving backward]. I just got my hands on it and came down in the end zone. It was something that we hadn't worked on."

The clock showed just 49 seconds remained in the game, and the Tigers went on to win 31–27, a victory that clinched Clemson's invitation to the Gator Bowl, the school's first bowl bid since 1959.

Jerry Butler made "The Catch" on November 19, 1977. It was a 20-yard pass from Steve Fuller with just 49 seconds remaining to give Clemson a 31–27 win over South Carolina in Columbia.

Butler was named first-team All-ACC that year and in 1978 became a first-team AP All-American. The No. 5 selection in the 1979 NFL Draft, he was named to the All-Rookie team in 1979, made the Pro Bowl in 1980, and played eight years in the NFL. Today, Butler continues to have a positive impact on the NFL as the director of player engagement for the Chicago Bears. He has had similar positions with the Cleveland Browns, Buffalo Bills, and Denver Broncos since he retired as a player.

The native of Ware Shoals, South Carolina, helps current Bears players with off-the-field tasks, from finances to counseling. "From the start, with rookies, I tell them I'm here to help," Butler said. "They have to believe that and know they can pick up the phone and call me at any time. And trust me, they do."

Butler's interest in player development was sparked when he was a player at Buffalo. Reggie McKenzie, a former teammate, constantly talked about using the off-season to prepare for life after football. Butler didn't think much of it at the time, but one off-season McKenzie stayed at Butler's house. The time he spent with Butler certainly had a positive effect. He could see firsthand how Butler was preparing himself for life beyond his playing days.

Butler's last season was in 1986. John Butler (no relation), the general manager at the time, needed someone for his new player development position. "It's just a passion for impact," Butler said. "I like to feel I made some type of significant contribution to a player's life. I understand the inside of the business and what role the athletes play in it. Not only that, but I also understand the responsibilities they have to their family and their community."

One of the stories Butler immediately calls to mind comes from his days in Cleveland. One of the Browns left college as a junior and had about 30 credit hours left to graduate. Butler found ways to help him through taking online classes and internships. Three months after he graduated, he got cut. "He came into my office and he said, 'I know this sounds stupid, but I want to thank you for pushing me, not to be a better athlete—to finish my degree. Because now I feel more confident about leaving out that door than I did coming through that door,'" Butler said.

"I'll never forget that. In that point in time, I realized that's my new trophy on the wall. They say, 'To give a man money, you're giving him part of your finances. But when you give him your time, you're giving him a part of your life.'"

In 2016 Butler was named the recipient of the Brian Dawkins Lifetime Achievement Award from the Clemson football program. It is presented each year to a former Clemson football player who has been successful in his professional career after his playing days are over.

Danny Ford's First Game

The 1977 and 1978 Clemson football seasons brought the Tigers program to the national football consciousness. They might be the most important consecutive years in Clemson football history.

The Clemson program had been without a bowl bid since 1959. The 800 rule had taken its toll on the program from a national perspective. The Tigers had won three straight ACC titles from 1965 to 1967, but lost at least four games in each of those seasons.

Clemson finally had a breakthrough season in 1977 with a Gator Bowl bid and a final top-25 national ranking. The 1978 team had 18 starters back, including ACC Player of the Year Steve Fuller and five other offensive players who would go on to start in the NFL. The starting defense had five future pros as well.

After stumbling at Georgia 12–0 (incredible to see the Clemson offensive lineup for this season and think they were shut out by anyone), the Tigers won the rest of their games in 1978 and had a 10–1 regular-season record with a No. 7 national ranking.

Had Clemson held out for an Orange Bowl bid they might have gotten it. These were different times, when bowl deals were struck in mid-November. But athletic director Bill McLellan didn't want to take a chance on getting left out in the cold and accepted a Gator Bowl bid to play 20th-ranked Ohio State (7–3–1) after clinching the ACC with a victory over Maryland.

After a 41–23 win over South Carolina in the season finale, a dominant rushing performance that saw three Clemson backs rush for 100 yards, Florida came calling for head coach Charley Pell. The Alabama graduate accepted.

Five days after Pell announced he was going to Florida, Danny Ford was named Clemson's head coach. Ford had been the offensive-line coach, though not the offensive coordinator, but he had the support of many of the players, who went to McLellan with their recommendation.

As was the case in 2008 when Dabo Swinney was named, the current athletic director really didn't need those recommendations from the players. Terry Don Phillips saw Swinney's abilities for many years as an assistant, and McLellan knew first-hand what Ford could do as well.

So, on December 5, 1978, Ford, at the age of 30, took over the Tigers football team. It was not on an interim basis for the bowl game, it was permanent. He was the youngest Division I head coach in the country. Ford had the luxury of a veteran team, especially at quarterback, where Steve Fuller could run the offense in his sleep.

Ohio State was coached by the legendary Woody Hayes, who was 65 years old and had already won three national championships, 13 Big Ten titles, and 205 games.

At a pregame press conference in Jacksonville, Ford was presented with a large container of Rolaids because taking over for this game with just 24 days to prepare was going to bring on a lot of stress. Hayes was presented with a pair of red boxing gloves. My, was that prophetic.

The contest was close for 60 minutes. Two efficient quarterbacks, Fuller for the Tigers and freshman Art Schlichter for Ohio State, ran their teams to precision. Schlichter actually had the better game statistically, connecting on 16 of 20 passes for 205 yards, with another 70 yards rushing. He accounted for over 75 percent of the Ohio State offense.

Clemson had a 17–15 lead with a little over two minutes left. It was third-and-5 at the Clemson 24. All the Buckeyes had to do was kick a field goal to win the game. But Ohio State had not been great in the kicking department that year, as the Buckeyes kickers had missed three extra points and were just 7-of-11 on field goals.

So on third-and-5, Hayes approved a pass play over the middle. It was a seemingly safe pass to running back Ron Springs. The hope was to put Springs on a Clemson linebacker and have him work for a first down in the middle of the field. Ohio State still had two timeouts left.

Schlichter faded back to pass and was rushed a bit by defensive tackle Steve Durham. Middle guard Charlie Bauman, dropped into coverage instead of rushing the passer and Schlichter never saw him as he threw the ball. Bauman stepped in front of Springs and intercepted Schlichter's pass at the Clemson 28, four yards behind the original line of scrimmage. He ran upfield toward the Ohio State sideline and was tackled as he was going out of bounds by Schlichter at the 36.

Bauman stood up after making the theft and was struck under the chin by Coach Hayes, who happened to be in the vicinity. Once Bauman was struck, a mêlée erupted on the Ohio State sideline, which carried over onto the field.

The game was televised nationally, and broadcasters Keith Jackson and Ara Parseghian were calling the game by watching the field, not their monitors. Neither of them acknowledged the punch to the throat by Hayes. A replay was shown, but it was from an end zone camera, and a player blocked out Hayes' swing.

After order was restored, officials lost track of where Bauman had run out of bounds. They marked off a 15-yard penalty against Ohio State for unsportsmanlike conduct from the 40, instead of the 36. The only thing the statisticians could do was give Bauman those four extra yards, or they would be lost in the statistical ozone. So he was credited with a 12-yard return for a run of eight.

After a Clemson running play, Hayes was given another personal foul, giving Clemson another first down at the Ohio State 27. The Tigers ran out the clock from there. Hayes was escorted off the field and never shook hands with Ford. But Ford was not upset. He was just thrilled with the win.

Ford and Bauman handled the postgame brilliantly. Ford really wasn't sure what had happened at the time. All he knew was that an official told him an Ohio State coach had hit one of his players. "I was hit, I don't know by whom," said Bauman in the locker room after the game. When asked again a few minutes later, Bauman said, "I'm not saying anything."

Jonathan Brooks, a Clemson defensive end, said, "A lot of players said Woody hit him. It looked like he did. I was in the middle of a whole bunch of people trying to get out of there."

Hayes did not appear at a press conference after the game, sending George Hill, his defensive coordinator, in his place. Hill said, "I didn't see it. I was there but still couldn't see. Whatever, it was certainly unfortunate."

After the game, Ohio State athletic director Hugh Hindman met with Hayes and asked him to resign. Hayes refused and told Hindman he would have to fire him. He did. The next day, December 30, 1978, when Hayes and the Ohio State team landed in Ohio, Hayes grabbed the airplane microphone and told his players to go home safely and to return to class on the first day of school for the next semester. He then said, "I am no longer the Ohio State football coach." He was then given a police escort to his home in Columbus.

Bauman was just a sophomore when this game was played, so he still had two more years of eligibility with the Tigers—two more years to handle questions from the media about the incident. But, to his credit, he remained quiet and classy about the incident. Ford was impressed with how he handled the situation as well, and still is today. For the 1978 season Bauman was presented with the Shingler Award, which is the Clemson team award given each year for sportsmanship.

Bauman was a college football fan growing up in New Jersey and had great respect for Coach Hayes. Hayes called him in February of 1979. "We had a nice conversation. He did not apologize, but I didn't ask for one," said Bauman.

Hayes passed away on March 12, 1987. He had been honored at the Ohio State graduation the year before with an honorary degree. He was beloved by his colleagues in all areas of Ohio State University who knew of his generosity when it came to his assistants. He often turned down raises and had the money distributed to his assistant coaches. His base salary in 1978, his last year, was just $43,000. When he passed away, his relatives found thousands of dollars worth of undeposited checks in pockets of suit jackets.

In a 2008 article, Bauman told the *Florida Times Union*, "He made a mistake. We all make mistakes. I mean, he didn't hurt me or anything."

When the two schools met in the 2014 Orange Bowl, Bauman respectfully declined all interviews. Bauman had a solid career at Clemson. He played all 47 games over four years, 18 as a starter. He finished with 153 tackles, 16 tackles for loss, and two fumble recoveries.

And, yes, one interception.

CHAPTER 9
NATIONAL
CHAMPIONSHIP
SEASON

Clemson's Manhattan Project

When football fans compare the college and pro games, one of the comparative assets attributed to the former is spirit. Oh, for the color and pageantry of college football. Teams at the university level have successfully utilized well-documented ploys since its beginning in 1869 to gain an edge, the intangible advantage called motivation.

In 1980, for the annual contest with South Carolina, the Clemson Tigers added to the college game's mystique by pulling off the most secretive plan since the Manhattan Project. The Orange Pants Project will live in the memories of Tigers fans forever, and based on the results, it will hold a special place in Clemson University history.

The history of Clemson's orange pants and the accompanying secrecy is a fascinating story. The idea was actually conceived by Len Gough, at the time the equipment manager and later assistant executive secretary of IPTAY. In the summer of 1980 he received samples of orange pants from various places. "I thought they would look super and we could use them as something special down the road," said Gough, a 1975 graduate of Clemson. "That summer I mentioned the idea to Coach Ford. He liked the idea but was not jumping up and down at the time and even said he was thinking about 1981 to use them."

The idea lay dormant until homecoming of 1980. "Kind of out of the blue, Danny came down to the equipment room to see the sample pair and asked if we could get a set for the South Carolina game [now only six weeks away]. I couldn't give him an answer right away, but we thought we should ask a couple of the players, some we could trust with a secret."

So the Wednesday before the homecoming game with Virginia Tech, Willie Underwood and Jeff Davis, two of Clemson's most respected team leaders, became the chosen two. Underwood, the model, recalled the meeting: "It was a complete surprise to me, we did not know what the meeting was about. I saw the pants and right from the start thought, *This is great*. The pair fit just right, even better than the pants I had been wearing all season. We needed something special for that game, and this was going to be the symbol. I was excited and so was Jeff, but Coach Ford said it was to be a surprise and that we could not tell anyone. It was a month and a half until the game, but we swore we would not tell anyone. We would see each other on campus during the days before the game and smile and ask each other, 'Did you tell anyone?'"

Underwood and Davis both did a fairly good job of not letting the cat out of the bag. Davis only spilled the beans to one person, his four-year roommate and fellow team leader Perry Tuttle.

"After the meeting with Willie, Len, and coach, Jeff came into the room and shut the door," said Tuttle. "He said, 'I'm going to tell you something you can't tell anyone. We are going to wear orange britches against South Carolina.' I thought, *How is this going to look?* But after I thought about it, I knew it was something we needed."

The decision to go with the pants actually was not finalized until November 3, 1980, the Monday after the Wake Forest game. That was cutting it close, but Gough and head athletic trainer Fred Hoover came to the rescue. "Fred was a friend of Hank Spires, the vice president of Russell Mills in Alabama, and we needed his connection to get them made in the 20 days left until the game," said Gough.

Getting cloth for 120 uniform pants is no easy task, and the cloth did not arrive at the plant until Wednesday, November 19, only three days before the game. "It was a panic situation that final week," said Gough. "They put it on as a priority-list item."

On Thursday the 20th the Mills company said the pants would be ready at noon on Friday, which meant the only way to get them to the game on time would be to fly down and get them. So that Friday Gough and pilot Earle Ambrose flew to Alexander, Alabama, to pick up the pants. At this point only 10 people still knew about the ploy.

"When we got there, they still weren't ready. We were asking a lot because we had ordered 120 pairs of custom-fitted pants. We waited patiently, and they were ready about 3:00 PM. It was getting tight, and we knew we had a late night ahead of us," said Gough. "Hank Spires then drove us back to the airport, and we got back to Clemson, with 40 boxes of pants in my vehicle. Our next task was to wash the pants. I took two pairs back to Jervey and washed them to make sure they did not shrink too much. They passed the test, and later that night at about 10:00 PM [assistant equipment manager] Bobby Douglas and I washed every pair, which is something we do with every new pair to get them into their natural condition."

Identification of the pants was the next step. Douglas and Gough started that tedious job at 7:00 AM the morning of the 1:00 PM game. They did not want to get the student managers involved because the secret had gone so well for so long. At this point, still only about 10 people knew what was going to be the surprise of the year just four hours later.

Gough and Douglas loaded the pants in a big hamper and covered the top with white towels for transportation to the stadium. "A few managers became suspicious when we brought out this extra hamper, but they still did not know what was happening."

While the pants were being transported to the locker room, the Clemson football team was at the Holiday Inn in Anderson finishing its pregame meal. At the conclusion of the meal, Ford informed the team of the secret pants and displayed a pair.

"When Coach Ford pulled them out of the box at the meeting the morning of the game, we knew we were going to win," recalled Tuttle. "The guys just went crazy. Coach said a few things, but he did not have to say anything really. We could not have been more fired up for the game."

At 11:10 AM Gough and the managers began unpacking the orange pants at the lockers. The Tigers were to warm up in the traditional white pairs, then change before the entrance via the hill for the final time in 1980.

Thus, the managers had to get two pairs of pants ready. Everything was going well until about 11:15 AM. "One of the managers brought in Paul Coakley [who worked for Clemson] to pick something up in the locker room," said Gough, who recalls the situation with a smile. "I felt bad for him, but we had to keep him in the locker room until we left for the last time. His eyes grew to twice their size when he saw the orange pants, and I just didn't want to risk South Carolina or anyone else finding out, so he stayed in Coach Ford's interview room area for an hour."

Everything went according to schedule for the rest of the pregame. The schedule to come off the field had been moved back five minutes to give the players extra time to change pants. "When they were putting on the pants, there was a constant buzz," said Danny Ford. "The players were beside themselves. I always made orange special in practice, especially in the spring and the fall for scrimmages. The team that got to wear

South Carolina's George Rogers never scored in four games versus Clemson's defense from 1977 to 1980.

Willie Underwood was the star in Clemson's 27–6 win over South Carolina in the season finale of 1980.

orange in the scrimmages was the team that was doing well. It had prestige, so orange already had a special meaning for them."

Every minor detail was taken care of in the minutes prior to the unveiling. For the coin toss, the Tigers sent out Eddie Geathers, who was injured, to represent the team at the toss, and he wore blue jeans. When the team went out of the locker room to board the bus, all the players went out through the prospect room so as few fans as possible would see them. The buses were moved right up to the door.

"When they were out of the locker room, I just went out to the side-line to see the reaction," said Gough. "The team stayed on the buses until South Carolina came on the field—we wanted them to see the full effect. When we got to the hill, it was like a rippling effect. People would see them at the end close to the hill and you could see the news pass through the stands."

The rest is history. Clemson went on to beat South Carolina that day 27–6. The Gamecocks were ranked 14th nationally entering the game and were led by Heisman Trophy winner George Rogers. But, appropriately enough, the star of the game was Underwood. The same man who had been selected to be the first to try on the Orange Pants had the game of his life with 17 tackles and two interceptions, including one returned for a touchdown. Those were the first two interceptions of his career, and he was named national defensive Player of the Week by *Sports Illustrated*. "That was the greatest game of my life," said Underwood. "You just felt so good in those pants. I swear you could run faster and jump higher in those things."

Clemson gained great momentum from that win over South Carolina game to end the 1980 season and went on to win the national championship with an Orange Bowl victory over fourth-ranked Nebraska. They wore those orange pants in that 22–15 victory as well.

Beating the Dawgs and Herschel Walker

"I am anxious to go up against the top back in the nation," said Jeff Davis. "Last year [1980], Herschel [Walker] was a freshman who played like a senior. But it's going to be different when he comes to Death Valley. He'll find that he won't be able to do as well against this senior." Davis showed his teammates he had the confidence to beat the defending national champions, a team that had never lost with Walker in its lineup.

In fact, Clemson's 13–3 victory that September 19 day would be the only regular-season loss of Walker's three-year career with the Bulldogs. Once again, it was the defense that carried the day for Clemson. The Tigers forced nine turnovers (five interceptions and four fumbles), and 35 years later that is still the Tigers record for turnovers forced in a game. The nine takeaways were recorded by nine different players, the best stat that shows that this was an all-around team effort. It gave Clemson 16 forced turnovers in two games, the best back-to-back takeaway total in school history.

Buck Belue threw five interceptions and lost a fumble for six of the nine turnovers. Walker had lost just one fumble his entire freshman season when he gained over 1,600 yards, an all-time NCAA freshman record. He had three fumbles in this game, two that were recovered by the Tigers defense, including one by William Perry when he seemingly just shoved Walker aside with his brute strength to scoop up the ball.

Walker would get 111 yards rushing on 28 carries, but he never reached the end zone. In fact, he would play three games against the Tigers in his career without scoring a touchdown, joining Heisman Trophy winner George Rogers of South Carolina with that career note against Clemson's defense.

This was a true rock'em-sock'em game from the outset, as the two teams combined for only 491 yards of total offense. Clemson had just 236 yards on the day, but still won by double digits. Field position was a big issue, and Dale Hatcher was an unsung hero, as he averaged 43 yards on seven punts.

Clemson scored 10 points in the second quarter, and they held up. An interception by Tim Childers set up the only touchdown of the day, an eight-yard pass from Homer Jordan to Perry Tuttle. Donald Igwebuike kicked two field goals, one in the second quarter and one in

Terry Kinard stops Herschel Walker, another Heisman winner who never scored against the Tigers. Clemson forced nine turnovers against Georgia in 1981, still a record for turnovers forced in a game by a Tigers team.

the fourth quarter. Georgia's only points came on a Kevin Butler field goal on the Bulldogs' first drive of the second half.

The Bulldogs had won 15 consecutive games, the longest active winning streak in college football at the time. Their No. 4 national ranking was the highest-ranked team Clemson defeated in Death Valley over the first 107 years of Clemson football, which was only eclipsed when Tommy Bowden's Tigers beat No. 3 Florida State in 2003.

When Rod McSwain intercepted a pass in the end zone with 1:08 left to clinch the win, the defense came off the field whirling their index fingers. At the time, they were giving notice that they had defeated last year's No. 1 team. But as it turned out, that celebration was a foreshadowing of things to come.

Tigers Are 10–8cious

Clemson's road to the national championship in 1981 included a classic game with North Carolina in Chapel Hill on November 7. It's considered to be one of the greatest games ever played in Atlantic Coast Conference history. It was eighth-ranked North Carolina against second-ranked Clemson, the first meeting of top-10 ACC teams in league history.

"The North Carolina game did more for us winning the national championship than any other game," said senior linebacker and captain Jeff Davis. "It was the ultimate test for us. We expected to win in Death Valley and we expected teams to already be behind when the whistle blew to start the game. But, to go into the backyard of a top-10 football team with everything at stake, and win, that did it for us. Remember, North Carolina had everything to play for. It's right there for them too. You can think there were people wondering, 'Can Clemson stay focused?' And we beat them in a fight. It was an all-out brawl. May the best man win! It was man-on-man."

With an ACC championship and a major bowl bid at stake, it was dubbed the biggest game ever in the state of North Carolina. "North Carolina came to play," defensive tackle and All-American Jeff Bryant said. "They were at home and they were a top-10 team. We both were striving for that goal, which was to win the ACC and take it further from there. It was a very physical game. I can remember being sore for a couple of days after that." It was also homecoming weekend in Chapel Hill and it was the last game at Kenan Stadium for UNC's seniors—a class that had helped the Tar Heels win an ACC championship the year before and beat traditional powers such as Texas and Michigan along the way.

To top things off, there were bowl representatives from eight bowl games in attendance, more than at any other game that afternoon across the country. *Sports Illustrated* had been at Clemson all week to chronicle the Tigers' magic run and was in Chapel Hill on that afternoon. ABC was broadcasting it as part of its regional coverage, but the week of the game they expanded the coverage to be carried to a much bigger area.

All of America's eyes seemed to be placed on this small school from the foothills of South Carolina. "Were we excited about the hype? Yes! We wanted the stakes high," said Jeff Davis. "It didn't get any better than this. This was another opportunity for us to do something in Clemson football history that had never been done. We took all of that into consideration. We would not have approached that game any other way because there was the crown jewel of college football standing right in front of us. We could almost touch it. The world was watching. We had a great opportunity. It was everything that a young man and a young student-athlete could want.

"North Carolina, for me, was a big game. I'm from Greensboro, North Carolina, and I wanted to beat them more than anyone else we played. This was my last opportunity to make a statement in North Carolina that I made the right decision in coming to Clemson."

With all of the hype and extra attention, Clemson head coach Danny Ford knew he had to do something to turn his team's focus to what was really important—beating the Tar Heels. He knew it was going to be tough too. "I was concerned about how we could play physically with this team," he said. "We were out-muscled in 1980, which did not happen too often with our football teams. Their game plan in 1980 was to out-muscle Clemson, and I think they did it." The Tar Heels scored a fourth-quarter touchdown to win 24–19 in 1980 in Memorial Stadium. "We knew that's what they were going to try and do again."

The game started as a defensive struggle and lived up to its billing. The score was 0–0 at the end of the first quarter. Jeff McCall had a game-high 84 yards before he left the game injured and scored the game's lone touchdown—a seven-yard run with 6:54 to play in the second quarter. Clemson led 7–5 at the half. North Carolina ranked second in the country running the football coming in, but Clemson held the Tar Heels to 84 yards on 42 carries. Stopping the run had been the Tigers' MO all season. With new defensive coordinator Tom Harper at the helm, Clemson led the ACC in rushing defense and ranked second in the country.

"We would put a goose egg on our [defensive] board before every game," Davis said. "We didn't do it as a mark or just to put something up there. No, we actually believed it. It was symbolic to us. You were not going to score on us. Even if you get in our territory, you might have a chance to get a field goal, but you can forget about scoring a touchdown on us."

North Carolina running back and three-time All-ACC selection Kelvin Bryant was in his first game back after arthroscopic knee surgery earlier in the season, and he gained just 31 yards on 13 carries, as did fellow running back Tyrone Anthony on eight carries.

Clemson's defense was stifling. No team that season learned that any better than the Tar Heels. Twice, North Carolina had first-and-goal inside the Clemson 10, and both times it was held to short field goals by Brooks Barwick.

Trailing 10–5, following a Donald Igwebuike 39-yard field goal, North Carolina took its second drive of the third quarter and marched down to the Clemson 4 thanks to a 21-yard halfback pass from Anthony to Griffin. But Davis and Terry Kinard stuffed Kelvin Bryant for a five-yard loss on the next play, and then quarterback Scott Stankavage threw incomplete on second and third down, forcing the Tar Heels to settle for a 26-yard Barwick field goal.

The Tigers led 10–8 at the end of the third quarter. In the fourth, North Carolina again had an opportunity to take the lead following a muffed punt at the Clemson 37. After gaining just four yards on first and second down, the Tar Heels' hopes of taking the lead were dashed when freshman nose guard William Perry broke through and sacked quarterback Scott Stankavage for a 10-yard loss. "With the kind of defense we had, we never panicked," defensive tackle Jeff Bryant said. "We are going to make the big play. It was always roll call to the ball."

Following a Clemson punt, UNC again moved into Tigers territory to the 39, but again the defense stiffened, with a tackle for loss and two incomplete passes. Unable to move the ball, Clemson punter Dale Hatcher then pinned the Heels deep in their own territory at the 2-yard line following a 47-yard punt with 2:19 to play, setting up the final dramatics in one of the biggest victories in Clemson history.

After moving the ball out from the shadow of their own goal post, the Tar Heels found themselves with a first down at their own 40 thanks to a 12-yard scramble by Stankavage on third-and-10 from the 2, a nine-yard pass to wide receiver Jon Richardson, and a 14-yard pass to Anthony. With just over a minute to play and one timeout left, the Tar Heels called a screen pass to fullback Alex Burrus. Stankavage threw the ball behind the line of scrimmage, and when Burrus went to make the catch, defensive end Bill Smith met him, knocking the ball to the ground. The ball rolled 15 yards backward toward the Clemson sideline, and that is where defensive tackle Jeff Bryant jumped on the football at the UNC 25-yard line. It appeared everyone thought it was an incomplete pass, except for Bryant, who hustled for he ball.

The pass was ruled a lateral, and by jumping on the loose football, Bryant secured Clemson's 10–8 victory in front of a then record crowd at Kenan Stadium of 53,611. Timely plays were the calling card of the 1981 defense. In 1981 Clemson ranked seventh in the nation in turnover margin and led the ACC in forced turnovers with what is still a school-record 41.

Jeff Bryant, who played 12 seasons in the NFL, had a stellar career at Clemson. But it wasn't until Tom Harper became the defensive coordinator in the spring of 1981 when he finally realized what kind of player he could be. Harper did wonders for Bryant's play. He not only helped him become sound fundamentally, he helped him with his technique.

He helped him become a better football player, and a better person. "Tom Harper was very instrumental in my development," Bryant said. "He was a great guy. I wish I had Tom Harper all four years. I'm thankful I had him when I did, though, because he really made a difference with me."

Bryant credited Harper's instruction as one of the reasons he stayed alert and recognized the lateral on North Carolina's final drive. "I was coming upfield pretty hard because I figured they were going to pass the ball. I had a good rush on, and I was about as deep as the quarterback," he said. "I noticed him throwing the ball, and I saw the hit, but I noticed he threw the ball behind him. Bill [Smith] made a great hit, and I saw the ball coming out, so my thinking was to rush over there and get on it because no one else thought it was a lateral. I thought it was one because of the angle I was at. I was right there behind the quarterback as he threw the ball."

Smith, who admits he did not know it was a lateral at the time, sometimes wonders about the what-ifs had Bryant not jumped on the loose ball. "Who knows what would have happened had we lost that game, but thank goodness we can say what-if all we want because we didn't lose it," he said. The next day, the *Greenville News* had in its headlines, in bold print, a very clever headline: "Tigers Are 10–8cious."

"We knew that anything was possible at that point," Bryant said.

With a victory over the eighth-ranked Tar Heels behind them, Clemson for the first time, admitted the possibility of going undefeated and playing for a national championship was on its mind. "It was important because we started thinking a little bit now about being undefeated," Davis said. "Until that point, we were not trying to touch it. There might have been a few rumblings here and there, but we were all about one game at a time. At that point, and where we were at, you were going to have to do something phenomenal to beat us."

Winning the National Championship

Affter Clemson defeated South Carolina 29–13 to close the regular season, the Tigers were still ranked No. 2 in the nation behind Pittsburgh and quarterback Dan Marino. (The future Pro Football Hall of Famer had actually narrowed his decision out of high school to Clemson and Pittsburgh, because he was considering playing both football and baseball.) But on Thanksgiving weekend, Todd Blackledge and Penn State trounced Pittsburgh 48–14, moving Clemson into the No. 1 position entering the bowl games.

Looking back, that was huge for the Tigers, because there probably would not have been a Clemson-Pittsburgh matchup as the teams had made deals with bowls prior to Thanksgiving. When Pittsburgh lost, it dropped like a rock in the polls, all the way to No. 10 by AP. So entering the bowl games, Clemson was No. 1, the seventh different No. 1 team in 1981 (still the most ever in one season), and Georgia was No. 2. That meant if Clemson won, it would be national champion. By the same token, had Pittsburgh also been undefeated heading into the bowls, Clemson could have gone 12–0 and not won the national title if Pittsburgh was also undefeated.

Nebraska was hoping for dominoes to fall, just as they had for Notre Dame in 1977 when the Irish went from No. 5 to No. 1 on January 1. Even though Tom Osborne's Cornhuskers had lost two games in the regular season, the Cornhuskers were ranked No. 4 entering the bowl games and were on an eight-game winning streak. They knew if they beat Clemson in the Orange Bowl, Pittsburgh beat Georgia in the Sugar Bowl, and Texas beat Alabama in the Cotton Bowl, they could jump all the way to No. 1 and give Osborne his first national title.

Despite Clemson's being the only unbeaten team in college football entering the bowl games, some still felt that Georgia could leapfrog the Tigers with an impressive victory over Pittsburgh and an unimpressive

Tigers victory over Nebraska. That might seem absurd since Clemson beat Georgia head-to-head, but Herschel Walker and the Bulldogs had a national following and had won the title the previous year. And they had won every game since losing to the Tigers back in September.

That is why the lead story in Clemson's media packet for the Orange Bowl was an article by the *Greenville News'* Dan Foster with the headline, "Herschel Would Vote for Clemson If Both Teams Win." Walker was just being honest, but we're sure Georgia head coach Vince Dooley wished he had not been quite that honest with Mr. Foster.

Even though Clemson was the only undefeated team in the nation and Nebraska had two losses, the Cornhuskers were a four-point favorite entering this clash that would be nationally televised, the only time all season someone in California could see the Tigers play. The Cornhuskers had great tradition and still do, and they had won two national championships in 1970 and 1971. They also had the third-best record in college football during the 1970s. In fact, they had won the 1971 national title in an Orange Bowl win over Alabama when Danny Ford was a Crimson Tide assistant, so Ford was trying to erase his own demons in the Orange Bowl 10 years later.

The media did not give the ACC much respect, calling it a "basketball conference." Ford's parting comment to the media after this game was, "Well, it's on to basketball season." (North Carolina did win the national title that March, the first time the conference won the two major titles in the same academic year.) Nebraska came in riding an eight-game winning streak, averaging 330 yards per game on the ground. They had just won at Oklahoma by a score of 37–14, only the second time in the last nine years they had defeated the Sooners. And they had a backfield that included Mike Rozier, the winner of the 1983 Heisman Trophy, and Roger Craig, who would go on to a successful NFL career with the San Francisco 49ers. They had played a tough schedule, with nonconference games against Iowa, Florida State, Penn State, and Auburn.

The Clemson players were excited enough prior to the game, but NBC held the start of the game 17 minutes due to the length of the Rose Bowl game between Penn State and Southern Cal. The game finally kicked off at 8:17 PM, and it did not take long for things to go Clemson's way. On Nebraska's first drive, and third play from scrimmage, Cornhuskers quarterback Mark Mauer fumbled and William Devane recovered at the Nebraska 33. Mauer had been the second-string quarterback for Nebraska much of the season, but was the starter in this game due to an injury to Turner Gill, who was a sophomore at the time.

"We had been forcing turnovers all year, and that play told us that this game would be no different," said Jeff Davis. "It gave us confidence." Clemson could not score a touchdown after the fumble, but Donald Igwebuike came on to boot his first of three field goals, this one a 41-yarder that would have been good from 60 yards. The Cornhuskers came right back and drove 69 yards for a score in just eight plays on the ensuing drive. They used a trick play to score, as Rozier threw a 25-yard halfback pass to Anthony Steels for six points. It was the only touchdown pass over All-American Terry Kinard over the last two years of his career.

Clemson added a field goal and trailed 7–6 after the first quarter, the eighth time in 12 games Clemson went to the second quarter without the lead in 1981. The second quarter was the most dominant for the Tigers in 1981, when they outscored the opposition 133–15 for the season, and this game was no different. A fumble, by Nebraska's Phil Bates, was recovered by Davis. This was his record fourth recovered fumble of the season, giving Clemson the ball at the Nebraska 27. A series of runs brought the ball to the 2, where Cliff Austin scored on a sweep. As a freshman in 1978, he scored what proved to be the winning touchdown in the 1978 Gator Bowl against Ohio State. In both bowl games that Austin scored a touchdown, Clemson allowed the opposition just 15 points. Those were the only two games between 1972 and 1990 that the opposition scored exactly 15 points.

It had been quite a day for Austin, who was trapped in an elevator for two hours in the Clemson team hotel that afternoon. Frank Howard was quoted in the *Miami Herald* as having said in the press box, "Well, Coach Ford told the players to stay off their feet as much as possible." Clemson held a 12–7 lead at halftime. While Clemson did not score on its first possession of the second half, it did record a touchdown on its second. The Tigers drove 75 yards in 12 plays on their best drive of the night. Homer Jordan connected with Perry Tuttle on a 13-yard scoring pass in the left corner of the end zone.

For Tuttle, it was his eighth touchdown catch of the season, establishing a school record. His post touchdown celebration was captured on the cover of *Sports Illustrated*, the first time a Clemson athlete had been pictured on the cover. That would remain the case until the 2015 season when Deshaun Watson, Shaq Lawson, and Wayne Gallman combined for four covers. That Tuttle TD gave Clemson a 19–7 lead.

Clemson forced a three-and-out on the next Nebraska possession, and sophomore Billy Davis returned the punt 47 yards to the Nebraska 22. It would be the longest punt return of his career. Igwebuike booted a 36-yard field goal to give Clemson a 22–7 lead. The Tigers had scored 19 consecutive points. On the first play after the kickoff, Mauer attempted a pass in the left flat. Johnny Rembert, a backup linebacker on this team who would go on to a 10-year NFL career, jumped in the passing lane and had the ball in his hands for an easy touchdown. But he could not hang on. Had he done so, this game might have turned into a rout.

Nebraska was a championship team and certainly was not down, even with a 15-point deficit. Mauer took the Cornhuskers 69 yards in eight plays, and Nebraska scored on a Roger Craig 26-yard run. It was the longest run all year against the Tigers. That's right, 26 yards was the longest run of the year versus the Tigers. Nebraska lined up to go for two points, but was penalized for delay of game. Much to everyone's surprise, they still went for two, and Craig scored from the 8 on a pitchout to the left. Momentum appeared to have shifted with over nine minutes left.

The momentum really shifted for Nebraska fans when it was learned about this time that Pittsburgh was going to beat No. 2 Georgia in the Sugar Bowl. Texas had already beaten No. 3 Alabama in the Cotton Bowl earlier in the afternoon. This meant a Cornhuskers victory over the top-ranked Tigers would in fact give them the national title. Clemson then went three-and-out, so Nebraska took over the ball at its own 37 down just seven points with 7:49 left.

But the Cornhuskers were called for holding on their first play, and a bad pitchout by Mauer on third-and-four forced a punt. Clemson then took over the ball with 5:24 left, and Jordan and the Tigers offense worked their ball-control magic. Nebraska could not stop Clemson's offensive line. The Tigers converted two important third downs, including a 23-yard run by Jordan on third-and-4 from the Tigers 37.

Jordan was dehydrated after this drive, and one has to wonder if he would have been able to come back for another possession. He was virtually carried off the field after the game and was given IVs. Even though he was voted Offensive MVP, you will not find any quotes from him after the game, because it was far past the media's deadline before he came out of the locker room.

Clemson ran the clock down to six seconds before giving the ball up. The Cornhuskers had one last chance from their own 46, but Andy Headen knocked away their final long pass, and Clemson became the first ACC team to win the national title since 1953. Clemson was the unanimous No. 1 team in the nation in both polls following its win over Nebraska, giving Clemson its first national championship in any sport. In addition to the AP and UPI polls, Clemson was also proclaimed national champion by the *Sporting News, Sports Illustrated, Chicago Tribune,* Football Writers Association, Football Coaches Association, and Washington Touchdown Club.

"All I can say is that Clemson has a great team," said Osborne after the game in his postgame press conference. "We want to congratulate them. Our inability to move the ball and commit five or six major penalties were a factor, but Clemson played great defensively. Clemson has the best defense we faced all year. Offensively, they did a great job, particularly in the first half when they dominated the line of scrimmage. I didn't think they could do that to us. Also, we couldn't contain their quarterback Homer Jordan. This is probably the most disappointing loss I've ever had. There was so much at stake, and I thought we were good enough to win. It was in our hands, and we let it get away."

"Are we No. 1?" asked Ford after the game. "Well, we're the only team in the country that beat the No. 2 team [Georgia], the No. 4 team [Nebraska], and the No. 8 team [North Carolina]. No matter what they say on the West Coast or in the Southeast, no one else did that this year. We just wanted to stay close to them in the first quarter and make sure it was close at the half. Our plan was to try to whip them in the fourth quarter. I think we did that. We reacted a little better than they did. We might have been more used to it. I'm glad it's over. Nebraska is by far the best team we played all season. I hope I'm not undercutting anyone on our schedule, but they were the best."

Behind the Scenes in 1981

George Dostal's Sign

In the summer of 1981 Clemson strength training coach George Dostal posted a sign in his facility, "1982 Orange Bowl: Clemson vs. Nebraska." At the time Nebraska had the best strength training program in the country, and he wanted the Clemson program to emulate the Huskers in that area.

Bob Bradley and a live tiger on Picture Day in 1981.

He posted the sign as a goal, a goal that seemed unrealistic at the time for a Clemson program that had had a 6–5 record the previous year. But he certainly proved to be a prophet by the end of the year.

A Live Tiger for Picture Day

On August 23, 1981, sports information director Bob Bradley held Picture Day at Memorial Stadium. A fan who owned a tiger had contacted the athletic department and asked if we were interested in having a live tiger present for the day. Bradley thought it would be a good addition that would attract some attention to the program, at least on the local level.

It was a big hit. The tiger was unusually tame as it posed with players for position pictures. Near the end of the session, Bradley got on all fours next to the animal. At one point the tiger started to lick Bob's ear. Bradley told all who were watching, "That tiger was whispering to me that the Tigers were going 11–0."

Trailing Wofford

Clemson did not look like a national championship contender a quarter into the season. The Tigers opened with Wofford, then an NAIA school that replaced Villanova on the schedule the previous April when the Wildcats of Howie Long dropped football.

The Terriers ran the ball successfully with a "wingbone offense" against Clemson's defense and took a 3–0 lead in the first quarter. Think of the odds you could have gotten against Clemson winning the national championship at the end of that first quarter when the score was 3–3.

Wofford gained 165 yards rushing against a Clemson defense that would rank eighth in the nation in defending the run at season's end. Only Nebraska would gain more rushing yards against the Clemson defense in 1981. But the Tigers won 45–10.

A Pulled Hamstring

Clemson played its first indoor game against Tulane in the Superdome in New Orleans in the second game of the season. During pregame practice, Tigers freshman punter Dale Hatcher wowed players and coaches on both teams by hitting the gondola above the field with a punt, something only Oakland/Los Angeles Raiders punter Ray Guy had been able to do.

Bob Paulling came off the bench to kick two field goals in Clemson's 13–5 victory. Paulling did not know he was going to kick that day until pregame workouts. Donald Igwebuike, the starter who was also a top goalscorer on the Clemson soccer team, was late for the team bus as it left the hotel. As he chased the bus down at the end of the parking lot, he pulled his right hamstring.

Second-Half Comeback at Kentucky

With Clemson's victory over Georgia and two weeks to talk about it, ABC decided to broadcast the Clemson-Kentucky game on October 3 to a large part of the South. It was an opportunity for Clemson to impress more poll voters, but the first half was dreadful. Clemson had just 65 yards of total offense, and Kentucky led 3–0 at intermission.

Danny Ford always told his teams (and the media) that the first five minutes of the second half were the most important of the game. He stressed that point to the team at halftime. The Tigers came out of the locker room and drove 83 yards in 13 plays behind a strong running game that featured Kevin Mack. Mack scored on an 11-yard run to give the Tigers the lead. Clemson went on to outscore Kentucky 21–0 in the second half and won 21–3.

Looking back, that first drive of the second half was the most important offensive possession of the 1981 season.

465 Pushups for Ricky Capps

Clemson's defense had been the dominant story of the 1981 season until the Wake Forest game on Halloween. The Tigers went 18 straight quarters without giving up a touchdown at one point at midseason. That changed with the 82–24 victory over the Demon Deacons. The Tigers never had to punt and were 12-for-12 on third down, the longest streak of third-down conversions in history.

The most memorable example of Clemson's domination took place in the fourth quarter when a Tiger wearing No. 44 scored on a 72-yard run. The Clemson media relations staff did not have any idea who it was, as there was no offensive player on the roster who wore No. 44. Bob Bradley called down to the sideline and found out if was Craig Crawford, who had never run the ball previously. That was the longest run in Clemson history by a back on his first carry until Mike Bellamy broke that mark in 2011 against Troy, when he ran 75 yards for a score on his first career carry.

That day in 1981 was one of physical exertion for the Tigers mascot Ricky Capps, who did 465 pushups—one for each point after every Clemson score. He could have done 76 more, but the Demon Deacons mascot felt sorry for him and actually came to the Clemson sideline and did the pushups for him after the Tigers scored their next-to-last touchdown.

Jane Robelot Invites Bear Bryant to Clemson Pep Rally

After the victory over Wake Forest, Clemson had an 8–0 mark and improved to No. 2 in the nation. The Clemson campus was at a fever pitch, and Danny Ford's popularity was at its zenith.

Jane Robelot, who would go on to fame with the CBS television network, was the senior leader of Central Spirit in 1981. Still noted for her ability to think outside the box to this day, Robelot wanted to have a pep rally for the upcoming North Carolina game, the first meeting of two top-10 teams in ACC history. This was a bit unusual because it was a road game. Jane wanted to promote this rally as a "Danny Ford Appreciation Rally."

Jane went to Frank Howard's office in the Jervey Athletic Center and asked him to call his good friend Bear Bryant and invite him to be the featured speaker at the rally. That's right, *the* Bear Bryant, Danny Ford's college coach at Alabama, who was still coaching the Crimson Tide. His team still was in the national championship hunt with a No. 5 national ranking at the time. Jane thought she had a shot to get the Bear because Alabama had an open date. What would Bear rather do Thursday night in November?

So Jane went to Frank Howard's office in Jervey and asked him to call the Bear. Not one to disappoint a pretty coed, Howard pulled out Bryant's direct line and called him on his speaker phone. "Hey, Bear, I am here with this pretty little girl who wants to invite you to come to our pep rally this week."

236

We know Jane would love to have a tape of that conversation! Jane made her pitch, which Bear politely declined but wished his protégé the best in Chapel Hill.

The McSwain Brothers

Clemson went to South Carolina ranked second in the nation with a 10–0 record. Talk about a tense situation. And when South Carolina scored the first touchdown of the game, it got worse. The McSwain brothers came to the rescue. Rod McSwain blocked a punt that was scooped up by Johnny Rembert, who raced in for a touchdown that changed the momentum of the game. McSwain and Rembert would later be teammates for the New England Patriots. In the second half, Chuck McSwain led a Clemson ground game that wrapped up the 29–13 victory. Chuck gained a career-high 151 yards in 25 carries and scored two touchdowns.

A Squirming Jim Phillips

Jim Phillips had been the voice of the Tigers since 1968, but he couldn't broadcast Clemson's biggest game in history.

In those days, bowl games had their own national radio contracts and did not allow local networks to originate the game. What a shame that we have no calls from Jim Phillips from Clemson's win over Nebraska. Jim attended the game but just squirmed in his seat, his voice silent.

Stockstill's Plan

When Andy Headen batted down Mark Mauer's long pass to clinch Clemson's 22–15 victory over Nebraska for the national championship, Tigers players put coach Danny Ford on their shoulders. In every picture beside him is Jeff Stockstill, a sophomore wide receiver and the brother of longtime assistant and current Middle Tennessee State head coach Rick Stockstill. Years later, Jeff confessed it was planned on his part. He knew that picture would live forever in Clemson history. He was right.

CHAPTER 10
CLEMSON LEGENDS

Mac McKeown

Located between Clemson's campus and the town of Pendleton is what could be described as a typical college hamburger stand that was created in the 1950s. It's a place where locals and students meet to talk about Tigers sports and other world events while enjoying a delicious meal.

However, this hamburger stand and curb-service diner had something more. It had a treasure and legend all its own—the owner, Harold "Mac" McKeown.

When you first walk into Mac's Drive In, it has the feeling of a special place. It's a place where the Clemson family meets. Looking at the multitude of pictures of athletes and sports heroes on the walls and the warm, friendly greeting from the former owner Mac, you couldn't help but feel right at home. After the first visit, you left knowing you had made a friend in Mac McKeown.

A conversation with Mac was priceless, and he knew exactly what to say to make people feel better after a long day or after a long grueling practice. He must have been an amateur psychologist.

There is no telling how many Clemson events and games people have watched there on the several televisions strategically placed around the restaurant over the years when the Tigers were on the road. You couldn't help but enjoy watching programs there along with the camaraderie of other Tigers faithful.

To many people there wasn't a better friend than Mac. No matter the situation, you would always feel better once you talked to him. If you didn't do well on your big test, or if that pretty girl you asked out for a date said no, a trip to Mac's would always be in the offing. It seemed as if a cheeseburger, an order of french fries, and a sweet iced tea could fix anything. Along with the food was a big smile from Mac and good advice so you would do better the next time.

Mac was a friend to thousands of people. It has been said, that they wouldn't give you a diploma from Clemson unless you had been to Mac's

Drive In. A lot of people believed this and they too, just to make sure they graduated, visited Mac's quite often.

One customer said that he made "the best cheeseburger this side of the Mississippi." When asked about the whole United States, he quipped, "I've never been on the west side of the Mississippi."

No matter where people were from, or what occupation they performed, he would turn on the Clemson hospitality and would always make people feel welcome. He never met a stranger.

There's no guessing at the number of famous Clemson celebrities and former Tigers players and their families you would see visiting Mac. When Moses Malone made his recruiting visit to Clemson in 1974, he had one of his meals at Mac's. When John Lucas played for Maryland in the 1974 ACC tennis tournament, he went to Mac's for his post-match meals.

There is an autographed photo hanging on the wall from former Tigers great Donnell Woolford of the Chicago Bears saying, "Thanks for everything, please send me a cheeseburger."

Many first dates of many married couples took place at Mac's Drive In. Former Clemson basketball great Bobby Conrad proposed to his wife, Ann, during his senior year. Conrad said, "I couldn't think of a better place to propose to Ann." And, he added, "In the days before cellphones, when my dad was looking to talk to me after a game, he called Mac's."

Perhaps the Clemson Alumni Office should set up a booth there on Fridays before a football game to greet the former students and athletes who visit and come back to campus—it was and continues to be that popular of a place. It was said that if you were there for 15 minutes on a Friday before a Clemson home football game, that you would see someone from the past that you haven't seen in several years.

Saying good-bye to a beloved figure, hero, and friend is never easy. Mac, although shying away from being singled out or being honored, deserves the salutes and all of the good thoughts and tributes that have come his way. He was honored over the years, and deservedly so, with the Order of the Palmetto by governor David Beasley and as a member of the honorary fraternity, Tiger Brotherhood, just to name a few.

His greatest and probably his favorite role was that of being a surrogate father to thousands of Clemson students who were away from home for the first time. He has given advice to that many people as well. He wouldn't want all of the fanfare. "I don't deserve all of this attention," would be the first thing he would say.

Mac passed away on December 30, 2009. Saying good-bye to a friend, mentor, and Clemson ambassador is never easy—it was hard for many.

Charlie Waters

One of the most popular football players at Clemson who made it big in the NFL was Charlie Waters. Waters played for what was known as "America's Team," the Dallas Cowboys, under legendary head coach Tom Landry.

"I remember coach Frank Howard and coach Art Baker recruited me when I was at North Augusta High School," said Waters. "Alabama, Georgia, and Tennessee recruited me along with a few other schools. Many of the schools I heard from wanted me to play defensive back and wide receiver, but I had my heart on playing quarterback. I chose Clemson since they wanted me to play quarterback. I loved the idea of playing in-state, and my brother Keith was already at Clemson playing on the baseball team. Coach Baker was a great man. I remember Coach Howard was a very tough coach and believed in hard, physical play. This really helped me in my career. I had a great run at Clemson, and I played quarterback and then was moved to wide receiver. Whitey Jordan is who I have to thank for moving me to wide receiver. This allowed me to become more athletic, and I was able to show my skills better. I believe this is why Dallas drafted me. They saw that I could be moved to another position. They weren't just interested in positions, they were looking at athletic ability."

In the spring of 1968 as a junior, he was competing with Billy Ammons for the starting quarterback job. When Ammons hurt his knee in spring practice, Waters won the position. The defending ACC champions started the season 0–3–1. When Ammons' knee healed, he took over the starting job, and Waters moved to flanker or wide receiver for the remaining 15 games of his college career. As a senior he caught 44 passes for 738 yards, which was a record that stood until Jerry Butler broke it in 1977.

A three-year letterman from 1967 to 1969, Waters was an All-ACC selection in 1969 at wide receiver as a senior. During his Clemson career, he caught 68 passes for 1,196 yards and 17.1 yards per catch, to go along with four touchdown receptions. He still ranks 10th all-time for yards-per-reception. Waters was drafted by the Dallas Cowboys as a defensive back in the third round of the 1970 NFL Draft. Although he nearly was released during training camp, his conversion was successful, and he became the backup to Cliff Harris at free safety. But, after Harris had to serve military duty late in the season, Waters started six games. He took advantage of the opportunity and had five interceptions that season. His performance was good enough to make the NFL all-rookie team as a free safety in 1970. The next year he was moved to cornerback, where he played for four years. Waters was eventually moved to strong safety in 1975 to replace Cowboys great Cornell Green, responding with three interceptions for 55 yards and a touchdown.

As a strong safety he became an All-Pro and, along with Cliff Harris, formed one of the best safety tandems of that era. He was like a coach on the field, with excellent instincts and the athletic ability to become one of the league's top defensive players of the decade. He was selected All-Pro twice (1977 and 1978) and named to the Pro Bowl three consecutive seasons (1976–1978).

Waters injured his knee before the start of the 1979 season and would sit out the entire year. He returned in 1980 and had five interceptions. After getting three picks in 1981, he retired with 41 interceptions, third-most in franchise history. His total matched his uniform number.

Waters played 12 seasons in the NFL, never experienced a losing season and only missed the playoffs one time during that span. He played in five Super Bowls and won two of them. He set the NFL record for most playoff interceptions with nine, including three in one playoff game, and has the unique achievement of blocking four punts over two consecutive games. He also was the team's holder for place-kicks.

"Playing for Coach Landry was a great experience. He was a disciplinarian, and I loved it. He had us so prepared. He was very detailed and very precise. He had an engineering background, and that is where his detailed approach came from. When he would draw plays on the board, it would be so detailed, down to the steps a player should take and would take. He was very intelligent. By the end of the week we knew more about our opponent then they did about themselves."

Waters was inducted into the Clemson Hall of Fame in 1981. He was also inducted into the North Augusta and South Carolina Athletic Hall of Fame. Waters retired and became an NFL and college football coach. He was the defensive coordinator for the Denver Broncos in 1993 and 1994 and then for the University of Oregon in 1995. Outside of football, he works with longtime teammate and friend Cliff Harris at Energy Transfer Technologies in the electricity and natural-gas delivery business.

Jim Phillips

Jim Phillips was the voice of Clemson football, basketball, and baseball from 1968 to 2003, one of the most beloved and respected broadcasters of his era. He was a hard worker with no ego. That was a common thread in testimonials from his ACC colleagues. Whether he was stopped by Brent Musburger, Dick Vitale (who ranked him on his website as one of his top 20 college basketball announcers in the nation), or a young announcer with a visiting student radio station, Phillips always gave the person the time of day and then some. He probably did as much for Clemson public relations in the 20th century as anyone this side of Bob Bradley.

And speaking of Mr. B, there were a lot of common denominators between Clemson's longtime sports information director and Phillips. They worked together for 32 years in the SID/broadcaster roles, so they learned from each other. Bradley was respected nationally in his field for his ability to represent Clemson in a professional manner with unparalleled credibility. Like Phillips, Bradley treated a media member for *Sports Illustrated* or the student paper with the same patience and decorum. Both men never met a stranger.

Both had incredible streaks of attendance that ended in the middle of a football season. Bradley worked 502 consecutive football games from 1955 to 2000, then passed away after battling cancer in the middle of the 2000 season. Phillips worked 401 Clemson football games and passed away just three days after doing the Clemson-Furman game on September 6, 2003. Phillips also had a streak of 499 consecutive basketball games broadcast at Littlejohn Coliseum. That's right, he was sick for the 500th game in the history of the facility in 2001 and missed the game.

Clemson fans are hard-working, down-to-earth people, and that is a reason both Bradley and Phillips fit in at Clemson. Even though Phillips grew up in Ohio and never had a southern accent, he had a way with Clemson people. We don't know how many people told us they would turn the radio on and scan the dial until they found Jim's voice, then they knew they had found the Clemson game.

There was one baseball game in 1999 when Jim was on his way to the field to do a postgame interview with coach Jack Leggett. He was stopped by a fan in a wheelchair who started to ask Jim questions about the game. Another fan interrupted and said, "Let Jim go, he needs to get to the field." But Jim responded, "No, Coach Leggett can wait a couple of minutes, I'm going to answer these questions."

When we think of Jim Phillips, the words that come to my mind are credibility, professionalism, and enthusiasm. At age 69, he was the only ACC broadcaster who worked football, basketball (men's and women's), and baseball. He might have been the only play-by-play announcer in the nation to do all four sports at the same time. But, he still worked as hard for a women's basketball broadcast as he did for a football game. Perhaps no one benefited from his overall love of Clemson athletes than women's basketball coach Jim Davis. Coach Davis would be the first to tell you that Phillips brought instant credibility to his program. When the Lady Tigers won the ACC tournament in 1999, who ran out on the floor to get in the front row of the team photo? Phillips had quite a smile on his face because he had finally broadcast his first ACC basketball championship.

Clemson fans, in attendance at the Middle Tennessee State football game on September 13, 2003, would not be surprised by the outward sign of affection for Phillips from fans all over the country. While the week had started in sadness, it concluded with an uplifting celebration of his life. From Central Spirit's development of a balloon that honored him to the Clemson team wearing *JP* on their helmets, a halftime video tribute complete with Jim's most famous calls in all sports that concluded with a standing ovation from 71,000 fans, the band spelling out *J-I-M* as it exited the field, and the performance of the Tigers team in a 37–14 victory, it was a memorable celebration of the man who will forever be the Voice of the Tigers.

The highlight of the day from a broadcasting standpoint took place when 83-year-old Bob Fulton, Jim's close friend of 36 years, and the voice of South Carolina athletics for 40 years, took over the play-by-play duties for a Clemson drive in the second period. Just as if it had been orchestrated from above, the Tigers went on a nine-play drive that culminated in a Chad Jasmin touchdown. When asked about broadcasting a Clemson touchdown, Fulton said, "Well, I broadcast a lot of Clemson touchdowns before, I just wasn't in the Clemson radio booth at the time."

Jim Phillips' impact on Clemson athletics was immense. When he passed away in 2003, every Clemson fan 40 years of age or younger had no other "Voice of the Tigers" in their memory bank. When he applied for the job at Clemson in the summer of '68, the only Frank Howard he knew was the American League home run champion of the Washington Senators. Now Phillips sits in the same Hall of Fame with Clemson's all-time athletic legend.

In 2013, on the 10-year anniversary of his death, the Clemson home broadcast booth was named in his honor.

Bob Bradley

The press box at Memorial Stadium was dedicated as the Bob Bradley Press Box on November 5, 1988, prior to Clemson's game against North Carolina. It was a joyous occasion as many of Bradley's former students and media members with whom he had worked as sports information director for 34 years came back to Clemson to celebrate his career and a 37–14 win over the Tar Heels that virtually clinched an ACC title.

In conjunction with that 1988 dedication, Bradley wrote "The Last Word" in the program that day, recounting some great stories in his over three decades of running the press box. One of Bradley's memories was about "Youth Day," and the experiences of a youngster who had a great day with a great seat and plenty to eat, thanks for the most part to Bradley. The story is an example of the Clemson family atmosphere, an atmosphere and spirit that Bradley had as much to do with as anyone.

Here is what Bradley wrote in that 1988 program article:

A number of years ago, one game each year was set aside as Youth Day. If you were a member of the Boy, Girl, or Cub Scouts, Future Farmers...any group...as long as you came as a group...members could get in for 10¢ each. And they would come by the thousands.

It wasn't unusual for a half dozen or more lost youth to be brought to the press box, only to be claimed by an anxious parent or sheepish chaperone. One game [in the 1950s] a few minutes before the first half ended, a security guard brought a little Cub Scout to the press box.

He had become separated from his group and didn't remember where he was sitting. In order to keep the little fella happy and his mind off being lost, we gave him some chicken, some soda pop and tried to keep him occupied with conversation.

We started announcing on the public address system that a lost Cub Scout was in the press box. At least a half dozen times the crowd was told this, but at game's end, he was still in the press box. After holding Coach [Frank] Howard's postgame press conference, which lasted over 30 minutes, he was still in the press box when I returned from the locker room.

Knowing his name and where he was from, we called the police department in his hometown of Belton, S.C., and asked if they knew this scout's parents. Sure enough, they did. We told the police that a state highway patrolman in Greenwood was getting ready to return to his home area and that he would bring the "cub" by the station in about 30 minutes.

We all thought that the lost child had come to the game in a school bus and wasn't missed by the group at the game. But we later found out that he had actually come to the game in a private car and the driver did not know he was missing until she pulled up to the front door of the boy's house in Belton and asked him to get out.

I doubt his parents had to feed him that night because he was eating our press food for most of the second half and we gave him a sandwich and a candy bar for the ride home.

The story had a happy ending as the policeman met the young man's parents at the police station by early evening. That story tells you all you need to know about Bob Bradley and the way he represented not only the athletic department but the school.

We tell many stories about the Clemson football tradition. The stories about Frank Howard, running down the hill, Howard's Rock, Banks McFadden, and Fred Cone, chances are those stories were first written by Bob Bradley. His southern charm helped relay the stories to the media, who then told the masses.

Bennie Cunningham

Bennie Cunningham was a consensus first-team All-America tight end at Clemson as a junior in 1974. That was the season the Tigers were 7–4 and had a 6–0 record at home with wins over Georgia, Georgia Tech, and South Carolina. He was also chosen to many All-America squads as a senior. He was a two-time first-team All-ACC pick and was selected to play in the Hula Bowl, Japan Bowl, and the East-West Shrine game.

In 2002 Cunningham was the only tight end at any school to be named to the ACC 50-Year Anniversary team. You could say Cunningham is regarded as the greatest tight end in Clemson history, and his career at Clemson had a lot to do with Clemson's rise to prominence in the 1970s. His success and the team's success in 1974 led to the recruitment of the players who were seniors in 1978, a Clemson team that finished sixth in the nation, the highest finish in school history at the time.

Cunningham's career at Clemson nearly never took place. He was more involved in the band as a youth than the football team. Before the start of the 1968–1969 school year, Cunningham was a tall skinny kid who played the clarinet in the band at the old Blue Ridge High School in Seneca, South Carolina. Though he enjoyed playing the clarinet, he did not like the work that went along with it.

What he loved to do was play football. Cunningham was a natural at it. He was lean, he was fast, and more importantly, he was good at it. So before his sophomore year of high school, Cunningham decided he was going to quit the band and play football instead.

A few weeks into practice, however, Cunningham realized football wasn't all it was cracked up to be. He discovered he hated practice. He didn't like the fact he had to condition his body and lift weights, and learning the playbook was like having extra homework.

He discovered he was working harder in football than he ever did in the band, so the week before the first game he told the coaches he was quitting the team. "I got fed up with football because I didn't realize how hard it was to play football," Cunningham said.

The coaches were puzzled by Cunningham's decision. Since the start of practice, he did nothing but succeed. They had already penciled him in as a starter, though he had never played the game before he came out for the squad.

But none of that mattered, he still quit the team.

That afternoon, Cunningham went back home and did his homework and studied like everything was okay. Life was good. He was getting what he wanted out of it, or so he thought. Later that evening, when his dad came home and discovered his son quit the team—it was time for a good heart-to-heart conversation.

"My father came to me upset and said, 'Listen, you quit the band because it was tough and now you have quit the football team because it was tough. I don't care what you do in life, there are going to be times when things get tough. You can't quit every time something gets tough,'" Cunningham recalled. "So that's when I decided to go back out for the team and prove to myself and everybody else that I can do this."

And did he ever prove it. After integration moved him to Seneca High School, Cunningham went on to become a three-time all-state player for the Bobcats, which led to Shrine Bowl honors and a football scholarship to Clemson.

During his time with the Tigers, Cunningham became the most decorated tight end in Clemson and ACC history. He became Clemson's first consensus All-American in 1974 and then the Tigers' first two-time first-team All-American the following year.

In 1976 Cunningham was taken in the first round by the Pittsburgh Steelers. He had a brilliant 10 years with the Steelers, where he amassed 2,879 yards and 20 touchdowns, as well as blocking for most of Franco Harris' 91 career rushing touchdowns. He played on a Super Bowl championship team. In 2007, when the Steelers celebrated their 75th Anniversary, Pittsburgh fans voted Cunningham to the all-time roster, the only tight end on the team.

While many stars of the 1977 and 1978 Clemson teams receive credit for Clemson's return to national prominence, Cunningham blazed the path, setting a foundation for greatness.

Terry Kinard's Greatest Game

Terry Kinard is one of three unanimous first-team All-Americans in Clemson history. He accomplished that feat in 1982 when he was named National Defensive Player of the Year by CBS Sports. He was the first Clemson football player to win a national award. Only Da'Quan Bowers has won a similar award as the 2010 recipient of the Bronko Nagurski Award.

Kinard received the honor at the Cotton Bowl in a nationally televised presentation by famed announcer Lindsey Nelson. Kinard was a first-team AP All-American in 1981 and 1982, the first two-time first-team AP selection in school history. He was a starter on Clemson's national championship team of 1981 when he had a team-best six interceptions.

In 2001 he was inducted into the College Football Hall of Fame, Clemson's first selection since 1959 when Banks McFadden was inducted. While Kinard had countless memorable games over his four years as a starter between 1979 and 1982, his finest might have come at Notre Dame as a freshman. Maybe it was fitting, as he would have his induction ceremony into the College Football Hall of Fame in South Bend, Indiana, just two miles from Notre Dame Stadium, 22 years later.

Notre Dame entered the game with a 6–3 record, but was unranked after having lost the previous week at Tennessee by a 40–18 margin. Still, the Irish under Dan Devine were just two years removed from winning the national championship, a season that included a narrow 21–17 win at Clemson. Clemson entered the contest with a 7–2 record and a No. 14 national ranking by AP. Even though Clemson was ranked and the Irish were unranked, Notre Dame was still the betting favorite in Las Vegas. The Irish were at home on Senior Day, and Notre Dame had lost just two games on Senior Day the previous 40 seasons.

Notre Dame had an outstanding passing game, led by Rusty Lisch, who was in his only year as Notre Dame's starting quarterback. He had served as a backup to Joe Montana off and on the previous three years. Clemson quarterback Billy Lott had served in the same capacity behind Steve Fuller for three years. Lisch's list of receivers included Pete Holohan, who went on to play more than 10 years in the NFL, tight end

Terry Kinard was a two-time All-American. He was named the CBS Sports National Defensive Player of the Year in 1982.

Dean Masztek, and freshman receiver Tony Hunter, the No. 1 receiver in the nation coming out of high school.

The Irish entered the game throwing for more than 200 yards a game, a high number in the 1970s, so it would be a challenge for Kinard and the Clemson secondary. Earlier in the year, Notre Dame had beaten South Carolina behind a 250-yard passing effort by Lisch.

Lisch started well by throwing for 140 yards in the first half, and combined with the running of All-America running back Vegas Ferguson, Notre Dame took a 10–0 lead. The margin almost grew to 16–0 just before halftime, but a holding penalty on Notre Dame wiped out the score. Notre Dame missed a field goal, and it remained 10–0 at halftime.

Clemson's' ground game, behind the strong option decisions by Lott, brought Clemson back. Lott's 26-yard run in the fourth quarter put Clemson in the lead 13–10, and an Obed Ariri field goal made it 16–10 with 8:30 left. Just a touchdown and extra point away from taking the lead, Lisch rallied his forces. He drove the Irish from their own 20 to the Clemson 25. On third-and-9, he threw a pass toward Hunter, but it was deflected, and Kinard grabbed the ball at the 3-yard line. He returned it to the 25.

Clemson had to punt the ball back, and the Irish took over, this time at their own 16 with 2:34 left. Devine called a trick play. Holohan had been a high school quarterback and threw a long pass downfield on a reverse. But Kinard was aware of the play and intercepted. He ran the ball back 40 yards to the Notre Dame 19.

The interceptions on consecutive possessions were the key plays in the final quarter. No Clemson defensive player would be responsible for two takeaways in the fourth quarter of a Tigers victory of seven points or less again until 2015. Incredibly, it came in the next Clemson–Notre Dame game 36 years later. In Clemson's 24–22 home victory over Notre Dame, B.J. Goodson had an interception and a fumble recovery in the fourth quarter.

The Tigers left Notre Dame in 1979 with a 16–10 victory, a huge win in Danny Ford's first full year as head coach. "You don't see many freshmen dominate the fourth period of a game at Notre Dame Stadium, but Terry Kinard did that day," said Ford.

After the game, Kinard was quoted as saying, "We knew they had that fake reverse play, and we weren't fooled by it. I caught it in the clear. We knew we were a better defense than what we had showed in the first half."

Kinard made a name for himself this day with those two interceptions, and he also had seven tackles. The game was not on live television, but Notre Dame had its national replay network in those days, and the game was shown on Sunday morning all over the country.

It was the first of many landmark games in Terry Kinard's Clemson career.

Woody Dantzler

ESPN has grown to almost too many networks to count since the network's inception in 1979. From an instant classic involving the most exciting college football game of the weekend on ESPNU, to a Sports Century showcase on ESPN Classic, the number of shows that highlight great performances and great athletes are just a click away on your remote control.

Since Clemson played its first football game on October 31, 1896 (a 14–6 win at Furman), there have been many great plays and great performances. While there will always be debate among Tigers faithful about what is the greatest performance on the gridiron by a Clemson player, almost all will agree Woody Dantzler's show against North Carolina State in 2001 would have to be at or near the top of any list.

Dantzler, a native of Orangeburg, South Carolina, had already had many games to remember in his two-plus seasons as starting at quarterback for Clemson before the game against North Carolina State. Just two weeks prior to the game in Raleigh, he had scrambled for 11 yards in overtime to give Clemson a 47–44 win against then ninth-ranked Georgia Tech in Atlanta. In that contest he rushed for 164 yards and passed for 254 for 418 yards of total offense against the Yellow Jackets. Following that contest he was named National Player of the Week by *USA Today*.

The previous year he led Clemson to a 9–3 record and No. 14 national ranking. In the final regular season game he completed a 50-yard pass to Rod Gardner to set up the winning score in the final seconds of a 16–14 victory. It is known as "The Catch II." Gardner gets a lot of the credit on the play for his ability create separation from two South Carolina defensive backs and make the catch. But Dantzler's pass was right on the money. Both players will live on as Clemson football legends because of that one play alone.

While that 2001 performance versus the Yellow Jackets is certainly one to remember, the game against North Carolina State on October 13, 2001, is one to never forget. Playing against a Wolfpack squad that featured future NFL Pro Bowl quarterback Phillip Rivers underscored the importance of scoring early and often. The Tigers, with Dantzler at the controls, did just that in the 45–37 victory.

The day started well for Clemson, even before kickoff. When the Tigers took the field in pregame warm-ups on a day that was perfect for football, Clemson was wearing purple pants on the road for the first time in school history. With the performance displayed by Dantzler that sun-drenched fall afternoon (23 rushes for 184 yards and 2 TDs, 23-for-27 passing for 333 yards and 4 TDs), it was clear that he more than enjoyed donning the purple pants. He accounted for a then ACC record six touchdowns.

North Carolina State head coach Chuck Amato summed it up best following the game when meeting with the assembled media. "I can't imagine there is a better player in America than Woody Dantzler," said Amato. "We must have set a record on missed tackles for him alone. He really put on a show today." After the game, Amato met Dantzler at midfield and told him, "You are the best player in the nation."

Early in the game, Dantzler got the scoring underway on a 55-yard scamper. The play is still easy to remember for Will Merritt, Clemson's starting offensive guard: "I had one of those rare plays in my career that I did exactly what I was supposed to do," recalled Merritt. "I pulled to the weak side and had a pancake block on a linebacker. I heard the Clemson crowd and thought that Woody had run behind me and the play had worked perfectly. I then looked up and saw him going down the opposite sideline. That summed up how the entire game went. No matter what play was called, Woody just made a play. As an offensive lineman,

"The Catch II"—Rod Gardner made a spectacular 50-yard catch with 10 seconds remaining to set up an Aaron Hunt 25-yard field goal with just three seconds left, giving Clemson a 16–14 win over South Carolina in Death Valley in 2000.

Woody made you look good whether you were doing what you were supposed to do or not. There are not too many Woody Danztlers that come along."

Tommy Bowden, who guided the Clemson program from 1999 until mid-2008, still remembers the effort Dantzler displayed against NC State. In that game against the Wolfpack, Dantzler surpassed 4,000 career yards passing and 2,000 career yards rushing, the first player in ACC history to accomplish the feat.

"Woody had an unbelievable game that day," said Bowden. "It seemed like everything we dialed up worked. You have to give credit to Woody. They just could not stop him. He just made so many plays. Woody was the type of player that you felt if you could keep getting him at bats, a home run was going to come. He hit some that day."

Dantzler, who earned his degree in marketing before his senior season, had a career of hitting home runs for the Tigers. Entering the 2016 season, he was still the only Clemson quarterback to rush for at least 160 yards and throw for 300 in the same game.

There is no other way to describe his performance in Raleigh that day. It was an instant classic.

Brian Dawkins

When Dabo Swinney decided he wanted to initiate an award to honor a former Tigers football player each year with a Lifetime Achievement Award for their performance on the field and their contributions in leadership and community service, it didn't take him long to decide who the first recipient should be. In fact, it was such a no-brainer that he decided to name the award after him.

"Brian Dawkins has represented this football program, this university, with distinction for over 20 years," said Swinney. "He had a terrific career at Clemson, then had an even better career in the NFL with

Philadelphia and Denver. But it was not just his accomplishments on the field, it was his character, his leadership, the respect that people have for him. For years I have dealt with NFL scouts, coaches, general managers, and I can't tell you how many times they have told me stories of Brian Dawkins."

Each year Swinney will first present the Brian Dawkins Lifetime Achievement Award at the Clemson Football Banquet in January. Then the recipient will be honored the following fall at a Clemson football game. Dawkins was on hand to first receive the award at the banquet honoring the 2012 team this past January. The 2016 recipient was all-time Clemson great receiver Jerry Butler.

"Brian Dawkins epitomizes this award," said Swinney. "What an impact he has had on the world of football. You could see the passion, the leadership every time he took the field. But off the field his impact on the Philadelphia and Denver communities was so strong. He was the 2008 Whizzer White NFL Man of the Year, an award that dates to 1966 when Bart Starr was the recipent. He has set the standard for this award. I am proud to have him be a representative of this program, and he continues to embrace this program. We are so fortunate to have him."

The best story written about Dawkins from a character standpoint was authored by Mark Meany, a producer at WPVI-TV in Philadelphia. It was published in 2012 when Dawkins' No. 20 was retired by the Eagles. He took us back to January 11, 2009, a day of celebration in Philadelphia because the Eagles had just beaten the rival Giants in New York to advance to the NFC Championship Game.

It was Meany's job to produce a postgame special on the game for his station, and Dawkins was to be his most important interview. The interview was to be done by Gary Papa, a television legend in Philadelphia who was dying of prostate cancer. (It would be the last game Gary covered.)

Here is what Meany wrote:

Dawkins emerged from the locker room barely able to walk, his face clearly reflecting the pain he was in. He asked me where we were going to do the interview. I explained that Gary was waiting for him, but it was a long walk to the other side of the stadium. That was as far as Gary could make it before he needed to sit and rest.

A quick discussion ensued between myself, Dawkins, and Eagles media relations manager Ryan Nissan. It was quickly determined that Dawkins was too hurt to make the walk. We would have to cancel the interview. That is, until I said one simple thing to Dawkins, "Gary's in bad shape, he's having a really rough day."

Dawkins looked me in the eye and said, "Let's go."

The walk down the hallway through the bowels of Giants Stadium took forever. Dawkins was limping and silent the entire way. We finally got to Gary, who was sitting down and still gathering his strength.

Dawkins walked up to Gary and helped him out of the chair.

Then the two embraced.

Both men, two of the toughest I've ever met, began to sob in each other's arms. It went on for what seemed like forever. I then noticed that through the entire embrace, Dawkins was whispering in Gary's ear.

I'm not sure that whispering can be described as intense, but that's what this was. Dawkins was giving Gary a pep talk, a pregame speech before a tough game. It was vintage Dawkins.

Dawkins played for the Tigers from 1992 to 1995. He is another of those great recruiting stories. Clemson had been recruiting Patrick Sapp, one of the most highly recruited quarterbacks in the nation out of Raines High School in Jacksonville, Florida. One of his high school teammates was Dawkins. Clemson assistant coach Rick Stockstill became impressed with Dawkins while watching Sapp and told head coach Ken Hatfield that they should take a look at him.

Dawkins and Sapp signed with Clemson on the same day in 1992. Sapp started at quarterback as a freshman, while Dawkins played on special teams. But in 1993 Dawkins moved into the starting lineup and made an All-ACC team each of his last three years.

His senior year, 1995, Dawkins had a breakout season, helping the Tigers to an 8–3 regular season and top-20 ranking. He led the ACC in interceptions with six, finishing eighth in the nation. He was a second-team All-American by the Associated Press and the *Sporting News*. He was named *Sports Illustrated* National Defensive Player of the Week against Duke when he had three interceptions in one quarter, the only Clemson player in history to do that.

A fierce tackler, something that was further developed during his professional career, Dawkins is still fourth in Clemson history in career tackles by a defensive back (251) and is third in school history in career takeaways with 15.

Dawkins was the No. 61 selection of the 1996 NFL Draft and went on to have one of the great careers in NFL history. A former Clemson player has never been inducted into the Pro Football Hall of Fame, but that will end in the near future as many feel Dawkins will be inducted soon after the five-year waiting period. He is eligible in 2017.

Dawkins was named to the NFL All-Rookie Team in 1996, and the awards did not stop. He was selected to nine Pro Bowls, more than any other former Clemson player, second-most of any safety in the history of the NFL.

Dawkins was named All-Pro after the 2001, 2002, 2004, 2006, and 2009 seasons. At the conclusion of the 2009 season he was named to the NFL's All-Decade Team for the 2000s. He is also the only Clemson grad to win the Whizzer White NFL Man of the Year.

Dr. R.C. Edwards

The 2009 season, Dabo Swinney's first full year as head coach, was the first time in 50 years that former Clemson University president Dr. Robert C. Edwards was not in Memorial Stadium to root on the Tigers. His passing on December 4, 2008, left a void in the Clemson athletic department, the university in general, and the Clemson community.

In the fall of 1978, one of this book's coauthors, Tim Bourret, had a daily morning task to interview a Clemson coach for the daily sports report. Two decades before the World Wide Web, the interview was made, usually about the upcoming football game, with a Clemson assistant coach, or head coach Charley Pell. Fans could call a phone number and listen to the interview. It was even played during the lunch hour on the local radio station.

By mid-October the Tigers were 6–0, ranked in the top 10 in the nation, and getting ready to play a very good NC State team in Raleigh. There were numerous media requests for that game, plus Tim was trying to finish the basketball guide. He got sidetracked on a Wednesday, and by 11:30 AM he still hadn't tracked down a coach for the interview.

Just before lunch, the phone rang in Tim's office. The person on the other end was using a speakerphone and sounded like the voice of God. "Mr. Bourret, I just wanted to let you know that the daily sports report has not been updated." Quickly, Tim realized the person on the other end was President Edwards.

"I will get right on that," he responded.

"Thank you very much, Mr. Bourret."

That was a lasting memory of Tim's first year at Clemson. It told him people really care about athletics at Clemson. That went all the way to the top.

Dr. Edwards had a profound, lasting impact on Clemson athletics. He was significantly involved in many facilities projects, including the expansion of Clemson Memorial Stadium to include an upper deck and profitable luxury boxes, and the construction of Littlejohn Coliseum. He championed the improvement of Olympic sports, and strongly endorsed the addition of women's athletic programs in the mid-1970s.

Dr. Edwards was omnipresent at Clemson athletic events. He missed just one of 242 football games during his 21 years as president. His final year (fall of 1978), he led the team down the hill prior to the South Carolina game.

We always had a seat for him in the baseball press box. We can't tell you how many times he met a team bus before it left for a road trip. And we aren't talking just the football team. Many times, he saw the women's basketball team depart from the Clemson House for a road trip even if the bus left at 5:00 AM.

He made his final appearance in that role on Friday, November 28, 2008, just five days prior to his death, when he greeted Clemson head coach Dabo Swinney and the entire football team from a stretcher provided by the local EMS. It was a moment Swinney will never forget. Dr. Edwards was on his mind in the closing moments of the 31–14 victory over South Carolina because he could visualize him watching from his bed at the Cottingham House, a hospice residence in Seneca.

Swinney and Edwards actually have a common bond. Edwards was hired as "acting president" in 1958 after president Robert F. Poole died in office. The "acting president" title was very similar to the "interim head coach" title Swinney took on October 13 before he was named head coach on December 1.

In 1963 Edwards directed Clemson through significant change when the university enrolled its first African American student, Harvey Gantt. There had been riots at other schools in the South during these times over the same situation, but there were no problems at Clemson. According to Gantt, "President Edwards was very fair to me. He seemed to be singularly interested in making sure the change was peaceful."

For years in retirement he came to the SID office on a Monday morning to pick up extra football programs for players who had been featured the previous Saturday. He then went to the locker room and put the extra programs with a handwritten note in each player's locker.

Today, thousands of Clemson graduates, many of them former student-athletes, have benefitted from the Clemson experience. That family atmosphere started at the top thanks to Dr. R.C.

Gaines Adams

In many ways, it was the saddest funeral any of us in the Clemson athletic department had attended. But, in many ways, it was also the most spiritually uplifting funeral we had attended. That was the feeling shared by over 1,000 mourners on Friday, January 22, 2010, when they left Rock Springs Baptist Church in Easley, South Carolina, after having attended services for former Clemson All-America football player Gaines Adams.

At the age of 26, and in the prime of his life both as a person and as a professional football player, Adams died suddenly on the previous Sunday morning in his hometown in Greenwood, South Carolina. That was why it was just so sad. There was still so much for him to accomplish, still so many lives for him to positively affect.

After an autopsy, toxicology reports found he had died of an enlarged heart, a cause of death seen before in many athletes. The week before, a college basketball player from the state of Indiana died of the same malady.

For those who knew Gaines Adams, that was a fitting way for him to leave us because figuratively, no one had a bigger heart than Gaines Adams. He would give you the shirt off his back. We saw an example of that during his senior year in 2006. One of the big stories of that season was the adoption of Fahmar McElrathbey by his brother Ray Ray, a redshirt freshman defensive back on the Clemson team.

Most Clemson fans remember that McElrathbey gained custody of his 11-year old brother because of a difficult home situation in Atlanta. When he first gained custody, NCAA rules prohibited the wives of coaches' families from helping Ray Ray get Fahmar to school. Just as importantly, Ray Ray could not receive financial help. By mid-September, the NCAA announced a special waiver that allowed Clemson to establish a fund to help the McElrathbeys and allow wives of Clemson coaches and administrators to give Fahmar transportation to and from school.

But in July and August, Ray Ray needed help from his teammates. After Larry Williams authored the initial story in the *Charleston Post and Courier*, Ray Ray's situation became a national story. Ray Ray told the media about players who had come to his aide. One of the first to do so was Gaines Adams. Gaines came to him and told him he thought what he was trying to do was a great thing and that he would help him any way he could. Just before school started, Gaines followed up and not only took Fahmar to get his school supplies, he paid for them. Often during that preseason, even on the morning after a two-a-day practice the previous day, Adams arose at 6:30 AM and would go to McElrathbey's off-campus apartment and take Fahmar to school.

This was a senior helping a freshman.

Adams' example led to other members of the team pitching in. Everyone figured if the star of the team was helping out, maybe the rest of the team should help out as well. One of the most emotional moments of Adams' funeral was the appearance of Ray Ray, who asked his now 15-year-old brother to stand. Ray Ray related to all in attendance the help Adams had given him when he was in his most difficult days of trying to adjust to being a "parent." Ray Ray was one of countless former teammates from Clemson who traveled to Easley for Adams' funeral and memorial service. Also in attendance were a planeload of players, coaches, and administrators from the Tampa Bay Buccaneers and Chicago Bears.

But the former teammate who must have been affected the most by this sudden death was Anthony Waters. Waters and Adams were like brothers. They came to Clemson at the same time as freshmen for the 2002 season. Both went through a redshirt freshman year together and began a bond that lasted through their respective Clemson careers and beyond. In 2005, as redshirt juniors, they led Clemson to a top-25 ranking in just about every defensive ranking and six victories in the last seven games to close the year with a top-25 overall national ranking. Both Waters and Adams were candidates to turn pro after the 2005 season, but they both decided to come back for their senior seasons.

"We wanted to be part of a change at Clemson," remembered Waters. "We wanted to be part of the class that changed Clemson football in every way. We were going to go to class, we were going to bring this program to another level by setting an example for those that came after us. Gaines and I talked about being the leaders of the class that made a difference."

The decision to come back had a big impact on the future of Clemson football. "Gaines' decision to comeback started a trend," said former Clemson head coach Tommy Bowden at the service. "Since then James Davis came back for his senior year, C.J. Spiller and now DeAndre McDaniel. They saw the example that Gaines Adams set. He saw it was important to come back and get the degree and to become the best player you can on the field."

Entering the 2006 season Clemson was ranked in the preseason top 25. With a recruiting class that included freshman C.J. Spiller, the sky was the limit. The Tigers got off to a great start with a 54–6 win over Florida Atlantic, but in the fourth quarter of that game, Waters suffered a torn ACL, an injury that ended his Clemson career.

"Gaines was very supportive of me when that injury happened," said Waters. "I was obviously very down. After I was told my senior season was over after just one game, he came to me and said he was going to play as hard as he could the rest of the year for me. That really did lift my spirits."

When you look at Adams' performance in 2006, he accumulated stats that would have been good enough for two players. He finished the year with 62 tackles, including 17.5 tackles for loss for 106 yards and 12.5 sacks for 87 yards. He had 25 quarterback pressures, six passes broken up, two forced fumbles, and three recovered fumbles.

His most memorable play as a Clemson Tiger took place at Wake Forest on October 7. With Clemson trailing 17–3, Wake Forest lined up for a 50-yard field goal on the first play of the fourth quarter. It looked like Clemson was headed for another loss at Wake Forest, who had turned into Clemson's nemesis at this time. But the ball was mishandled by the Wake Forest holder. When Adams hit him, the ball popped into the air. Adams tipped it to himself, like a basketball player would trying to control a rebound. He then caught the ball and raced 66 yards for a score. Instead of trailing 20–3, Clemson was now down just 17–10.

The play totally changed the momentum of the game, and Clemson went on to a 27–17 victory over a Wake Forest team that would win the ACC championship. That play was named one of the top four game-changing plays of the year by ESPN. At the end of the year, Adams was named a unanimous first-team All-American, just the second in school history. He was a finalist for the Chuck Bednarik Award (national defensive player of the year), named the ACC Defensive Player of the Year, and was second in the voting for overall ACC Player of the Year behind Georgia Tech wide receiver Calvin Johnson (who also attended Adams' funeral).

In the spring, Adams was the No. 4 selection of the NFL Draft by the Tampa Bay Bucs, tying Banks McFadden (1940 draft) as the highest draft pick by a Clemson player. That draft day was the culmination of years of hard work for Adams. He had played eight-man football under former South Carolina quarterback Steve Tanneyhill at Cambridge

Academy in Greenwood. How many NFL players played eight-man football in high school?

"Two things come to mind when I think about Gaines Adams," said Bowden. "The first thing I think of is that smile. He was never in a bad mood, even when we were walking out to the practice field. I always thought there was something wrong with him, he used to smile on his way to practice. The other characteristic I think of is patience. Here is a guy who played eight-man football, so he had to have patience to go to a prep school to get better. Then when he came to Clemson we asked him to redshirt. Then his first two years he had the patience to work hard as a second-team player. Then, with people telling him he would be a late first-round draft pick, he had the patience to come back for his senior year."

The maturity and patience that served Adams so well over his 26 years on earth came naturally. In Bowden's eulogy, he told of the relationship Adams had with his parents. It had to be a story that brought peace and pride to Mr. and Mrs. Adams in such a trying time. "When I met with Gaines and his parents about whether or not to turn professional prior to his final year," Bowden said, "it occurred to me who his best friend was. It was his father, Gaines Sr. You could see the strong relationship he had with his parents, and their ability to set an example for Gaines was the reason he was such a fine young man who had the patience to make the right decision."

The funeral concluded quite a week for Waters, as he went from the emotion of losing one of his best friends to playing in the NFC Championship Game for the New Orleans Saints. Then, three weeks later, he was a Super Bowl champion.

"When Coach [Chris] Rumph called me from Clemson to tell me Gaines had passed, I just couldn't believe it," said Waters. "I went off and broke down for a while. Then I just went on YouTube and watched his highlights when we played together at Clemson. I don't know a better person than Gaines Adams. I thought about all we had been through together at Clemson. I thought about all the games and all the practices. I thought about all the times we went to Mac's Drive In together. I thought about how we pushed each other to be better. I thought about his family and how close they were. I also thought about how he told me how he would play the 2006 season for me after I got injured. Well, that is what I am going to do for him. The rest of my NFL career I will be playing for Gaines Adams."

CHAPTER 11
DOMINATING THE 1980s

The Balloon Game

During the 1983 season, student-body president Mark Wilson came to athletic director Bill McLellan with the idea of breaking the existing *Guinness Book of World Records* mark for a balloon launch. Wilson thought it would be quite a spectacle as the Tigers ran down the Hill prior to the Maryland contest, Clemson's final home game of the season.

Showing his great organizational skills, and with the fundraising help of IPTAY members, Wilson bought 250 miles of string, 400 tanks of helium, 195 balloon fillers, and somehow got 3,000 Clemson students (without the use of social media) to come to the stadium at 7:00 AM for the 1:00 PM game.

The balloons were ordered from Jim Wauldron of the WinCraft Company of Winona, Michigan, and arrived on Wednesday before the Saturday game. Balloons were filled by 11:30 AM, and at 12:57 PM as the cannon sounded, the Tigers descended the Hill while 363,729 balloons ascended to the heavens.

From the press box, the brilliant sun-splashed day turned black, something out of an Alfred Hitchcock movie. IPTAY collected $28,000 from private donations, and the excess money raised was donated to Cooper Library on campus.

And yes, Clemson won the game by a score of 52–27.

There were reports that some of the balloons landed in Lumberton, North Carolina, over 200 miles away. The 83,000 fans were at a fever pitch from the opening kickoff. Maryland was ranked No. 11 in the country, but quarterback Boomer Esiason and company were no match for the Tigers that afternoon.

Longtime legend and former head football coach Frank Howard, who would sit in the press box during home football games, was very impressed with the balloon launch. "We set a Guinness world record on the day when 43,000 fans had Tiger paws painted on them," said Howard. "At the Maryland game here in 1983 we also got into the

The Balloon Game in 1983

Guinness Book of World Records by releasing more than 363,000 helium-filled balloons as the team came down the hill before the game. You talk about spectacular sights. That topped them all."

The Legend of William Perry

William Perry might be the most legendary figure in Clemson history. He was a larger-than-life figure who helped the Tigers to the national championship as a freshman, a top-10 finish in 1982, and an 11th-place finish in 1983. The Tigers were 22–1–2 in his career at home.

He continued his legendary status as a member of the Chicago Bears from 1985 to 1992. Just as happened in his first year at Clemson, the Bears won the championship in his rookie season of 1985. And his play on offense claimed national headlines throughout the year, which culminated in a one-yard touchdown plunge in the Super Bowl against the New England Patriots.

No defensive player has scored a touchdown on an offensive play in the Super Bowl since. That is just one of many unbelievable facts and stories about "the Fridge."

Wake Forest Game 1984

We could do a top-10 list of greatest William Perry plays, but you really need to see the video to believe them. His most incredible play took place as a senior against Wake Forest on November 3, 1984.

Clemson was leading 13–0 in the second period when the Demon Deacons faced a fourth-and-1 at the Clemson 43. Danny Ford thought Wake Forest might go for it on fourth down, so he left his normal defense on the field. That meant Perry was on the field as the middle guard, going head-up over the snapper. Perry bull rushed with such force that he sent the blocking back airborne so that Wake Forest's Harry Newsome punted the ball off his rear end. The ball caromed backward all the way to the Clemson 21, or 36 yards downfield from the line of scrimmage where Jeff Wells recovered for the Tigers.

After a meeting in the press box, we decided to give Perry a blocked punt, even though no part of his body touched the ball. But his pure strength caused the blocked punt, and he was thus credited with a 36-yard punt return, the only 300-pounder with a punt return in Clemson history.

Lunch at McDonald's

The most often quoted story about William Perry during Clemson's 1981 national championship season concerned his infamous lunch visit to McDonald's with teammate Perry Tuttle. Over time and the magic of the media's frenzy and inflation, writers wrote that he spent $55 at the fast-foot chain in Clemson in one sitting. According to Tuttle, then a senior, he offered to treat the then true freshman to lunch. The bill between them was $22, still a sizeable amount for two people in 1981.

William Perry won a national championship at Clemson and a Super Bowl with the Chicago Bears in his first year on each team.

Athletic Accomplishments

Yes, Perry could dunk a basketball and dive off a diving board. You name it athletically, he could do it. He really did go for a swim in Fike one summer day and nearly broke the diving board.

During the off-season, he would play pickup basketball games in Fike. He even played in some games against Barbara Kennedy, Clemson's greatest women's basketball player ever, who was in school at the same time. Whether he weighed 295 or 350, he could still dunk, it was amazing. Prior to his senior year, he reported at 350 pounds. "Why come to camp in shape? That's what camp is for, to get in shape," he once said.

A photographer from *Sport* magazine was sent to campus to take a photo of Fridge dunking. A few days before the photographer appeared.

Perry assured us he could still do it, even though we had seen on the training room chart that he was still over 350 pounds. But, sure enough, on the day we shot the photo in the Jervey Gym, he dunked until the photographer ran out of film.

Never Injured

While his weight fluctuated, his health did not. You might have thought that at some time he would have suffered a pulled muscle, suffered a knee problem, something. But, according to now retired head trainer Fred Hoover, Perry missed just one practice in four years, due to a knee strain his sophomore year.

He went to the workout in a yellow jersey, but that was the only practice he sat out in four years. When it came to games, he was always there. He played 45 consecutive games at Clemson after never missing a game in four years of high school. He then played every game his first three years in the NFL, meaning he went 11 straight years without ever missing a football game.

Growth Spurt

Perry grew so fast his senior year of high school that his thighs increased from 31 inches to 33 inches during the season. By the end of the year, his high school coach had to take two pairs of football pants to a seamstress, who sewed them together to create a pair of pants that Perry could fit in.

The Perry Poster

The William Perry Growth Poster was the most interesting and publicized promotion the Clemson sports information office has ever undertaken. The idea actually came from a printing salesman named Jeff Pratt, who worked for Sports Graphics, a company that was coincidentally based in Chicago.

Pratt had done a life-size poster of Paul Molitor, then a young baseball star with the Milwaukee Brewers. He had seen a story on Perry and thought he would be a good subject for a life-size poster. We jumped at the promotion and ordered 4,000 posters—2,000 to send to the media and high schools in Clemson's recruiting area (then allowed, now against the rules, probably thanks to this project) and 2,000 to sell to the general public. The project cost a little over $10,000, and at a sales price of $5, we were just hoping to recoup our costs over the course of the remainder of the season.

We unveiled the poster during homecoming weekend 1984 (October 20 against Duke), selling the posters out of what is now the Clemson ticket office at Memorial Stadium. The interest was incredible when we started selling the posters at Tigerama on Friday night. We sold all 2,000 posters in 15 hours and had the money (in cash) needed to pay for the project before we had even received a bill.

The Nickname

Perry's nickname, "the Refrigerator," started on an elevator in Mauldin Hall on the Clemson campus in September of 1981. The elevator was crowded as it landed on the second floor. Ray Brown, then a defensive tackle for the Tigers wanted to get on, but faced Perry in the front of the elevator and determined that there was not enough room for him.

Brown said, "William, you take up almost the entire elevator. I'm going to start calling you 'G.E.' because you are as big as a refrigerator."

Later in the week. Brown related the story to Clemson SID office student assistant Jeff Rhodes (who still works on the football stat crew 38 years later), who in turn mentioned it to sports information director Bob Bradley. Bradley first used the nickname "G.E." in an October 1, 1981, press release prior to the Kentucky game. Later in the year, Bradley changed the nickname to "the Refrigerator" because he didn't want the NCAA to penalize Clemson for endorsing a corporation.

The rest is history.

Michael Dean Perry

When William Perry was a freshman and sophomore at Clemson, Tigers fans in his hometown of Aiken, South Carolina, said, "If you think he's good, wait until you see his brother."

Clemson had the fifth-best record in college football in the decade of the 1980s, and the Perry brothers had as much to do with it as any two players. From the time Michael Dean was a freshman, when he had 15 tackles for loss starting alongside his brother William (who had an NCAA-best 27), until his senior year when he was a first-team All-American and Outland Trophy finalist, Michael Dean was a leader.

"The memories I have of playing at Clemson are all good," said Perry. "I had a great five years there [he redshirted in 1983]. I think the one moment that stands out will be playing with my brother for the first time. We were playing against Appalachian State in 1984 in the opener, and he got a sack and I recovered a fumble that day. It was a great start to my career in Death Valley."

Michael Dean concluded his career by leading the Tigers to a top-five-ranked defense, a 10–2 overall record, and an ACC championship in 1987. He was named ACC Player of the Year that season and concluded his career with conference records tor tackles for loss (61) and quarterback sacks (28).

Both records had been held by William, and Michael Dean broke each mark by just one. At the conclusion of his career, Perry's height (6'1") was a question mark among pro scouts, so he wasn't drafted until the 50th selection of the 1988 draft. But Perry went on to an NFL career with the Cleveland Browns and Denver Broncos that would be considered among the best ever among former Tigers in the NFL.

When the Carolina Panthers played in Death Valley in 1995, Perry and the Denver Broncos played the Charlotte-based team in an exhibition game. "It didn't seem like a whole lot had changed except I dressed in the visitors' locker room," said Perry with a laugh.

Michael Dean Perry broke brother William's ACC records for tackles for loss and sacks, and went on to a six-time Pro Bowl career.

Before the game Perry said he had to provide plenty of information about Clemson traditions to his Broncos teammates. "All of them asked me if I was going to go up the hill and rub the rock," Perry said with a laugh. "I told them I didn't think so. I wasn't even tempted. That's something special just for Clemson players," he explained.

He was a six-time Pro Bowl selection, more than any other former Tigers defensive lineman. The *Sporting News* selected all-time teams for NFL franchises, and Perry was chosen as one of the starting defensive linemen on the Cleveland Browns all-time team.

NORMAN HAYNES

Linebacker Norman Haynes is remembered by Clemson fans as having his top two games as a Tiger against the team from his hometown, the University of Georgia. The native of Athens had 14 tackles in Clemson's 31–28 win at 20th-ranked Georgia in 1986, a game that was decided on the last play—a 46-yard field goal by David Treadwell. It was just the second Clemson win in Athens since 1914.

Haynes went on to lead the 1986 ACC champion in tackles with 74. At 5'9" he is the shortest player to lead Clemson in tackles.

The next year, Treadwell was at it again with a 21-yard field goal with just two seconds left that gave Clemson a 21–20 win in Death Valley. It was the first time Clemson had beaten the Bulldogs in consecutive games since a seven-year run from 1900 to 1906. Haynes led the defense again in that 1987 game with 12 tackles in 49 plays. He played 28 games in his Clemson career and had just two in which he had at least a dozen tackles. Both were against Georgia in those consecutive legendary victories.

Haynes is also known for a less publicized distinction. He is the only Clemson football player to get hurt on Picture Day…twice.

In 1986, 155 players attempted to get on bleachers for the team picture. But it was a tight squeeze, so during the lineup Haynes was inadvertently forced off the side of the bleachers from six rows up and sprained an ankle on the landing.

The next year, larger bleachers were ordered, but on the hot, sunny day, bees attempted to join in the team picture. Just before the first set of photos was taken, Haynes was stung on his lower lip. Almost immediately, he reacted and his lip grew to three times its normal size in a matter of minutes. He endured the swelling, posed for the team picture, then went into the training room with head athletic trainer Fred Hoover.

Haynes survived two titanic physical games against Georgia but didn't last to the end of Picture Day prior to those seasons.

Perry Tuttle

The most iconic image of Clemson's 1981 national championship is All-America wide receiver Perry Tuttle adorning the front cover of *Sports Illustrated* after Clemson's 22–15 victory over Nebraska in the Orange Bowl.

When a reunion was held for the 1981 national champions in 2011, each player was presented with a coin marking that season. The image on the back of the coin was the same picture of Tuttle from the *SI* cover.

Thirty-five years later, and despite the adoption of a more sophisticated passing game in the last 15 years, Tuttle is still in the top 10 in school history in receiving yards, receptions, and touchdown catches. He was the only active Clemson student-athlete to appear on the cover of *Sports Illustrated* until 2015 when Deshaun Watson (twice), Wayne Gallman, and Shaq Lawson were all on *SI* covers.

Tuttle came to Clemson from Winston-Salem, North Carolina. Many of the yards, receptions, and receiving touchdowns Tuttle amassed came against the team from his hometown. In fact, a look at his career stats shows that he had at least one touchdown reception each of his four seasons against Wake Forest, the only receiver in Clemson history to catch a touchdown pass against the same school four years in a row.

He had 10 receptions at Wake Forest in 1980 for his career high in catches in a game, and had 161 receiving yards against the Demon Deacons in 1981 as a senior, his career high in yardage for a single game. He finished his career with 23 receptions for 394 yards and five touchdowns against the Demon Deacons, his career high totals against any opponent.

"People used to think I didn't like Wake Forest and I just got fired up to play them," said Tuttle. "But that wasn't the case at all. I like Wake Forest and their players. I just had great games against them because I had so many friends and family in the stands. My freshmen year it seemed like my entire high school team and coaching staff came to that game in Winston-Salem." Tuttle responded with his first career touchdown on a 42-yard pass from Steve Fuller.

"I remember it like it was yesterday. It was an underneath route and Steve Fuller put the pass right in my hands. It was my favorite pattern because it put me in the open field. I made a few moves and went to the end zone." Clemson defeated the Deacs 51–6 that day on the way to an 11–1 season and No. 6 final ranking.

The next year, 1979, Tuttle had four catches for 52 yards, including a 10-yard touchdown from Billy Lott. It was actually an upset victory for the Tigers, as Wake Forest came into that game ranked 14th in the nation and had already defeated Auburn and Georgia.

Tuttle's roommate Jeff Davis scored on a 17-yard interception return, and it would be the only game over four years that Tuttle and Davis scored a touchdown in the same game.

As a junior at Wake Forest, Tuttle had a career-high 10 catches for 124 yards, including a 22-yard touchdown pass from Homer Jordan, a score that put Clemson up 33–7 in the fourth quarter. Wake Forest made an incredible comeback and cut the margin to 35–33 before the Tigers got the victory.

The 1981 game at Clemson on Halloween was another outstanding day for Tuttle as he finished with seven catches for 161 yards and two scores. He caught a 75-yard touchdown pass from Jordan and a 25-yard scoring pass from Mike Gasque, giving Tuttle five touchdowns from four different quarterbacks in his career against Wake Forest.

Clemson has not had a scoring day like it since, as the Tigers won 82–24. "We just hit on everything that day," said Tuttle. "They never stopped us on offense." He was right. Clemson was 12-for-12 on third down and did not punt once.

When looking back on his career against the Demon Deacons, Tuttle had one conclusion: "I just felt so comfortable playing against them because I just felt I had so many people close to me in the stands. I wanted to do well for them, the people who had raised me and my high school friends."

Tuttle became a first-round draft choice in 1982 and played with the Buffalo Bills and Atlanta Falcons before going to Canada for a productive career that included a Grey Cup championship and a few all-league selections. He is still regarded as one of Clemson's most popular players. And to this day, he still signs a lot of those *Sports Illustrated* covers.

Jeff Davis

During Clemson's magic run through the 1981 season, the Tigers' defense was known as a hard-hitting bunch that played football the way it was meant to be played. They were rough and tough. If there was a blade of grass to defend, they defended it, and usually they were successful in doing so.

The defense got its attitude from its captain, senior Jeff Davis, who led the team in tackles, forced fumbles, and fumble recoveries. "He was the best I ever had," said Ford. "No linebacker I played with or coached hit as hard as he did." With Davis leading the way in 1981, the Tigers finished second nationally in scoring defense, seventh in rushing defense, seventh in turnover margin, and eighth in total defense. Clemson led the ACC in total defense, rushing defense, scoring defense, and interceptions.

The 1981 defense forced what is still a school-record 41 turnovers, with some of those coming after their own offense had turned the ball over. "There were times when our offense would turn the ball over, and as we were walking onto the field, I would find Homer [Jordan] and tell him, 'Don't sit down. We're going to get you the ball right back.' Then we would go out there and do it," Davis said.

The North Carolina native was a first-team All-American, MVP of the ACC, and Defensive MVP in the Orange Bowl victory over

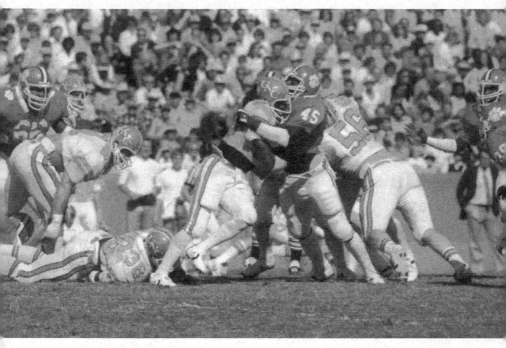

Jeff Davis (45) had 175 tackles and was a first-team All-American in 1981. He had a career-high 24 tackles against North Carolina in 1980.

Nebraska, the game that clinched the national title for the Tigers. He was a fifth-round draft pick of the Tampa Bay Bucs and played for them from 1982 to 1987. He led the Bucs in tackles and was the captain of the team for four seasons.

Along with being in the Clemson Ring of Honor, Davis was inducted into the Clemson Hall of Fame in 1989 and the South Carolina Hall of Fame in 2001. His greatest honor may have come in 2007. In May, Davis came back from a lunch meeting with a donor prospect and discovered an unusual box on his desk. He was not expecting a package from anyone, but when he saw the return address on the outside of the box, he became excited. "What in the world is this?" recalled Davis. "There was an expectation when I saw the return address was the National Football Foundation and College Football Hall of Fame. What do I have here?"

Davis had known it was the time of the year when the College Football Hall of Fame announces its new class. He had been a finalist each of the last two years, but he had not been selected. "They had not sent me a box telling me I had not gotten in before, so I had a hunch this might be some good news." It was. Inside the box was a formal letter telling him he was one of 14 members of the College Football Hall of Fame class of 2007. "It was an awesome feeling, a unique feeling," recalled Davis, who is the second member of the 1981 national championship team to be inducted into the Hall of Fame. (Terry Kinard, who was also a member of Clemson's 1978 freshman class, was inducted in 2001. It is the only ACC recruiting class to have two Hall of Famers.)

"I wasn't very focused the rest of that day," said Davis. "My mind was going in a million different directions. It has really made me reflect on my time at Clemson. It made me reflect on my family, growing up, my wife Joni, and our six children. It made me reflect on my coaches, high school and college. It really has made me reflect on my whole life. It makes you remember where you came from and who helped you along the way. It is important to remember the journey, not just focus on the result."

Davis grew up in a family that was dominated by females. That might not be all bad, but the baby boy of the family can get spoiled. It is certainly not the upbringing that often lends itself to being a tough middle linebacker. But fortunately for Davis, he had a mother and grandmother who kept him on the right track. "I didn't meet my father until I was 33," said Davis. "We have a very good relationship now, but when I was growing up, it was my mother, my grandmother, and my sisters. My grandmother and mother always talked about me being a man, even when I was a young kid. They knew I lacked a male influence, so they tried to instill that attitude in me. Being selected for the College Football

Hall of Fame and other accolades I have won is a true testament to their caring and direction I received when I was growing up."

While mom and grandmother did a great job with Davis in his formative years, Davis will be the first to tell you that his coach at Dudley High School in Greensboro, North Carolina, Jonathan McKee, had a strong impact on his character and thus his leadership qualities. Davis' ability as a leader has as much to do with this national honor as his tackle totals. It also has to do with his success in all aspects of his life. "Coach McKee died in 2006, and when I received that box I wanted to call him and share it with him, but I couldn't," said Davis. "It paralyzed me for a moment. But he knew it. He always expected greatness from me. He had enjoyed many of my other accomplishments. He treated me like a son. When I think of my leadership qualities, they all go back to him. I needed a male presence in my life, and he provided that when I was young. He empowered me with leadership. He brought structure to my life through athletics."

Receiving the box from the Hall of Fame also made Davis reflect on his experience at Clemson and his teammates. "I grew up in Greensboro, the heart of Tobacco Road. But when I visited Clemson [for the 1977 Notre Dame game in Death Valley], I became enthralled with Clemson. I thought this is the place God thought I should be. I am glad I was in agreement with Him."

While Davis gives credit to his coaches and teammates, his accomplishments were extraordinary on the field and off. When you meet Davis, you can see that he is a man of resolve and consistency, and that carried over to his everyday life. In his four-year career, he played 40 games, including the last 35 as a starter. He had 30 career double-figure tackle games in those last three years, and he led the Tigers in tackles 25 times. The stats and accolades are impressive, but when Clemson players and coaches reflect on Davis, they remember his leadership, character, and integrity. While he showed those traits over his first three years at Clemson, they did not come to the forefront until the summer before his senior season.

"The summer before my senior year, Coach Ford told me to meet him at the Holiday Inn one afternoon at lunch," recalled Davis. "He wanted to have a private meeting to talk to me about being the leader of the 1981 team. He thought I had the ability to do that, and he let me know he expected that from me."

Davis' qualities as a leader were sensed by his teammates and the head coach, and they were a big factor in Clemson's drive to the national title. "Jeff certainly ranks up there among the best leaders I ever coached," said Ford. "We had so many outstanding young men. I hate to single one out. But I can't think of a better leader than Jeff Davis. He was what you want in a leader...someone who leads by example and someone who leads with his voice. He always backed up what he said."

"Jeff was the heart and soul of our defense," said Bill Smith, starting defensive end on the 1981 team and now a member of the Clemson board of trustees. "He led by example, and he always came to practice and to games with a work ethic that was contagious to his teammates. Jeff not only affected his teammates by getting the most out of them on the field, but he has been equally effective in showing us how to live our lives off the field since he finished playing. He is a man of strong Christian values with unwavering integrity. I am proud to call Jeff my teammate and friend."

After six productive years in the NFL in Tampa Bay, Davis sensed it was time to turn the page on his playing career and enter a new stage in his life. He thought about going into coaching, but he knew that would involve a difficult decision. "I wanted to be a coach [when I finished playing]," he said. "I wanted to be a coach at Clemson. But I couldn't see how I could be a dad and coach at the same time, because the hours were just too long and there was so much travel due to recruiting. I had to pick between being a dad and being a coach. I chose being a dad. I thought about coaching so I could have an impact on young student-athletes, but I picked having an impact on my own kids. Who you are at home is the true measuring stick of your value. Not growing up with a dad made me more sensitive to that role."

Today with wife Joni (they both graduated from Clemson in 1984), they have six children, including twin boys who are members of the Clemson football team. "I want to have a great impact on my children and give them an opportunity to bring their lives to another level. I want them to be able to navigate life's obstacles at a high level. I don't want them to have to go outside our house to find a mentor." Davis has had a positive effect on more than just his children. He has continued to have a profound effect on Clemson University and future student-athletes through his work in fundraising and the Call Me Mister Program.

The Call Me Mister program is a program in South Carolina that recruits African American males to become secondary school educators. From its humble beginnings, there are now more than 100 graduates of the program who are teaching in schools throughout South Carolina. "I am very proud of that program," said Davis, who is no longer the director but is still involved. "We lack African American teachers in this state, and those young men can provide role models for our youth. It has been enjoyable to watch the program grow. What you give is more important than what you receive. I don't want to be known as just a football player. I want my kids to believe that I made a difference."

A special day came in 2001 when Davis received a $100,000 gift for the program from Oprah Winfrey's Angel Network. Davis has been successful as a fundraiser and representative of Dabo Swinney's program at Clemson. He has a sound message that is easy for him to recite. He just tells his personal story. "My mother and grandmother couldn't afford to send me to any university. I couldn't have come to Clemson without IPTAY. Those IPTAY members who paid for my scholarship in the 1970s are hopefully continuing to realize the dividends from their investment. When I tell my personal story, hopefully people see they can have the same impact on a young person's life today. The investment an IPTAY member makes in Clemson can be very rewarding. You are helping a young person realize his potential in life just like I did many years ago."

Davis was undersized as a linebacker in his playing days. But he never let that hold him back. He is being rewarded for his success on and off the field. It is a success story that continues today. Sometimes, great gifts come in small packages.

Homer Jordan

Clemson's 1981 national championship team was full of leaders. Jeff Davis, Perry Tuttle, Jeff Bryant, Terry Kinard, and others provided a core of leaders that set a strong tone for the rest of the team before the season even started.

Among those who looked to those elder statesmen for guidance was junior quarterback Homer Jordan. Entering his second year as the starter under center for the Tigers, some might have expected Jordan to become more of a vocal leader on the 1981 team. But the signal-caller knew his role and embraced it, deferring instead to a respected group of seniors. "I said very little back then," the Athens, Georgia, native said. "I did what I was supposed to do to keep the guys going. I'm not a holler guy and a screamer. My best way to lead was just to do my job. I lived right next door to Jeff Davis and Perry Tuttle, so I was right behind them everywhere they went. I was a young guy trying to do what they told me to do. That was such a strong class for us. Without that senior class, I don't think we could have done what we did. That whole senior class just led the way."

In head coach Danny Ford's offensive scheme, the quarterback simply had to manage the football and move the chains. Jordan ably completed the task on a regular basis, completing almost 55 percent of his passes for 1,630 yards and nine touchdowns. He also rushed for 486 yards (good for third-best on the team) and six touchdowns, giving him more than 2,000 yards of total offense during his junior campaign.

Facing defending national champion Georgia on September 19, 1981, was a thrill for Jordan. Being a native of Athens, Jordan took all three of his showdowns with the Bulldogs personally. In 1981, of course, the Tigers prevailed 13–3, largely thanks to Jordan's eight-yard touchdown pass to Tuttle in the second quarter. It ranks as one of the quarterback's proudest days as a Clemson student-athlete. "That was a big game for us," he said. "We played well that game, and it kind of set the tone for the season. We knew that we had all these guys coming back, so if we could beat Georgia, we could make a run and go undefeated. Our defense had a great day. It was the key victory to our season."

Jordan's Tigers were the model of consistency during the 1981 season, largely in part to Ford's tough-minded approach to football. It is said that the young head coach's practices were more difficult than games, so Saturday was physically the easiest day of the week for the football team. "It wasn't as hard on the quarterback, but the other guys, they never eased up on them [in practice]," Jordan recalled. "I'm glad it was tough, because those linemen made my job easy."

After the Tigers blazed through the regular season undefeated, they faced off against Nebraska in the Orange Bowl. Hype is often a factor in championship scenarios, and sometimes teams can lose focus. But according to Jordan, Clemson never wavered thanks to the combination of Ford's steady hand, senior leadership, thorough preparation, and keeping things simple and consistent. "We treated it as a normal game," Jordan explained. "We knew we had a good team. We knew what type of team we had. We were pretty confident in what we could do. No one there probably thought we should have been there or believed in us. But we believed in ourselves and in our coaching staff, and we played that way."

To this day, the bonds formed in the trenches on the practice field and on the field of play remain from that special team. Jordan still keeps tabs on many of his teammates, and he looks forward to every reunion in Tigertown when he can spend time with the ones with whom he shared college football's crowning team achievement. "That's probably what helped us win that season," the former quarterback said of the team's camaraderie. "Thirty-five years later, we still stay in touch with each other. It shows you how close we were as a team. That's probably the main reason why we did what we did—the lifetime relationships we built."

That was never more present for Jordan than in February of 2016 when Jordan's wife died from cancer. Fifteen of his former teammates came to the funeral. "When you go to Clemson, it's like home," Jordan stated. "That's what it felt like when I was being recruited. That made my decision for me. The people were very nice, and they are still that way today."

Gary Cooper

October 3, 2015, is a date we will remember for a long time. It was the day Notre Dame came to Clemson to play a football game for just the second time. It was a thrilling game that came down to a two-point conversion with just seven seconds left as Clemson won 24–22. Clemson probably would not have reached the national championship game without the win.

But we will also remember that day for some sad news Clemson Nation received just after the conclusion of the *ESPN College GameDay* program. Just after noon Woody McCorvey informed the administration that former Clemson receiver Gary Cooper had died.

Woody had talked about bringing Cooper to campus for a game so he could serve as an honorary captain for a Clemson game. He had not been to a game at Clemson since 1991. If someone were to ask us who was the most underrated football player in Clemson history, Gary Cooper would be at the top of the list.

If you browse the ACC football record book, you will find Gary Cooper's name as the fourth entry on a significant chart. He holds that rank in ACC history for career yards per reception (minimum of 70 catches) with a 20.2-yard average on 79 career receptions for 1,592 yards and 11 touchdowns. Just *below* him on the list is former Georgia Tech receiver Demaryius Thomas, now an All-Pro receiver with the world champion Denver Broncos.

You won't find Sammy Watkins, Nuk Hopkins, or Perry Tuttle on the list. They are all well below Cooper in this category. "Gary Cooper had great height, strength, and speed," said McCorvey, an associate athletic director in the Clemson football department, who was Cooper's position coach from 1986 to 1989. "There is no doubt if he played at Clemson today he would put up some incredible numbers in this system. We were a team that was built on the run, but Gary could break a long play as a receiver or a runner."

In 1988 Cooper caught a 61-yard touchdown pass from Chip Davis on an end-around pass against Florida State. He outran a Seminoles secondary that included Deion Sanders. It was Clemson's best trick play in years, but it didn't get the notoriety it deserved because Florida State executed the "puntrooskie" to perfection in the fourth quarter and won 24–21. That was the story of Cooper's career. He never got the acclaim he deserved.

Later that season at Maryland, Cooper scored a pair of touchdowns on end-around plays, one of 52 yards in the first quarter, and one of 20 yards in the fourth quarter that iced the game and the ACC championship for the Tigers. No Clemson receiver has rushed for two touchdowns in the same game since. For his career, Cooper averaged nine yards per carry. In 1988 Cooper touched the ball 21 times and averaged 26 yards per play.

"Gary gave us an advantage because he played the Z-position and had a size and speed advantage on the defensive backs who had to cover him," said McCorvey. "When he caught the ball, he made something happen. He was like Sammy Watkins in that he attacked the football when he went to catch it."

After gaining 504 yards receiving as a senior in 1989, Cooper was drafted by the New Orleans Saints and was the last receiver cut before the 1990 season. He then went to Canada and played for the Montreal Machine of the World League of American Football.

After that season he returned home to Georgia. On June 1, 1991, he received a phone call from the Kansas City Chiefs, who signed him as a free agent. The day before he was to leave for Kansas City, he was driving on wet pavement in Georgia and was involved in an automobile accident. Cooper's injuries were significant, as he suffered traumatic brain injuries. He would never walk again.

After a long rehabilitation, Cooper went to a college near his home town of Ambridge, Pennsylvania. He earned his degree in accounting, but the remaining years of his life were difficult as there were many complications as a result of the accident. The complications from a respiratory infection became too grave on the day Clemson beat Notre Dame.

We tell Gary's story for two reasons. One, current players need to appreciate the time they have playing a game they love. Two, Clemson fans need to remember Gary Cooper and what he did for Clemson football in the 1980s.

He was a heck of a player.

Danny Ford

It was the first week of December 1978, and Danny Ford came into Bob Bradley's sports information office carrying a copy of the *Atlanta Constitution* sports section. Other members of the sports information department happened to be in the office as Bradley had been busy on the phone all day with writers from all over the Southeast who were wondering if rumors of Charley Pell's departure to the University of Florida were true.

The Atlanta newspaper had written an article that Ford would be a strong candidate to replace Pell if he left for the home of the Gators. But there was a typo in the article, which should have read, "Highly regarded Clemson offensive line coach Danny Ford is a strong candidate to succeed Pell if he goes to Florida." The typo came in the second word. The writer had typed a *t* in the word *regarded* instead of a *g*. Ford asked Bradley, "Bob, can I sue?" In classic Bob Bradley style, he responded, "Well, coach, you are going to have to prove them wrong first!"

Pell decided to take that Florida job on December 4, 1978, and Ford succeeded him. Ford "proved them wrong" for the next 11 years at Clemson. He wrote a résumé that culminated on August 31, 2013, with his induction into the Clemson Ring of Honor, the highest award bestowed by the Clemson Athletic Department.

Clemson's 1978 team had posted a 10–1 record in the regular season and won nine in a row and an ACC championship. The Tigers were ranked seventh in the nation and accepted an invitation to play Ohio State and future Hall of Fame coach Woody Hayes in the Gator Bowl just 24 days after Ford was hired.

No pressure, Danny!

"I really didn't know how to be a head coach," said Ford in his classic humble manner. "I just made some decisions on penalties that night. We had some great coaches and some great players."

Ford certainly had some great players help him in that first game, a 17–15 win over the Buckeyes. His roster included Steve Fuller, Jerry Butler, and Jeff Davis, all of whom plus Terry Kinard (who did not play due to injury) preceded Ford into the Ring of Honor.

The victory received even more acclaim than normal because Woody Hayes punched Clemson middle guard Charlie Bauman after he made a game-deciding interception late in the fourth quarter that allowed the Tigers to clinch the two-point win on national television. In the chaos of the moment and the chaos that followed the game, we learned a lot about Danny Ford. At age 30, he had the maturity of a 20-year veteran coach the way he handled the situation.

Ford had a unique ability to motivate his players. He was a disciplinarian who worked his team hard. In the days before the 20-hour rule (maximum hours of practice and meetings) we have today, he would be known to start a practice over again after the team was an hour into the workout if things weren't going well.

Two-a-days in August camp? How about three-a-days? He was tough, but his players respected him.

That hard work and respect went hand-in-hand in his ability to get the Tigers ready for highly ranked opponents coached by legendary coaches. In his 11 years as Clemson head coach, he led the Tigers to a 21–7–1 record over coaches who are now in the Hall of Fame, a 75 percent winning percentage.

That list includes Dan Devine of Notre Dame, Joe Paterno of Penn State, the aforementioned Woody Hayes of Ohio State, Barry Switzer of Oklahoma, Vince Dooley of Georgia (four times), Tom Osborne of Nebraska, and Bobby Bowden of Florida State. That record does not include a 5–1 combined mark against Frank Beamer and Steve Spurrier, who most certainly will some day join the Hall of Fame as coaches.

Of course the 22–15 victory over Osborne's Nebraska team in the 1982 Orange Bowl was the pinnacle of his coaching career because it brought a national championship, the first in any sport in Clemson history. Just 33 years old at the time, he is still the youngest FBS coach to win a national championship.

"We just took each game one at a time," said Ford. "We didn't look ahead, and people really didn't think we could do it. We never became No. 1 until Penn State beat Pittsburgh the Saturday after Thanksgiving. Our regular season was already over."

Jeff Davis confirmed that approach during the 1981 season. "Coach Ford did a great job of making sure we took it one game at a time. Now, when we beat North Carolina in Chapel Hill when we were both in the top 10 and we moved to No. 2, it got a little harder to do. But he kept us grounded."

The 1981 season is still one of the most unusual in college football history from an upset standpoint nationally. Seven different teams were No. 1 during the course of that season, still the most in one season in college football history.

It was a special night in Miami on January 1, 1982. There were some moments that day that made Ford figure it would not be Clemson's night. In the afternoon, Cliff Austin was stuck in an elevator at the team hotel for two hours. That night he would score an important touchdown in the second quarter.

Nebraska was ranked fourth in the nation entering the game, while Clemson was No. 1, Georgia No. 2, and Alabama No. 3. Alabama lost in the Cotton Bowl earlier in the day, 14–12, then Pittsburgh beat Georgia 24–20 while the Clemson-Nebraska game was in progress. Which meant that if Nebraska beat Clemson the Cornhuskers would have vaulted all the way to No. 1. Many Clemson fans worried that would give Nebraska extra motivation. But Ford's defense dominated most of the game. When Andy Headen batted down a desperation pass, Clemson had the title.

Obviously, that victory over the Cornhuskers was the highlight of Ford's career in terms of on-field results. But there were many other significant seasons and victories. He would lead Clemson to six bowl victories in all, still the most in Clemson history and the second most in ACC history. Five of the bowl wins were over coaches in the Hall of Fame.

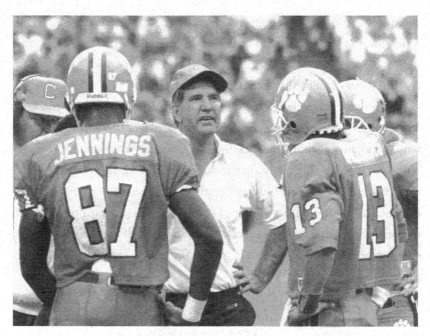

Danny Ford won five ACC titles and had seven top 20 seasons, including the 1981 national title.

He had 20 wins over top-25 teams, still the Clemson record. He led Clemson to a streak of 41 consecutive weeks in the top 20 in the late 1980s. Seven years he led Clemson to a top-25 final ranking. He coached 26 All-Americans and 71 first-team All-ACC players. He finished with a record of 96–29–4, a 76 percent winning mark that is third in ACC history behind Bobby Bowden (whom he beat the last time he faced him in Tallahassee, Florida, in 1989) and Jimbo Fisher.

Ford is proud of all of his former players, but he must hold some extra pride for those who went on to successful NFL careers. Ten former players won Super Bowl rings.

Many of Coach Ford's former players were at Clemson on August 31, 2013, when he was inducted into the Ring of Honor. It proved to be a special night for Ford and Clemson football in many ways. The ceremony was quite a celebration as former Clemson baseball coach Bill Wilhelm was also inducted. Ford and Wilhelm helped Clemson dominate ACC football and baseball in the 1978–1989 era, and it was fitting that they were inducted together.

"I am very appreciative of this honor," said Ford. "I feel a coach is less deserving of something like this than a player. They are the ones who did all the blocking and tackling. The coaches just try to direct them and draw up the plays. My first thoughts are to all the players, assistant coaches, the fans, the support staff people, the trainers and managers, the SID staff, and Jim Phillips (voice of the Tigers for Ford's entire career), who helped make us successful on the field. If they look up in the stadium and see my name and it gives them pride for what we accomplished, I am for it."

The ceremony took place 10 minutes before kickoff. Clemson fans were in the stands well before kickoff, which led to a very special moment for national television when the Tigers ran down the hill.

It was also an evening of eerie similarities. Clemson's winning touchdown was scored by No. 81 Stanton Seckinger. A key recovery in the end zone was made by C.J. Jones, who wears No. 38, the number Wilhelm wore. The victory over the fifth-ranked Bulldogs was the sixth for Swinney against a team ranked in the top 11, tying him with Ford for the most top-11 victories in Clemson coaching history.

"I am so happy for Coach Ford," said fellow Alabama alum Swinney. "It was a special night, and everything was so fitting. So fitting that he was inducted prior to a Clemson-Georgia game because those games were just legendary when he was the coach here. It was a great moment I know. Winning the national championship is the greatest accomplishment in this program's history, and we are all trying to get there. Coach Ford established a standard. He told Clemson that you can do it here. I have always had great respect for Coach Ford. He's always gone above and beyond to help our program."

CHAPTER 12
CLEMSON,
A SPECIAL PLACE

There's Something in These Hills

by Joe Sherman, Class of 1934

Times when so many things seems to be coming unglued are disquieting times. These are disquieting times.

It always intrigues me how nearly any specific condition of nearly any specific time can find some application in a book that, essentially, was handed down to us by word of mouth through century after century.

I believe it says somewhere, "I will lift up mine eyes unto the hills from whence cometh my help."

My thoughts are wandering through these upper South Carolina hills that shelter the university that forms common bonds for many thousands of people who have studied here or taught here or worked here.

There's something in these hills that has touched every one of them, something that has rubbed off on them in varying degrees, something that has built within the breasts of all Clemson men and women an enduring spark akin to an eternal pride.

There's something in these hills. It was here when a handful of fledgling faculty members greeted a relatively small band of 446 students more than 106 years ago. That was shortly after convict labor had competed an administration building and clock tower that still dominate these Blue Ridge foothills with a timelessness and serenity that impart inspiration and strength anew each time they are looked upon.

There's something in these hills that has endeared itself to an endless procession of administrators, teachers, students, secretaries, and workmen. Hundreds of names pass through my consciousness, names of people who gave selflessly of themselves to build the institution nestled here and who at one and the same time mined the priceless something the hills contain and returned to them still more of it.

I have my names and I see once more the faces and feel again the beloved personalities that go with them. If you will but close your eyes and drift awhile, you too will recall the names and faces and personalities of those who meant the most to you while the privilege of being among them was yours.

There's something in these hills, and from them we have drawn the power to transcend the stresses and strains that tug away that make things come unglued in these disquieting times, the power to cut through such modern concepts—and such modern facts—as generation gaps, communication gaps, and ideological gaps.

Where is the generation gap when an alumnus who spent four years in these hills before the turn of the century says, "Next to my church and my home, I love Clemson University beyond all other institutions this side of Heaven," and when a graduate-to-be says, "Excepting only my parents, Clemson has meant more to me and done more for me than anything that has touched my life"?

There's something in these hills that has bound together a man over ninety and a boy under twenty, something has given them common ground on which to stand and a start toward bridging, and eliminating, any gap or any stresses or any strain that might try to make unglued whatever they seek for themselves as they move out of these hills into the mountains, the plains, the oceans, the forests, the skies, and the storms of life.

We have all drawn from these hills something to suggest to youth that those over thirty can be trusted and to indicate to those over thirty that the qualities of youth are as sound today as they ever were.

There's something in these hills that brings together and binds together and holds together men and women of all persuasions, of all heights, sizes, weights, and cultural backgrounds—something that cuts across every difference, spans every gap, penetrates every wall—something that makes a man or a woman stand taller, feel better, and say with high pride to all within earshot, "I went to Clemson."

There's something in these hills, and I suspect that's what it is—the ability of an institution through the unending dedication and greatness of its people—its administration, its faculty, its staff, its students, and its alumni—to impart to all it touches a respect, and admiration, an affection that stands firm in disquieting times when things around it give impressions of coming unglued.

Yes, there's something in these hills where the Blue Ridge yawns its greatness.

ACKNOWLEDGMENTS

We'd like to extend special thanks to the contributors to the Clemson Football Game Programs: Al Adams, Brent Breedin, William Qualkinbush, Sanford Rogers, Kyle Tucker, and Will Vandervort; and photographers Mark Crammer, Earle Martin, Jim Moriarty, and Bob Waldrop.

SOURCES

Bourret, Tim (2008). *Clemson Football Vault*. Atlanta: Whitman Publishing.

Blackman, Sam, (1999, 2013). *Clemson Where the Tigers Play*. New York: Skyhorse Publishing.

Blackman, Sam and Tim Bourret. Clemson Football Media Guide (printed annually). Clemson, South Carolina: Clemson University.

Blackman, Sam and Tim Bourret. Clemson Football Game Programs (printed for each Clemson home football game). Clemson, South Carolina: Clemson University.